WOMEN'S ECONOMIC WRITING IN THE NINETEENTH CENTURY

WOMEN'S ECONOMIC WRITING IN THE NINETEENTH CENTURY

Edited by
Lana L. Dalley

Volume II

Routledge
Taylor & Francis Group
LONDON AND NEW YORK

First published 2023
by Routledge
4 Park Square, Milton Park, Abingdon, Oxon OX14 4RN

and by Routledge
605 Third Avenue, New York, NY 10158

Routledge is an imprint of the Taylor & Francis Group, an informa business

British Library Cataloguing-in-Publication Data
A catalogue record for this book is available from the British Library

Library of Congress Cataloging-in-Publication Data

Names: Dalley, Lana L., 1976- editor.
Title: Women's economic writing in the nineteenth century / edited by Lana Dalley.
Description: New York, NY : Routledge, 2023. | Includes bibliographical references and index. | Contents: v. 1. — v. 2. — v. 3. — v. 4.
Identifiers: LCCN 2022052308 (print) | LCCN 2022052309 (ebook) | ISBN 9780367336417 (set) | ISBN 9780367336561 (v. 1 ; hardback) | ISBN 9780367336585 (v. 2 ; hardback) | ISBN 9780367337247 (v. 3 ; hardback) | ISBN 9780367337254 (v. 4 ; hardback) | ISBN 9780429321054 (v. 1 ; ebook) | ISBN 9780429321078 (v. 2 ; ebook) | ISBN 9780429321504 (v. 3 ; ebook) | ISBN 9780429321511 (v. 4 ; ebook)
Subjects: LCSH: Women economists—History—19th century. | Women–Economic conditions—19th century.
Classification: LCC HB75 .W7876 2023 (print) | LCC HB75 (ebook) | DDC 330.082—dc23/eng/20221102
LC record available at https://lccn.loc.gov/2022052308
LC ebook record available at https://lccn.loc.gov/2022052309

ISBN: 978-0-367-33641-7 (set)
eISBN: 978-0-429-32101-6 (set)
ISBN: 978-0-367-33658-5 (volume II)
eISBN: 978-0-429-32107-8 (volume II)

DOI: 10.4324/9780429321078

Typeset in Times New Roman
by Apex CoVantage, LLC

Publisher's Note
References within each chapter are as they appear in the original complete work

CONTENTS

VOLUME II

ACKNOWLEDGMENTS

Most of my work on *Women's Economic Writing in the Nineteenth Century* took place during the COVID-19 pandemic; reading and sorting through hundreds of historical texts about women and economics while simultaneously learning to teach online and to (temporarily) homeschool my four children made me think anew about the contingencies of women's economic lives. The toll of the COVID-19 pandemic on women's work and their economic stability has been devastating; the precariousness discussed by many of the nineteenth-century female writers in this volume thus feels especially trenchant in this particular historical moment. I am deeply grateful to the community of editors, scholars, students, and family whose support allowed me to continue my scholarly work, even under such trying circumstances.

I would like to thank my editor, Simon Alexander, and the Routledge production team for their patience and encouragement, even as I pushed deadlines to accommodate my increased responsibilities at home. I received significant institutional support to complete this project from my home institution, California State University, Fullerton (CSUF), including a research sabbatical, a SURE-A student-faculty research grant from the Office of Research and Sponsored Projects, and a Gregory, Cheryl, and Katheryn Wirzbicki Grant for Student-Faculty Research from the CSUF English Department. I am deeply grateful for the time and resources this support granted me to work on the project. I would also like to thank my three student research assistants, Sara Camacho, Layal Messelmani, and Sela Pastrana, who tirelessly helped me read and cull materials.

And finally, to my children, Eli, Finley, Sawyer, and Dashiell, and my husband, Tristan – thank you for always cheering me on, for making me feel like my work matters, and for giving me the space and the time to write my own economic story.

GENERAL INTRODUCTION

Women's Economic Writing in the Nineteenth Century establishes a tradition of women's economic writing and contextualizes that tradition within the broader social and historical context of the period. Until now, women's economic writing has largely been treated as isolated, unusual, or a deviation from the norm. This collection demonstrates just how common it was for women to write about economics in the nineteenth century and establishes various throughlines and trajectories within their body of work.

The work in this anthology spans the course of the long nineteenth century, here defined as starting in the late eighteenth century and ending after the first World War, and includes female writers from around the world, although most selections are from British and American writers. The selections in this anthology also demonstrate how women's economic writing in the nineteenth century crossed the boundaries of genre. The "woman writer" was a burgeoning institution in the nineteenth century, and women were increasingly visible as novelists, poets, essayists, and dramatists. They were less visible, though, within domains of knowledge considered masculine, like economic theory; women were writing and participating in those domains of knowledge, even though their participation was often obscured by the prominence of male writers in the field. Within the canon of women's economic writing in the nineteenth century, a tension emerges between the economic methodology that emphasizes abstraction, as found in economic theory, and the humanistic tradition of representing individual stories, as found in imaginative literature. The selections in *Women's Economic Writing in the Nineteenth Century* showcase the wide variety and range of economic writing by women in the period; selections include didactic tales, fictional illustrations, poetry, economic theory, social theory, reports, letters, novels, speeches, dialogues, and self-help books.

The economic landscape of the nineteenth century was deeply shaped by social and political changes like the Industrial Revolution, the expansion of empire, the abolition of slavery, the various innovations in print culture, the rise in consumerism, and the campaign for women's rights. Modern economic theory emerged as a serious field of study in the nineteenth century, and it gained cultural clout throughout the period. The publication of Adam Smith's *An Inquiry into the*

Nature and Causes of the Wealth of Nations in 1776 ushered in political economy as the dominant economic theory, until the marginalist revolution of the 1870s shifted the focus away from the laborer and production and toward the consumer and consumption. Despite the growing authority of economic theory throughout the nineteenth century, women were woefully underrepresented, not only as economists but also as subject matter.

The scope of classical political economy was quite broad – encompassing moral philosophy and dealing with many aspects of everyday life – but its scope did not extend to women, who are virtually absent within early economic theory, and rarely did it extend to the domestic sphere, in which women were ideologically (and often literally) seated. Very few women were writing economic theory – or were considered economists – in the nineteenth century, and political economists had very little to say about the economic facets of women's lives. Indeed, if we limit our scope to the economic theory of the period, we will see an incomplete record of women's participation in economics. More importantly, it looks like women did not have much to say and were not impacted by – or interested in – economic theory. This anthology refutes that claim and demonstrates that representation must be sought elsewhere, in women's writing on the subject.

Women's marginal status within nineteenth-century economic theory is a result of the ideological (and, for some middle- and upper-class women, actual) relegation of women to the domestic sphere and the simultaneous devaluation of domestic work within the capitalist ethos. Economic Man (*Homo economicus*) is the key actor in economic theory; political economists imagine men as rational economic actors and rarely even place women within their economic landscape. As political economy became an increasingly relevant and important "science" in the nineteenth century, it became a key framework for making sense of and describing the world; the absence of women within this framework reinforced the separate spheres ideology that confined women to the domestic sphere.

Women clearly had a stake in economics – both the economics of the nation and the economics of the home – even if that stake has often been underrepresented or ignored. As contemporary feminist economists have shown, women and women's issues continue to be scarce within the discipline of economics. The selections in this collection demonstrate that female writers have long been trying to rectify this scarcity and to open the discipline of economics to women's voices and concerns. If we expand the scope of analysis beyond economic theory to other genres that address economic issues, we obtain a broader picture of economic writing and thinking in the nineteenth century, and we see how women's literary traditions were shaped by and inclusive of the emerging economic discourses and practices.

At the same time that political economy was gaining cultural authority, the women's rights movement was gaining steam and a woman's "place" within society was being reimagined. Throughout the century, several legal and social changes contributed to this reimagining of woman's role, including the expansion of work opportunities, the opening of higher education institutions for women, and revisions to married women's property laws. Political economy became a common language for mainstream liberal feminists of the period to use when advocating for the expansion of women's rights. Liberal feminists often upheld the notion that women's character is decidedly moral and domestic, which enables them to offer something new (and necessary) to the marketplace without threatening the work of men. In this way, they rendered domestic values as compatible with, rather than at odds with, economic values and posited sexual difference within the marketplace as simply another facet of the division of labor. Female writers often emphasized the liberating possibilities of the changing economic landscape, and they used the language of economic theory to do so. At other times, female writers demonstrated the problematic position of women within the liberal economic scheme when narratives of female economic empowerment are disrupted or stalled by contemporary gender expectations.

The way we think about women's relationship to economics is partly a result of lived experience and objective measures; we can, on the one hand, quite easily quantify women's participation in the economy and the discipline of economics. What is less easy to quantify is women's discursive relationship to economics – the way in which women's economic lives are talked about, described, and represented. And yet, these discursive practices come to shape the more tangible quantifications of their economic lives. In the nineteenth century, women's writing was often the site of these discursive formations, helping to form attitudes about women and economics that persist into the twentieth and twenty-first centuries. *Women's Economic Writing in the Nineteenth Century* provides a cohesive picture of these discursive formations and thus helps readers to better understand women's historical relationships to economics.

The anthology is divided into eight themed sections: political economy, feminist economics, domestic economics, labor, philanthropy and poverty, consumerism, emigration and empire, and self-help. Each section begins with an introduction that tells a story about female writers' relationships to the section theme and then provides an overview of the selections contained therein. While some overlap between sections is inevitable, the units are meant to help readers navigate the numerous selections in the anthology and gain a more comprehensive understanding of various traditions of women's economic writing. *Women's Economic Writing in the Nineteenth Century* offers readers a much-needed contextual framework and charts a chronology for the study of female writers' engagements with economics in the nineteenth century; in so doing, it paints a more robust and accurate picture of women's writing in the period.

Part 2

FEMINIST ECONOMICS

Editorial Headnote

Feminist Economics

The field of feminist economics formally emerged in the 1970s, as more economists began to critique then-standard methodologies in economics and to argue that gender should be a fundamental category of analysis and consideration within the discipline. Contemporary feminist economists argue that gender bias is hard baked into the field of economics and that its methodological approaches need to be profoundly revised. As a field, then, feminist economics proposes radically different approaches to collecting data and interpreting it.

The emergence of feminist economics was simultaneous with the rise of second-wave feminism in the 1960s and 1970s. Both movements shared concerns about the political nature of the domestic sphere, women's economic autonomy, and women's subjugation under patriarchal capitalism. Nearly a century earlier, many of these concerns were being expressed by female writers, albeit somewhat differently. As Edith Abbott's and Mabel Atkinson's essays in this section demonstrate, the women's rights movement of the nineteenth century was decidedly economic; both writers delineate a tradition of women's work within the field of economics. Abbott offers a revision of Harriet Martineau's study of women's employment in 1836, and Atkinson unpacks the economic dimensions of the women's rights movement, frequently citing imaginative literature as evidence for her claims. Eleanor Marx Aveling similarly cites imaginative literature as evidence (in her case, Olive Schreiner's *Story of an African Farm*) to make her argument that the abolition of private property is the most promising means of promoting gender equality. At a time when women's participation in the labor market was strongly discouraged and women's dependence on men in marriage was highly encouraged, women's rights activists imagined and advocated different ways of being for women. For them, economic independence was the key to living a life of dignity and fulfillment, and paid labor was instrumental to women's liberation. (As the selection in the labor section in volume III of this Anthology demonstrates, there was another strand of women's economic writing that focused on the exploitative and damaging nature of the paid work available to women.)

DOI: 10.4324/9780429321078-1

Within the dominant liberal feminist paradigm, paid labor was often conceptualized as universally beneficial and desirable for women; selections in this section by Harriet Martineau and Clara Collet extol the personal, social, and political benefits of women's labor. In 1859, the British Society for Promoting the Employment of Women was formed in an effort to expand such opportunities for women, and Barbara Leigh Smith Bodichon's report offers an overview of the organization's efforts in its first year. Elizabeth Garrett Anderson and Matilda Gage emphasize women's suitability for specific careers, nursing and inventing, respectively, and argue that women's efforts need to be recognized and remunerated. Frances Abbott makes an early argument for equal pay, suggesting that educated women need to be paid fairly for their work; Margaret Bateson advocates for women being paid money for their labor, rather than simply being paid in room and board, because learning to manage money will contribute to the growth of their character. However, as selections by Anna Julia Cooper and Fannie Barrier Williams demonstrate, expanded work opportunities did not reach all women equally; black women were often excluded from the efforts of early feminism, and they consistently experienced higher barriers to paid employment and more risk of exploitation.

In their attempts to expand the scope of economics, the writers in this section established a tradition of feminist economic writing that made gender a fundamental category of economic analysis and, in many cases, encouraged new and different approaches to existing economic problems.

1

"INDEPENDENT INDUSTRY OF WOMEN," *DAILY NEWS*

Harriet Martineau

Source: Harriet Martineau, 'Independent Industry of Women', *Daily News*, 17 November 1859

For a good many years now the subject of the independent industry of women in Great Britain has come up at shorter intervals, and with a more peremptory demand on the attention of society. From the day when the *Song of the Shirt* appeared there could be no doubt that the industrial condition of women would occupy attention as we see it doing now. The founding of the Governesses' Benevolent Institution, the controversies about factory employment for women, the movement in favour of women and watchwork, the opening of a few Schools of Design to women, and of an annual exhibition of pictures by them, and the successful footing they have established in various department of Art, have all pointed to the awakening of that wide interest in the subject which we witness now. The *Edinburgh Review* of last April contained a full narrative of the actual state of female industry in this country; and at the Social Science Meeting at Bradford, a paper read by Miss PARKES excited so much interest that the discussion has been kept up, and does not seem likely to drop at present.

Discussion about what? This is an important thing to know in a case in which so much sentiment is involved, and so much prejudice, and so much sense, and so much goodwill. What is the precise mischief to be taken in hand? and what is to be done to cure it?

Miss PARKES's paper was abundantly clear and definite. She tells us the truth that a multitude of the daughters of middle-class men are neither educated nor provided for like their brothers; and that if they do not marry, they must work (unprepared by education as they are) or starve. The terms demanded on behalf of women are that parents shall either educate their daughters so as to fit them for independent industry; or lay by a provision for them; or insure their own lives for the benefit of their daughters in the day which will make them fatherless. This is very simple and clear. It is also very interesting; and, as a natural consequence, we hear of sympathy, in the form of advice and suggestions,

DOI: 10.4324/9780429321078-2

in all directions; and of various establishments, existing or proposed, with more or less of the charitable element involved for the relief and aid of industrial women of the middle class. Under such circumstances there must be a melancholy waste of effort, unless we ascertain betimes what it is that is wanted, and how the want may be met, with something like concert and business-like faculty. Looking at the matter from a practical point of view, the conditions of the case seem to be these.

It is supposed by persons whose attention has not been particularly called to the subject, that the women of Great Britain are maintained by their fathers, husbands, or brothers. It was once so; and careless people are unaware that we have long outgrown the fit of that theory of female maintenance. It has been out at elbows at least since the war which ended with Waterloo. From the last Census Report we learn how things were eight years ago-before the last war which has much increased the tendency of women to maintain themselves. In Great Britain, without Ireland, there were in 1851 six millions of women above twenty years of age. More than half of these work for their living. Does this surprise our readers? If it never occurred to them before, they will be still further impressed by the fact that two millions of women, out of the six millions, are independent in their industry-are self-supporting, like men. So far is the theory of women being maintained by their male relatives from being now true. But how do these women work? and how far do they succeed in maintaining themselves? for it is universally understood that women are paid less than men for the same kind and degree of work. Society has been a good deal surprised by the disclosures in the Divorce Court of the amount of effectual female industry, proved by applications for protection of earnings from bad husbands. That women should maintain themselves and their children seems a matter of course when they are unhappily married; and the revelation has caused a good many people to perceive that there is a good deal going on in middle-class life which they were unaware of. It may strike some observers that the matter has far outgrown the scope and powers of charitable societies, and that the independent industry of Englishwomen has become a fact which must be recognised by the law, and which must itself essentially modify middle-class education throughout the kingdom.

What, then, are these three millions and more of working women doing? and especially the two millions who are industrial in the same sense as men? There were in 1851 nearly 130,000 employed in agriculture, without reckoning the farmers' wives and daughters, who usually have their hands full. This is also exclusive of the widow-farmers, who are numerous. Nearly half of the independent class of workers are dairymaids. The ores and clays of the mining districts afford occupation to 7,000, now that female labour has ceased (ostensibly) in coal-pits. It does not seem to be ascertained how many women are employed in the catching, curing, and itinerant sale of fish. Jersey oysters alone maintain 1,000 women, and this may give some notion of the scores of thousands so employed all round our coasts. The country districts, however, afford the greatest number of all in the department of domestic service. Nearly two-thirds of our maid-servants are country born; and there are considerably more than half-a-million of them altogether. They constitute a fourth part of the independent workers. We employ no fewer than 400,000 maids-of-all-work. Other female servants amount to above 180,000, without reckoning the large class (about 51,000) of charwomen.

There are many thousands of shopkeepers, but they are for the most part the widows of the men who had the business before them; and it is too common a thing to see them marry their assistants in the business, from their own inability to keep the books, and manage the financial part of their concerns. The Divorce Court and the police courts, all the year round, afford evidence of this weakness and ignorance among women who have had a good business as innkeepers or shopkeepers. There are 14,000 of this class, butchers and milk merchants; 8,000 waggon or hackney-coach proprietors; 10,000 beer-shop keepers or victuallers, besides 9,000 innkeepers. These are the independent proprietors, excluding the wives, who are yet the mainstay of the industry in houses of entertainment and many branches of retail trade. With all this shopkeeping by women, there are no more than 1,742 shopwomen. This is a fact eminently worthy of consideration. The function is one which occurs first to almost everybody's mind, when female industry is discussed, as one precisely fit for women. The failure may be partly owing to the jealousy of the men, who have hitherto engrossed it, and partly to the well-known prejudice of purchasers in favour of shopmen; but it is no doubt in part ascribable to the inferiority of women in the special training required; and especially in accounts and bookkeeping.

Manufactures maintain a million and a quarter of the women of Great Britain. More than half a million are employed on dress; that is, in millinery and laundry-work, exclusive of shoemakers' wives, who amount to nearly 100,000. Losing sight of the great field of female labour, because female industry is so completely established there, we are apt to say that there is no choice for a middle-class woman who must work but between the needle and tuition. The milliner's work-room and the school-room, we are wont to say, afford the only alternative. Yet we find in the Census returns "Teachers, Authors, and Artists," all lumped together, their collective number being under 65,000, exclusive of nearly 2,000 set down as "miscellaneous." Independent proprietors of lands, houses, or incomes are declared to be under 173,000.

Considering these figures in relation to each other, we strive at some sort of notion of what is wanted -first, to provide for a certain proportion of women now left helpless or miserable on the death of fathers, or under the accidents of fortune; and next, to improve the quality of existing female industry, so as to render it more effective for the support of the individual, and the benefit of society. We do not conceive that any appeal to fathers to provide better for their daughters, in comparison with their sons, will be of much practical use (however just and right) till the women have established the fact of their own capability, and their will to be independent. All sorts of people have to show what they can do before obtaining free scope to do it; and, antecedently unjust as this seems, it is a fact, and to be taken into the calculation. Women need not object to this, judging by what they have lately achieved for themselves under manifold disadvantages. They have won a good position in many departments of literature and art; and there is a good prospect of their soon occupying what we have repeatedly insisted on as their proper place in the medical profession. The thing would be done at once (as it is already in the United States), if the decision rested with our wisest physicians and most enlightened heads of households. We see women now entering in increasing numbers on new methods of industry, introduced by the progress of science and art. We see them in the telegraph offices and at railway stations, transmitting reports with remarkable accuracy, and selling railway tickets-if not yet in charge of the signals, like French women. The arts of design for manufactures are open to them; and this is a wide and profitable field of labour. As authors and artists there is no hindrance in their way when they can prove their capability. No doubt, the counting- house, the shop-counter, secretaryships, and indeed any trade, and the medical profession will afford them entrance, notwithstanding a good deal of jealousy and prejudice, if they can make themselves valuable enough to defy obstacles. The practical question is how to establish the fact of the capacity. The fitness which exists may be called out and put to use by such associations as those which we see proposing to register applicants for work and for workers, and to train young women to mechanical fitness for certain occupations. These efforts are good as far as they go; and we are always glad to hear of them. The educational preparation which is necessary to make effective workers of either men or women is a deeper and wider affair of which we must speak another day. Our present object is to show that it is mere waste of time to speak for or against the industrial independence of Englishwomen-above one third of their whole number being already established in that destiny. A smaller number of women are passing miserable lives under the wreck of the old theory that women are not self-supporting. These sufferers are not supported: they cannot support themselves, and they form the most prominent of our "uneasy classes." The old theory can never be reinstated in practice, and the question is how best to obey the natural laws of society, which now compel women to work.

The first step is to perceive that the problem is now simply an educational one. This is the point which the facts of the last Census seem to us to establish. The next step will be to provide the education specially required.

2

"REPORT OF THE SOCIETY FOR PROMOTING THE EMPLOYMENT OF WOMEN"

Barbara Leigh Smith Bodichon

Source: Barbara Leigh Smith Bodichon, 'Report of the Society for Promoting the Employment of Women', *English Woman's Journal* Vol. IV, No. 33, November 1860, pp. 146–51

"As this is the first formal report issued by the Society for the Employment of Women, the Committee have thought it desirable briefly to state its origin and objects before proceeding to give an account of its past efforts and indicate its aims for the future.

"Nearly two years ago a few ladies, feeling deeply the helpless and necessitous condition of the great number of women obliged to resort to non-domestic industry as a means of subsistence, consulted together as to the best way in which they might bring social position and influence to their aid.

"They resolved on the formation of a society which should have for its object the opening up of new employments to women, and their more extensive admission into those branches of business already open to them.

"The Committee found that they were dealing with a question which more or less affected one-half the female population of the country. While truly anxious to secure new openings for female industry, they felt that a great responsibility rested upon them in the choice of occupations fitted for the physical strength and suited to the general powers of women. They resolved therefore to proceed by means of experiment. The advocates of extreme opinions might advance the theory that all professions and trades ought at once to be thrown open to both sexes, on equal terms. But with theory they resolved to have nothing to do. There is a great crowd of women dependent on work; the two points of the case were – what can *they* do? what can *we* do for them? Another preliminary question arose, at what point in the social scale is this wedge of experiment to be inserted? and after due deliberation they felt that they must endeavor to begin somewhere in the lower ranks of the middle class. For highly educated women we could for a time do nothing; women of

DOI: 10.4324/9780429321078-3

no education could do nothing for us; that is to say, we could open up no new channels for the labor of the former, and our experiments would have failed owing to the inefficiency of the latter. But we felt convinced that in whatever direction we made an opening, the pressure on all ranks of working women would be lessened: the low class governess would become the first class tradeswoman, and the poor sempstress would find her services better paid as her more intelligent or favored companions were withdrawn from competition in starvation to competition in skill.

"Printing was suggested as a suitable employment for women, and on inquiry we found that several experiments on a small scale had been tried in various places, and with sufficient success to tempt to further effort in the same direction. From personal trial several members of the Committee found that composing could easily be accomplished by girls, while they decided that the heavier parts of the business must remain in the hands of men. The Committee felt that to make any business self-supporting, to make it a fair money speculation, capital was required, and an amount of superintendence and management which they knew it was impossible for a Committee to give. A well-known friend of the cause offered to embark a certain amount of capital in starting a printing office, in which women only were to be employed. The Committee selected and apprenticed to the office five girls, at a premium of £10 each. This was all the money help the Society could afford to give; they were justly afraid of incurring responsibility in the matter, but on that responsibility being assumed by others, the Society brought all its influence to bear, in order to promote the success of the undertaking.

"The Committee would acknowledge the great assistance rendered by Lord Shaftesbury and others, on behalf of the Victoria Press, whose success is mainly due to the influence of the Society. We must not omit to mention that our late able and energetic secretary is the manager of the office, and has now sixteen girls under her judicious care, who have attained a considerable degree of efficiency. They now print the ENGLISH WOMAN'S JOURNAL, a monthly periodical devoted to the interests of women.

"A still lighter and more suitable employment has been found in law-copying; and the Committee undertook the responsibility of opening a law stationer's office in Portugal Street, Lincoln's Inn. Ten female clerks are employed in this office, having learnt the simpler parts of the business in a few weeks in a manner satisfactory to their employers. The necessity of a paid superintendent, with all the other expenses of a pretty large establishment, have trenched largely on the funds of the Society. A lady who has taken a most prominent part in the movement has offered to advance £200 if our present superintendent will undertake to conduct the business and work it for her own profit and that of the clerks. The Committee agreed that this offer be accepted, and have referred it to the managing committee to arrange the details.

"The Committee consider that by this means the funds of the Society will be set free for other purposes, and that it is their province to open up new branches of business, leaving them to be conducted by others in the ordinary way of trade. The law clerks have done a very fair amount of business during the time they have been at work, but further capital is required for its extension and support, and the Committee think it will be on a more satisfactory footing as a private enterprise.

"The Committee were desirous of extending the employment of women as book-keepers and cashiers in shops. They found that the great obstacle to their progress in this direction was the ignorance of women of the higher branches of arithmetic; and resolved to open book-keeping classes, in which the daughters of tradesmen might be qualified for clerks and cashiers, and the higher branches of book-keeping. One of the ladies of the Committee undertook to establish, at her own risk, a middle class school, and the Committee agreed to give her a grant of £40, on condition that morning and evening classes for book-keeping were established in connexion with her school.

"The school has a certificated teacher, but as it has been so short a time in operation, the Committee are not prepared to state the result of this experiment.

"With regard to the future course of action to be adopted by the Society, the Committee have to suggest the desirability of finding an outlet for the emigration of a class of educated women.

"The number who might take advantage of an opening of this kind would at first be comparatively limited; but the inquiries made by the Committee prove that such an outlet exists, while it is rendered unavailable by the want of the necessary agencies. The Committee would be glad to avail themselves of any opportunity for the furtherance of a middle class female emigration. The following statement affords testimony to the desirability of taking advantage of the opening thus afforded.

"Disparity of the Sexes in Victoria. – Some remarkable facts respecting the disparity of sexes in this colony are disclosed in the census of 1857. Sir Henry Barkly, the Governor, in noticing these facts, says in a despatch: – 'It now appears that though considerable improvement in this respect took place between 1854 and 1857, yet that the effective disproportion at the latter period was far more serious than would be deducible from the fact of there being 163 males to every 100 females in the entire population. Since tabling the portion of it above the age of twenty years, there were no less than 217 males to that number, the proportions below that age being pretty nearly equal. There were 88,355 unmarried men of twenty years of age and upwards to 12,545 unmarried women of corresponding ages; or, to raise the age of marriage for men to twenty-one, and lower it to fifteen for women, there was still an excess of 61,859 bachelors, not too add 5,112 widowers. Even this comparison, however, fails to convey a full sense of the evil as it affects the goldfields, where it appears that the percentage of unmarried men is, to that to be found in the seaport towns, as 61 to 39; or, to state the case in another form, where the bachelors are to the spinsters in the proportion of more than 20 to 1. There are, moreover, 8,096 married men, chiefly in the mining districts, whose wives are not in the colony. It has been alleged, during the agitation of the land question, that this state of things is attributable to the difficulty of buying small allotments suited to agricultural purposes (for the miner's right itself sanctions a certain area for residence), but this idea is not borne out by the figures, which manifest an extraordinary disposition on the part of the gold-diggers, despite the unsettled nature of their pursuits, to enter into matrimony. This may be judged from the fact that only 9 per cent. of the women on the goldfields above twenty are unmarried; while in Great Britain the proportion who marry under that age is only 2½ per cent. 30 per cent. of the girls between fifteen and twenty are here married.'

"The Committee also recommend that the attention of the Society should be directed to securing the employment of women in such light and suitable occupations as hair dressing and hair working; and as far as possible in every trade by which the requirements of ladies are supplied.

"In conclusion, the Committee are able to say, that however far their efforts may have fallen short of any expectations which may have been formed, however little they may have been able to accomplish of the great task which lay before them, they have succeeded far beyond their anticipations in securing the adherence of public opinion in favor of the cause, and this it appears to them is no small matter. It is on public opinion that the matter mainly rests, for it is the public and not the Society that must find employment for women. All that can be done by a Society is to act as pioneer, to make experiments, to inaugurate efforts. The rest remains to be accomplished by the real impetus of the movement: namely, its necessity, its justice, and its expediency, acting through the ordinary economic laws, with which mere benevolent interference is temporary and futile."

* * * * * * *

The reading of the report was followed by Miss Parkes's paper, "A Year's Experience in Woman's Work," and a paper by Miss Emily Faithfull on the "Victoria Press," both of which were given in the last number of the Journal. Some discussion then arose upon the question of training readers for the press, a branch of the business which we would gladly see in the hands of educated women, and which is peculiarly suited to them. Carried on in a room appropriated to the purpose, and usually occupied by the reader only, there is nothing to jar upon the feelings of the most fastidious, while the work is light and amply remunerative. A good reader for the press, conversant with English only, readily obtains an engagement at two guineas a week, while the knowledge of French, German, and Italian, adds considerably to the market value of his services. The discussion had regard to the amount of practical knowledge of printing necessary to make a good reader, not to the fitness of the employment for women, concerning which the feeling was unanimous. The employment of women as sellers of railway tickets, clerks and cashiers, was warmly supported, and Mr. Duncan M'Laren (late Lord Provost of Edinburgh) stated that about three years ago young women were introduced with great success into the business with which he is connected, and that at the present time there are thirteen young women employed selling in important departments.

Mr. Campbell Smith said he should like to see ladies following the example of Miss Elizabeth Blackwell, and becoming doctors. He thought that science and morality would alike be served by the general introduction of women as practitioners for their own sex.

Mr. Hastings, after an indignant and manly protest against certain gross and anonymous attacks upon the movement and its promoters, said, he had urged upon the Social Science Association Council to support and defend the principles of these ladies. He was glad to say the Association had taken the matter up, and in a little time and in a quiet way it would be seen that they really were acting in earnest. He advocated the emigration of females to our colonies, where the disproportion of the sexes is frightful. The public might safely support the movement, and it was in excellent and most judicious hands.

The President expressed his appreciation of the principle embodied in the employment of female labor, and his gratification that the Association had energetically taken up the subject. He had to state that the discussion must now cease, as the whole question was to be renewed to-morrow at a special meeting in a separate section.

Miss Louisa Twining read a paper on "Workhouse Inmates." Twenty-five years' experience of the poor law, and recent statistics of pauperism, had shown that there were many practical points upon which improvements could be made. The labors of Jonas Hanway in improving the English workhouse were adverted to. Previous to 1760 the mortality in workhouses was positively frightful. Prisons were often more comfortable than workhouses. The nurses had frequently no qualification but that of physical strength – had no knowledge of the art of nursing – and became intoxicated whenever they could get drink. The paper urged the necessity of improvement in nurses, more regular and careful superintendence by official medical men, &c.

Miss Twining read also a paper by Miss Cobbe on "Destitute Incurables in Workhouses." The paper detailed the painful position of incurables in workhouses, and suggested a greater amount of kindness and comfort. Of the 80,000 who will this year die in England of consumption, dropsy, and cancer, there are tens of thousands wearing away the last minutes of their agonies in the workhouse. The comforts proposed, though trifling, would greatly alleviate suffering.

Mr. Duncan M'Laren believed if women were taken into all and every one of our public institutions it would be better for all. Having had considerable experience in public institutions, hospitals, &c., he was struck with the want of administrative and superintending women. He thought that in every workhouse there should be a female committee, the same as the existing committee of management, and that all the female servants should be appointed and supervised by ladies. Were their duties carefully defined, he trusted so much to the tact of women, that he was sure that in one year they would do as much good as a governor could do in seven. He thought the public were under a deep debt of gratitude to Miss Twining and the ladies who were associated with her. He should like to see committees appointed by the Legislature.

Dr. GILLAN thought there was a heroism about the ladies who had come forward to defend and explain such subjects. There should not only be practical nurses, but sympathizing ladies to superintend them. Who would grudge a halfpenny in the pound of assessment to make workhouse inmates comfortable? Humanity, justice, and Christianity called for this. After listening to the papers of the ladies who had spoken, he did not think the subject could be neglected in a Christian land. He trusted the suggestion of Mr. M'Laren would receive the attention of the Legislature.

3

"VOLUNTEER HOSPITAL NURSING"

Elizabeth Garrett Anderson

Source: Elizabeth Garrett Anderson, 'Volunteer Hospital Nursing', Paper read at the Tenth Annual Meeting of the National Association for the promotion of Social Science, Manchester, 1866

Read at the Tenth Annual Meeting of the National Association for the promotion of Social Science, Manchester, 1866.

THE question of hospital nursing is one which has received, during the last ten years, considerable attention, and which excites interest among people not immediately connected with hospital administration.

It may be noticed, in the first place, that in the discussion of the question, no doubt has been raised as to the value of good nursing. Thanks to Miss Nightingale, most people have some notion of what nursing should be; every one wishes it to be good, and every one agrees that, to be so, it should be in the hands of trustworthy and intelligent women. Unanimity even goes a step beyond this; for those who are in a position to decide upon the merits of our present system, agree in saying that it wants reform. The point of divergence is reached when we ask for a plan upon which the reform shall be based. Hospital nursing, like most other employments, may be undertaken in either of two ways; that is, in what may be briefly described as the commercial way, where the work is chosen primarily for the sake of the income to be gained by doing it, or in the philanthropic or religious way, where the work is done gratuitously. The words "commercial" and "religious" must be understood as referring only to the motive for the choice of an employment, not necessarily to the spirit in which it is done. Commercial work may be done religiously, or religious work commercially.

The commercial method is that which has till quite recently prevailed in all our hospitals. The main point at issue between those who discuss the question of hospital reform is whether it shall be continued, or whether it shall give place to the religious or volunteer method.

DOI: 10.4324/9780429321078-4

It will clear the ground for the consideration of this question, to state briefly the distinctive features of the present system and its rival.

In the majority of English civil hospitals the nursing department is under the control of the matron. Choosing the nurses, and overlooking them, form two of her most important duties.

The nursing staff consists of two classes: the head nurses and the under nurses. The former are in some hospitals called sisters, to distinguish them from the under nurses. These are again divided into night and day nurses. The head nurses are responsible for from thirty to fifty patients; they give medicines, attend to the surgical dressings, receive the medical directions for each patient, keep order in the wards, serve out the dinners, and see that the actual attendance upon the patients is given by the under nurses. As a rule they are skilful, experienced, kindly people, very well suited to their work. They usually belong to the lower section of the middle class, are the widows of small tradesmen or clerks, or less frequently they have been confidential domestic servants. Their salary varies from 20*l.* to 50*l.* a year, with board and residence.

The under nurses wait upon the patients, assist the sister in her duties, and in many cases clean the wards. One nurse is found to be enough for fourteen or fifteen patients, so that every head nurse has two or three under nurses beneath her. The latter are, as a rule, vastly inferior to the head nurses both in intelligence and character. They are commonly below the class of second or even third rate domestic servants; if they were not nurses, one would expect them to be maids-of-all-work, scrubs, or charwomen. They receive about 10*l.* or 12*l.* a year, with partial board, or board wages. From them again there is an apparent descent to the night nurses. I believe it is apparent only, and that actually they are much on a level, the night nurses seeming worse only because more is required of them, and because they are left for several hours entirely without supervision. When they do not live in the hospital, they eke out their scanty incomes by working the greater part of the day, and consequently they come to the hospital hoping to be able to sleep the greater part of the night. On the whole, ordinary hospital nursing may be described as a mixture of good, indifferent, and bad – the head nurses being often very good, the under nurses fairly good when under supervision, and bad when left without it.

In contrast to this, the volunteer method puts the nursing department into the hands of ladies who, having elected to do the work, are interested in doing it well. The main difference is, that the control no longer rests with the matron, and that at least the higher part of the nursing is done gratuitously. The head nurses are replaced by ladies to whom the under nurses are directly responsible. At King's College and University College Hospitals in London, where this method has been introduced, there is but one opinion as to the immense improvement in the nursing since the change was effected. The *Lancet* has recently given emphatic testimony on the same point. Referring to the volunteer help given during the cholera epidemic, it says, "The nursing by ladies is the very best nursing that England has yet seen;" and it prophesies that we cannot long refuse to adopt a system "which embodies intelligence, the keenest sympathy, refinement," and, it might have added, "economy." In fact, the advantages to the patients and to the hospitals are so great and so obvious, that it is astonishing to find any one blind to them. It is *all* gain to them to get in the place of paid servants, ladies who are willing to do the work for nothing in a peculiarly admirable manner. But admitting the superiority of ladies as nurses, it is still possible to question the wisdom of asking them to take up nursing as a profession. No amount of medical testimony in favour of their fitness for the work is of much avail when we are asking, "Is the work fit for *them?*" The *Lancet* says it is, apparently on the ground that the volunteer cholera nurses, in spite of very hard work, continued in excellent health. And in truth the "health and strength" argument, as it may be called, is entirely with those who advocate nursing by volunteers. There is very little room for doubt that most ladies would find the work of hospital nursing positively invigorating. Constant exercise in large and airy wards, employment of the kind which prevents morbid introspection or continuous mental exertion, absence of anxiety, regular and early hours, simple diet, and a life at least much less dull than that of most single women, combine to form a sum of conditions under which the health of most ladies would rapidly improve. The volunteer nurses in the cholera hospitals were by no means above the average standard of health, and among them there was but one opinion as to the hygienic effect of the work. One lady who had suffered daily from neuralgia for seven years, lost it entirely from the day she came to the hospital; several agreed in saying they took more food in a day than they had before taken in a week, and in all there was the unmistakeable look of healthy vigour. But the argument drawn from these facts has less weight when we reflect upon the beneficial influence of any regular work done with spirit and interest. It tells strongly in favour of doing something, but it does not decide what it is best to do. The question remains, "Is it for the advantage of the whole community that hospital nursing should be accepted as an unpaid profession by women of the educated classes?" To answer this, it is necessary to consider the subject of unpaid *versus* paid labour somewhat broadly, not merely with reference to the special point at issue.

It will probably be conceded that wherever the circumstances of society and of the individual permit a choice of work, there are two points to be considered; namely, the appropriateness of the individual for any special work, and of that particular work for him. A small amount of thought shows us that these two points require consideration in a kind of inverse proportion. The quality which our American friends have named "faculty" fits its possessor to acquire skill in doing almost anything he attempts to do, but the power of doing small things well ought not to be used as a fetter to bind him perpetually to the doing of them. The same is true of women. A lady who, with very little training, does hospital nursing in a first-rate way, is, *à priori*, likely to be able to do much more difficult things; and the question is whether it is desirable, for the sake of saving money to the hospital, to limit her permanently to work of so subordinate a character? What we want to know is, if hospital nursing can *only* be done well by gentlewomen, – if the qualities which fit them for many employments pledge them, as it were, to *this?* For it must be remembered that, in virtue of their position and their advantages, cultivated women are bound to discriminate in the choice of work. As education multiplies power, the moral obligation of making a choice is also increased. If the highest work is to be done at all, those capable of doing it must be content to leave the easier work to others, to recognise that they are bound not to do it, but to leave it undone for the sake of those to whom it is the highest possible. True social economy demands not only that every one should do something, but that every one should do his *best.* The advantage of getting moderately easy work exceptionally well done for nothing is apparent only if those who do it are prevented from doing other equally useful work for which those whom they displace are entirely unfit. It is generally admitted now, that in a well-ordered household the mistress ought not to do the domestic work herself, if she can afford to keep servants; although in virtue of her superior refinement she is peculiarly capable of doing it well. For experience has shown that when she gives up her time to petty domestic businesses the higher duties of her position get neglected; so that as there are appropriate people glad to do her cooking and dusting as a means of getting their living, her duty is to see that *they do* them, and to reserve herself for work which they cannot do. I would suggest that what is true of domestic management is true also of hospital nursing. Admirably as ladies can nurse, the actual work of nursing is not much more appropriate to them than that of cooking or dusting in their own homes. It is not true that hospital nursing cannot be well done by women of inferior rank and culture, and therefore it cannot be entirely desirable that those of a higher class should spend their time in doing it.

The difficulties in the way of good hospital nursing would, I believe, be completely removed, by the introduction of two reforms into the old commercial system. In the first place the scale of wages should be uniformly raised to the present maximum rate. In the official report on hospitals made to the Privy Council in 1863 by Dr. Bristowe and Mr. Holmes, much of the improvement observed in the nursing at St. Thomas's Hospital is attributed to the higher salaries given to the nurses since the Nightingale training institution was associated with the hospital. The reporters state that while the old rate of wages was, for the head nurses £40 to £50 a year without board, and for the under nurses 10*s*. to 13*s*. per week, without board, the present rate is £50 and £21 respectively, *with board*, and that this higher scale has been sufficient to gain for the hospital the services of a very superior class of women. Respectably clever women will not take the post of under nurse at the present minimum rate of hospital pay, and of course where the salaries are so low that none but intemperate charwomen will think of taking them, the nursing is as bad as intemperate charwomen can make it. The wages should be sufficient to attract respectable women of the rank of good domestic servants, that is, they should be somewhat above that which the people who are wanted could get in service, as an under nurse's life is necessarily less comfortable than that of most domestic servants.

In the second place I would suggest that the supervision, now confined to the day, should be extended to the night. Nursing requires more thought and attention than the routine work of domestic servants; and, therefore, even fairly good under nurses should have over them one who would give them even more than the supervision which a careful mistress gives to her servants.

It is not easy to see why the superior work of supervision should be done by unpaid labourers. It is the kind of work which many women, who have to support themselves, could do exceedingly well; and the keen demand for remunerated work, among women of the educated class, makes it desirable to open as many such situations as possible.

The amount of employment thus opened would not be great, as probably not more than 200 such situations could be offered to women if all the hospitals in the United Kingdom agreed to use the services of paid lady superintendents. Excluding workhouse infirmaries, there are only about 100 hospitals (having more than fifty beds) in England, Scotland, and Ireland. Two or three of these in the rural districts are too small to require more supervision than the matron ought to to be able to give, and this is the case also with a few of the special hospitals in London. On the other hand, several of the large metropolitan hospitals could perhaps employ three ladies, so that the rough calculation of two for each hospital containing more than fifty beds, will not be far from accurate.

It may be said that the objections here expressed to ladies doing the work of the head nurses does not apply to those who, though very much in need of employment, are not likely to do anything higher than nursing. It sounds very plausible to say, "Here are a number of unemployed women, pining for work, not in need of payment, glad indeed to do the work of a head nurse for nothing, and not at all likely to enter into any more difficult work. Surely they may offer to give their time to the service of the sick poor?"

I admit that to say No, sounds somewhat hard, but the hardship is removed by the simple expedient of their taking the salary which should rightly go with the work. It is not fair to the women to whom work is bread, for those to whom it is luxury, to come into the market and cheapen its price by giving what the others have to sell. The notion that there are crowds of women eager to do hard work for nothing, very much increases the difficulty of those who have to live by their work. It would be far better that it should be accepted as a point of honour among women, as it is among professional men, to take without question the salary or fee which belongs to any post or work even when the recipient is not without some private income. The difficulty of spending the extra money need never be great or permanent, or the salary could be returned indirectly to the hospital.

But it may farther be asked, Why have not ladies the right to give their services when the hospital physicians and surgeons give theirs?

The answer to this is, that the cases are in no degree parallel. True, the medical staff usually receive no payment for their services, and even where a medical school is connected with the hospital, the fees received by its teachers are too small to be of any moment. But, on the other hand, the immense advantage of hospital practice far more than repays any one enjoying it, for the time and labour it costs; the amount expended being indeed very much less than it would be in the case of a lady who made the wards her home.

Perhaps the only class of volunteer nurses to whom the objections now raised do not apply, are those to whose exertions we owe the recent renewal of the discussion; those namely who come forward to give extra help in times of emergency. But there is no reason, because the ordinary staff of nurses are paid, why in times of sudden and unusual difficulty extra volunteer help should not be both offered and accepted. To help heartily for a month or two is very different from taking the routine work as an unpaid profession. In fact it may fairly be doubted if the whole benefit of the help in the cholera wards would have remained, had volunteer nurses been quite *en règle* in the hospitals. Their presence was *then* all the more valuable because no one could take it quite as a matter of course; half the good they did (and it would be difficult to say *how* much this was) in cheering and encouraging every one, was due to the fact that neither the patients, the medical officers, nor the regular nurses were accustomed to their presence; the stimulus was felt the more from its being a novelty.

Briefly recapitulating, in conclusion, the opinions now expressed, it is contended: –

1. That hospital nursing can be very well done by women of the lower middle class.

2. That the payment necessary to secure the services of appropriate people need not exceed 50*l*. a year for the head nurses, 21*l*. a year for the under nurses, with board and residence.

3. That each head nurse thus paid could, if the size and arrangement of the wards permitted it, attend to not less than fifty patients, and every under nurse, in ordinary circumstances, to fourteen or fifteen.

4. That the influence of a lady superintendent over the nurses would be exceedingly good, as combining the principal advantage of the volunteer method with the advantages of the present system.

5. That the office of lady superintendent is one which should be held by a trained and qualified person, and that a salary should be given which a lady of the educated class would be glad to take; for instance not less than 150*l*. with board and rooms.

6. That the employment which a general adoption of this plan would open to educated women is too limited to justify its advocates in thinking of nursing as a profession for ladies, in the sense in which the word profession is commonly used. Two hundred such situations represent the maximum number ever likely to be offered, and the probable number would be very much below this.

4

"WOMAN AS AN INVENTOR," *THE NORTH AMERICAN REVIEW*

Matilda Joslyn Gage

Source: Matilda Joslyn Gage, 'Woman as an Inventor', *The North American Review*, Vol. 136, No. 318, May 1883, pp. 478–89

No ASSERTION in reference to woman is more common than that she possesses no inventive or mechanical genius, even the United States census failing to enumerate her among the inventors of the country. But, while such statements are carelessly or ignorantly made, tradition, history, and experience alike prove her possession of these faculties in the highest degree. Although woman's scientific education has been grossly neglected, yet some of the most important inventions of the world are due to her. Hon. Samuel Fisher, while Commissioner of Patents, said: "Any sketch of American inventions would be imperfect which failed to do justice to the part taken by woman" The New York "Times," in an editorial upon woman's inventive genius, says: "The feminine mind is, as a rule, quicker than the masculine mind; takes hints and sees defects which would escape the average man's attention. Women frequently carry the germs of patents in their head, and cause some rude machine to be constructed which serves their purpose. If women would fix their minds on inventions, it is entirely probable that they would distinguish themselves in this line far more than they have done hitherto." The "Scientific American" testifies of the inventions of women for which they solicit patents, that "in their practical character and in their adaptation of means to effect a definite purpose, they fully equal the same number of inventions made by men."

Ancient tradition accords to woman the invention of those arts most necessary to comfort, most conducive to wealth, most promotive of civilization. Man's first needs are food, clothing, and shelter, and to woman tradition assigns their present practical forms. Isis in Egypt, Minerva in Greece, Surawatí in India, the mother of the Incas in Peru, and several empresses of China, have alike been worshiped because of their inventive genius. Diodorus, speaking of the worship paid to olden gods and goddesses, says: "The inventors of things useful and profitable to man's well-being were as a reward of their deserts thus

DOI: 10.4324/9780429321078-5

honored by all men with everlasting remembrance." He adds, that the gods of Egypt were of two characters: first, the supernatural, or purely spiritual gods; second, "most beloved and most worshiped," those human beings who had been of especial benefit to the world, and who after death were enrolled among the gods. Foremost among these secondary gods he places Isis. To her was attributed the invention of bread-making, and the foundation of agriculture; previous to her time the Egyptians lived upon uncooked roots and herbs. She also taught the art of healing and the manufacture of flax, and laid the foundations of Egyptian literature. Down to the time of Galen many medicines bore the name of Isis. So famed were the medicines of Egypt that the prophet Jeremiah mentions them, and Homer sang their praises. The potion Nepenthes, which lulled sorrow, given by Helen to Telemachus, was obtained in Egypt by the wife of a Trojan hero. Isis also invented the art of embalming; through its means the Israelites were enabled to keep their oath to Jacob, and take his body with them when they fled from Egypt, nearly four hundred years afterward.

Athens, a name synonymous with all that is beautiful in art or generous in culture, a city that still holds power over men's hearts, was under the special protection and guidance of the feminine inventor and goddess Minerva, who, as Pallas Athene, was one of the most ancient religious conceptions of the Greeks. Regarded as the inventor of every kind of work usually done by woman, she was equally deemed the originator of agriculture and mechanics; the inventor of all tools of man's handicraft; of musical instruments, and of the arts; of war chariots; of shipbuilding, and the breaking of horses. Ceres not only gave corn to the Greeks, but, under the name of Thesmophoros, was revered as the first law-giver. Letters, attributed to the Muses, look back to a feminine source for their invention. Divination, that art which ruled the actions of heroes and turned the fate of empires, with its sibyls, priestesses, oracles, and books, has come down through history as originating with woman. To the Amazons the javelin, shield, and battle-ax were attributed; even the toils and nets of the hunter are also ascribed to woman.

But, leaving the realm of tradition and half-mythical history, we still find woman accredited with some of the earliest and most useful inventions. That she was the primitive artist is quite universally conceded. To her, as the one to prepare the food, the invention and ornamentation of pottery is ascribed. Among savage races it is still easy to trace the inception and growth of this art in woman's hands. The most ancient Chinese writers accord the invention of spinning to Yao, wife of the fourth emperor, and the discovery of silk to Si-ling-chi, wife of the Emperor Hoang-ti, four thousand years before Christ. This country was long known as Ser, or Serica – the land of silk. Its later name of China originated from Sien Tshan, under which appellation, as goddess of silk-worms, Si-ling-chi is still worshiped. When the word China is spoken, it is in perpetual honor and remembrance of this woman inventor. The unparalleled duration of Chinese civilization and the prosperity of that country are largely due to silk, the secret of which was for ages kept from other nations; and which formed an export of extraordinary value, its weight in gold being paid by Roman emperors for a garment. The culture of the mulberry, the rearing of silk-worms, and the manufacture of silk in various forms, are still the great staple domestic industries of this people, to whom cotton was unknown until within the last eight hundred years.

Aristotle was the first European writer to mention silk, yet it was not until a thousand years after his time that the secret of its manufacture became known to the West. It is now, however, an article of great commercial value to many nations. The worth of its raw material produced in France alone is computed at $32,000,000 yearly, and the profits upon its manufacture at $12,000,000. Gauze was the invention of Pamphile, a woman of Cos, who, shortly after the introduction of silk into Europe, Penelope-like, unraveled its web, re-manufacturing it into a transparent fabric known to Roman ladies as "Coa vestis," and to moderns as coan or gauze. One of the most diaphanous fabrics of the ancient world, familiarly designated as "The Woven Wind," it was yet possessed of sufficient strength to take colors, and bear embroidery of silk and gold thread.

Under the forms of velvet, crape, gauze, satin, foulard, pongee, plush, and lace, silk, largely contributing to the wealth of the world, has shaped the policy of states. As lace, its use dates only from the middle of the eighteenth, century. No other fabric requires such delicate manipulation. Upon the white varieties not even every woman can work, as the breath itself must possess exquisite purity. Those who have what is locally termed the *haleine grasse*, i. e., greasy breath, are compelled to confine themselves to the manufacture of the black varieties.

Silk is possessed of the qualities most sought by manufacturers: delicacy, luster, strength, and a capability of taking any color desired. It is the strongest of all fibers, exceeding that of hemp or flax. By a law of eternal fitness, spinners strive for a thread like a woman's hair, "long, fine, strong, and vibrant." As a source of wealth, lace, equally with silk, has largely influenced state policy. The value of the finest thread lace when wrought in points is enormous, far exceeding that of precious stones. No other art, it is said, is capable of bringing about such an extraordinary increase in value from a material worth as little as flax in the unwrought state. The early records of this art are lost in the mists of antiquity, but there is no doubt that woman was its originator. At the exposition of woman's work in Florence, a few years since, visitors were greatly interested in a specimen of the magnificent lace known as "Puleto di Venezia" (Venetian Point). Its stitch, lost since the thirteenth century, has recently been rediscovered by Madame Bessani, a humble workwoman, to whom the Italian Minister of Commerce accorded letters patent, with exclusive control of her discovery for fifteen years. The importance of Madame Bessani's invention to Italy is incalculable, opening to that country an immense source of revenue and political power.

Pillow-lace making, which brought this elegant addition to the toilet within the reach of all, was the invention of Barbara Uttmann, of Saxony, at a period when that country was on the verge of financial ruin. The art spread with great rapidity, and Belgium soon derived an immense revenue from it; and although three hundred years have since elapsed, lace still continues to be its great source of wealth. Nor has its influence upon other countries been less beneficial: not only did wealth accrue to England through its introduction there, but a great moral change for the better soon appeared as one of its effects.

To Mheural Nisa, best known to English-speaking peoples through Moore's "Light of the Harem" as Nourmahal, is the world indebted for its priceless Cashmere shawls, the manufacture of which gives employment to thousands of men and women, and forms one of the principal sources of revenue in India. To her, also, we owe that most exquisite and costly perfume, Attar, or more properly, Atyr of Roses. Her husband, the great conqueror Jerunzebe, most passionately attached to her, through his love, and for the benefits she had conferred upon her country, caused her name and the title "Light of the World" to be struck on the coins of India. He built to her memory that fairy temple on the banks of the Jumna known as the Taj Mahal, which travelers vie in describing as all that is most light, graceful, exquisite, and picturesque in architecture. With Kamejo, a woman worker in bronze, the decorations in relief, so much used by Japanese artists, originated. Wood-engraving, the pioneer of all other forms of engraving, was the invention of the Cunio children, twin sister and brother, at Ravenna, Italy, in the thirteenth century. The discovery of cotton as a textile fiber, ascribed in the East to Semiramis, was in America attributed to the mother of the Incas, who taught the Peruvians its manufacture. The Caftan, or Eastern robe of honor, also known as "Semiramis's Gown," was ascribed to that Eastern heroine, – an invention for the purpose of concealing her sex when journeying to meet her husband. The right to wear this garment has for ages belonged only to potentates. It was one of the emblems of exalted rank chosen by Haman, when consulted by Ahasuerus as to the marks of distinction to be shown "the man whom the king delighted to honor."

The straw industry of the United States owes its origin to Miss Betsy Metcalf, who, in 1798, made the first straw bonnet[1] ever manufactured in this country. Within twelve years thereafter the State of Massachusetts alone produced half a million dollars' worth of straw goods. That State now produces six million hats and bonnets annually; a great deal of straw is also manufactured in other States.

The most remarkable invention of the age, in its industrial, social, and political influence, – the cotton-gin, – owes its origin to a woman, Catharine Littlefield Greene, widow of General Greene, of Revolutionary memory, with whom the idea originated. The cotton-gin heads the list of sixteen remarkable American inventions that have been adopted by the world.

After the close of the war General Greene settled in Georgia, where he soon died. The great difficulty of separating the seed from the cotton was at that time the staple subject of conversation among planters. To separate a pound of the black seed from the lint was a day's task for a negro. The white variety, much more valuable, from its greater tenacity, was scarcely at all cultivated. It was the regular custom of the planter's family to unite in this work every evening, and a fortune was prophesied for the person who should construct a machine capable of doing the work. After a conversation of this character between some guests at her house, Mrs. Greene conceived the idea of such a machine, and intrusted its construction to the hands of Eli Whitney, then boarding with her, who possessed the usual New England facility in the use of tools. The wooden teeth at first tried not doing their work well, Mr. Whitney wished to abandon the machine altogether; but Mrs. Greene, whose faith in ultimate success never wavered, would not consent; she suggested the substitution of wire. Within ten days from the first conception of Mrs. Greene's ideas, a small model was completed, so perfect in its construction that all succeeding gins have been based upon it.

This invention produced an extraordinary increase in the culture of cotton. Instead of the single pound cleaned by hand, three hundred pounds were now daily separated from the lint at the same cost. Not only did the languishing industries of the South receive a sudden and stable impetus, but every part of the world felt the influence of this woman's idea. It may be asked why Mrs. Greene, then a widow, did not take out the patent in her own name; but to have done so would have exposed her to the ridicule and contumely of her friends and a loss of position in society, which frowned upon any attempt at outside industry for woman. Through her second husband, Mr. Miller, she afterward assumed a subordinate interest in it.

A very slight investigation proves that patents taken out in some man's name are, in many instances, due to women. A recent noted instance of this kind is Miss Louise McLaughlin's invention of underglaze painting on pottery. Miss McLaughlin, desiring that all artists should share in its benefits, explained her process to every person who asked her, and even wrote a book giving this information. But a certain man, seeing its value, took out a patent upon it, thus prohibiting even its inventor from using the fruit of her own brains. The Burden horse-shoe machine, turning out a complete shoe every three seconds, was a woman's invention. At a renewal of the patent, in 1871, it was claimed that thirty-two million dollars had been saved to the public during the fourteen years of its use.

A third great American invention, the mower and reaper, owes its early perfection to Mrs. Ann Harned Manning,[2] of Plainfield, New Jersey, who, in 1817–18, perfected a system for the combined action of teeth and cutters, patented by her husband, William Henry Manning, as "a device for the combined action of teeth and cutters, whether in a transverse or revolving direction." Mrs. Manning also made other improvements, of which, not having been patented, she was robbed after her husband's death by a neighbor whose name appears in the list of patentees upon this machine. Mrs. Manning also invented a clover cleaner, which proved very lucrative to her husband, who took out the patent. Nor was she the only woman whose thought has been turned toward agricultural machines. The name of Elizabeth Smith, also of New Jersey, appears in 1861 among the list of patentees upon an improvement to the mower and reaper, whereby the knives could be adjusted while the machine was in motion.

The smallest inventions sometimes prove the most lucrative. A San Francisco lady, inventor of a baby carriage, received fourteen thousand dollars for her patent. The paper pail, the invention of a Chicago lady, yields a large income. The gimlet- pointed screw, the idea of a little girl, has realized millions of dollars to its patentee.

Among recent inventions of importance by women, are a spinning machine, capable of running from twelve to forty threads; a rotary loom, doing three times the work of an ordinary loom; a volcanic furnace for smelting ore; an improved wood-sawing machine; a space-saving clothes-mangle; a chain elevator; screw-crank for steamships; a fire-escape; a device for correct pen-holding, invaluable in schools; a wool feeder and weigher, one of the most delicate machines ever invented, and of incalculable benefit to every woolen manufacturer; a self-fastening button; a portable reservoir for use in case of fires; a process for burning petroleum in place of wood and coal for steam generating purposes; an improvement in spark-arresters, to be applied to locomotives; a danger-signal for street-crossings on railways; a plan for beating cars without fire; a lubricating felt for subduing friction[3] (the last five all bearing upon railroad travel); a rapid change box, a marvel of simplicity and convenience, invaluable at railway stations and ferries, the invention of a girl of sixteen; syllable type with adjustable cases and apparatus; machine for trimming pamphlets; writing-machine; signal rocket, used in the navy; deep-sea telescope; method of deadening sound on elevated railways; smoke-burner; satchel-bottom bags; bag-folding machine, etc., etc. Many improvements in sewing machines have been made by women; as a device for sewing sails and heavy cloth; quilting attachments: the magic ruffler; threading a machine when upon a full run (an idea scouted by male machinists); an adaptation of machines for sewing leather, etc. This last was the invention of a practical woman machinist, who for many years carried on a large harness manufactory in New York City.

Systems for improved drainage; for better ventilation; for forcing water to great heights and distances; a thousand household appliances, etc., are the fruits of woman's inventive genius; but they must be passed by, as this paper is designed simply to attract public attention toward a subject upon which much ignorance and misapprehension exist.

The deep-sea telescope, invented by Mrs. Mather, and improved by her daughter, is a unique and important invention, bringing the bottom of the largest ships to view without the expense of raising them into a dry-dock. By its means wrecks can be inspected, obstructions to navigation removed, torpedoes successfully sought for, and immense sums annually saved to the marine service.

A machine which, for its complicated mechanism and extraordinary ingenuity, has attracted much attention both in this country and Europe, is that for the manufacture of satchel-bottom paper bags. Many men of mechanical genius long directed their attention to this problem without success. Miss Maggie Knight, to whose genius this machine is due, received a compliment from the Commissioner of Patents upon its entire originality. Most inventions are but an improvement upon some preceding one. She refused fifty thousand dollars for it shortly after taking out her patent. Miss Knight has since invented a machine doing the work of thirty persons in folding bags, and herself superintended the erection of the machinery at Amherst, Mass. The Eureka street-sweeper, the invention of a Hoboken lady, owes its origin to the fact of this lady's dress having been spattered with mud by a clumsy machine one day in New York. Possessed of a mechanical genius, she determined to try her hand upon a sweeper that should do its work more perfectly. Her success was great, and her invention a vast improvement upon all its predecessors.

The remarkable invention of Mrs. Mary E. Walton, for deadening the noise of elevated railroads, has occasioned much comment. Edison and other inventors had for six months unsuccessfully striven to accomplish this end, when Mrs. Walton brought forward a device which was at once adopted by the Metropolitan and other elevated railways. The benefit to human health and life likely to accrue from this invention can scarcely be realized. The evil effects of persistent noise upon the human system are very great, and an invention tending to lessen its force confers a benefit upon mankind. A prominent New York physician says: "We see very little of the gentle decline of old age in New York City. The constant din of travel and traffic, borne for a time without evidence of injury, suddenly shows itself in a shattered nervous system and imminence of dissolution." Since her noise-deadener, Mrs. Walton has taken out, both in this country and England, a patent for a smoke-burner, that she considers much more valuable. By this device all smoke from a fire, furnace, or locomotive is consumed, as also the dust caused by railway trains, and the offensive, unhealthful odors emitted from factories, gas-works, etc. When in England, Mrs. Walton received the congratulations of British officials for it, as one of the greatest inventions of the age.

While passing by woman's discovery in science, where the names of Hypatia, Maria Agnesi, and Caroline Herschel shine, mention must still be made of the aquarium, the invention of Madam Jeanette Power, one of the most eminent naturalists of the century. It was used by her in making curious scientific discoveries. The value of the aquarium to marine zoology is incalculable. Not only can rare species from the Indian, Arctic, and Pacific oceans be brought into close comparison, but the subject of embryology can be studied, and the great Darwinian problems of evolution and permanence of type are likely to be solved by its instrumentality.

Medicine, even in modern times, owes much to woman. It was to her knowledge of this art that woman's persecution for witchcraft in the middle ages was largely due. Through Madame de Coudray's invention of the manikin, a knowledge of physiology has been much more widely diffused than would otherwise have been possible. Many delicate and important surgical instruments owe their origin to woman, as also the adaptation of wax for recording medical observations. Dr. Hunter was indebted for the illustrations of his greatest work to the observations of a woman preserved in wax.[4]

Chemistry offers an infinite resource to the inventor in a field whose exploration has scarcely begun. A Prussian governess recently invented a new fulminate for needle-gun cartridges, and the Government is experimenting with it with a view to its purchase. From this lucrative field woman is largely debarred through that prejudice and injustice which still deprives her of full opportunities for scientific education.[5]

But among woman inventors the name of the celebrated sculptor, Harriet Hosmer, must not be passed by. Miss Hosmer has succeeded in producing marble from limestone, closely simulating the finest antique varieties. This process had long been unsuccessfully sought by the Italian Government. But her most valuable invention is that of the permanent magnet as a motive power. Scientific men and practical machinists deem this one of the most important inventions of the century, and its influence upon the world as likely to be far-reaching and extraordinary. No such power was known to inhere in the permanent magnet until Miss Hosmer's discovery, to which she gave fifteen years of study and experiment.

The national value of patents, and the relation of invention to civilization, are subjects that receive marked attention both in England and the United States. A paper upon the latter topic, read in London, in 1881, before the Society of Engineers, forcibly represented the loss sustained by the nation through the obstacles placed in the way of inventors, upon whose genius, this paper claimed, England was dependent for holding her place among the nations.

The inventions of a nation are closely connected with the freedom of its people. During the reign of George III. the average yearly number of patents taken out in Great Britain was but fourteen. At present the average is five thousand, while in the United States it is eighteen thousand. This difference is directly traceable to the progress of freedom and education. While, as has been shown, many of the world's most important inventions are due to woman, the proportion of feminine inventors is much less than of masculine, which arises from the fact that woman does not possess the same amount of freedom as man. Restricted in education, industrial opportunities, and political power, this is one of many instances where her degradation reacts injuriously upon the race. The majority of inventions are the result of much consideration and self-reliant thought. Inventors must not only possess full freedom to exercise their powers, but there must also be a certain welcome and protection to their ideas. Deprived, as woman is, of political power, she has to face contempt of her sex, open and covert scorn of womanhood, depreciatory allusions to her intellectual powers, – all tending to hamper the expression of her inventive genius.

Nor is woman by law recognized as possessing full right to the use and control of her own powers. In not a single State of the Union is a married woman held to possess a right to her earnings within the family; and in not one-half of them has she a right to their control in business entered upon outside of the household. Should such a woman be successful in obtaining a patent, what then? Would she be free to do as she pleased with it? Not at all. She would hold no right, title, or power over this work of her own brain. She would possess no legal right to contract, or to license any one to use her invention. Neither, should her right be infringed, could she sue the offender. Her husband could take out the patent in his own name, sell her invention for his own sole benefit, give it away if he so chose, or refrain from using it, and for all this she would have no remedy.

It is scarcely thirty years since the first State protected a married woman in the use of her own brain property. Under these conditions, legally incapable of holding property, and trained, as she has been, to seclusion, dependence, and abeyance of thought, that woman has not been an inventor to an equal extent with man is not so much a subject of surprise as that she should have invented at all.

While every invention, however small, develops new industries, provides work for a multitude of people, increases commercial activity, adds to the revenues of the world, and renders life more desirable, great inventions broaden the boundaries of human thought, bring about social, religious, and political changes, hurrying mankind on to a new civilization. Lecky forcibly shows the loss to the world from the celibacy and martyrdom of the best human element in the past. No less is the darkness of the world kept more dense, and its civilization retarded, by all forms of thought, customs of society, or systems of law which prevent the full development and exercise of woman's inventive powers.

NOTES

1 The Rhode Island Society for the Encouragement of Domestic Industry possesses a *facsimile* of Miss Metcalf's original bonnet. It was woven of seven straws.

2 Sister of Mrs. Clemence S. Lozier, M. D., Dean of the Women's Homeopathic College in New York.

3 Took the first prize at the fair of the American Institute.

4 Mademoiselle Biheron.

5 A lady who won the chemical prize at the University of Edinburgh, over 240 competitors, was not permitted to receive it on account of her sex.

5

"THE WOMAN QUESTION," *WESTMINSTER REVIEW*

Eleanor Marx Aveling and Edward Bibbins Aveling

Source: Eleanor Marx Aveling and Edward Bibbins Aveling, 'The Woman Question', *Westminster Review*, Vol. 125, January 1886. pp. 207–22

The publication of August Bebel's *Woman – Past, Present and Future* and the issue of a translation of the work in English, make any attempt to explain the position of Socialists in respect to the woman question timely. The reception that the work has met with in Germany and in England renders such an attempt imperative, unless our antagonists are willing to misunderstand us, and we are willing to remain passive under the misunderstanding. The writers of this article have thought that the English public, with that fairness which is said to be its special prerogative, would give hearing to the views, the arguments, the conclusions of those who call themselves Socialists. Thus, whatever opinions may be held by that English public as to the conclusions, its opinions will at least have a basis of knowledge. And the writers have further considered that the treatment of such a question as this is as its best when it is that of a man and a woman thinking and working together. In all that follows they desire it to be understood that they are giving utterance to their own opinions as two individual Socialists. Whilst they believe that these opinions are shared by the majority of their fellow-thinkers and fellow-workers in England, on the Continent, and in America, they are in no sense to be understood as pledging their Party to all, or necessarily to any particular one, of the propositions put forward . . . .

The truth, not fully recognised even by those anxious to do good to woman, is that she, like the labour-classes, is in an oppressed condition; that her position, like theirs, is one of merciless degradation. Women are the creatures of an organised tyranny of men, as the workers are the creatures of an organised tyranny of idlers. Even where this much is grasped, we must never be weary of insisting on the nonunderstanding that for women, as for the labouring classes, no solution of the difficulties and problems that present themselves is really possible in the present condition of society. All that is done, heralded with no matter what flourish of trumpets, is palliative, not remedial. Both the oppressed classes, women and the

 DOI: 10.4324/9780429321078-6

immediate producers, must understand that their emancipation will come from themselves. Women will find allies in the better sort of men, as the labourers are finding allies among the philosophers, artists, and poets. But the one has nothing to hope from man as a whole, and the other has nothing to hope from the middle class as a whole.

The truth of this comes out in the fact that, before we pass to the consideration of the condition of women, we have to speak this word of warning. To many, that which we have to say of the Now will seem exaggerated; much that we have to say of the Hereafter, visionary, and perhaps all that is said, dangerous. To cultured people, public opinion is still that of man alone, and the customary is the moral. The majority still lays stress upon the occasional sex-helplessness of woman as a bar to her even consideration with man. It still descants upon the *natural calling* of the female. As to the former, people forget that sex-helplessness at certain times is largely exaggerated by the unhealthy conditions of our modern life, if, indeed, it is not wholly due to these. Given rational conditions, it would largely, if not completely, disappear. They forget also that all this about which the talk is so glib when women's freedom is under discussion is conveniently ignored when the question is one of women's enslavement. They forget that by capitalist employers this very sex-helplessness of woman is only taken into account with the view of lowering the general rate of wages. Again, there is no more a *natural calling* of woman than there is a natural law of capitalistic production, or a *natural* limit to the amount of the labourer's product that goes to him for means of subsistence. That in the first case, woman's *calling* is supposed to be only the tending of children, the maintenance of household conditions, and a general obedience to her lord; that, in the second, the production of surplus value is a necessary preliminary to the production of capital; that, in the third, the amount the labourer receives for his means of subsistence is so much as will keep him only just above starvation point: these are not natural laws in the same sense as are the laws of motion. They are only certain temporary conventions of society, like the convention that French is the language of diplomacy.

To treat the position of women at the present time in detail is to repeat a thousand-times-told tale. Yet, for our purpose, we must re-emphasise some familiar points, and perhaps mention one or two less familiar. And first, a general idea that has to do with all women. The life of woman does not coincide with that of man. Their lives do not intersect; in many cases do not even touch. Hence the life of the race is stunted. According to Kant, "a man and woman constitute, when united, the whole and entire being; one sex completes the other." But when each sex is incomplete, and the one incomplete to the most lamentable extent, and when, as a rule, neither of them comes into real, thorough, habitual, free contact, mind to mind, with the other, the being is neither whole nor entire . . . .

Whether we consider women as a whole, or only that sad sisterhood wearing upon its melancholy brews the stamp of eternal virginity, we find alike a want of ideas and of ideals. The reason of this is again the economic position of dependency upon man. Women, once more like the labourers, have been expropriated as to their rights as human beings, just as the labourers were expropriated as to their rights as producers. The method in each case is the only one that makes expropriation at any time and under any circumstances possible – and that method is force.

In Germany at the present day the woman is a minor with regard to man. A husband of *low estate* may chastise a wife. All decisions as to the children rest with him, even to the fixing of the date of weanings. Whatever fortune the wife may have he manages. She may not enter into agreements without his consent; she may not take part in political associations. It is unnecessary for us to point out how much better, within the last few years, these things have been managed in England, or to remind our readers that the recent changes were due to the action of women themselves. But it is necessary to remind them that with all these added civil rights English women, married and unmarried alike, are morally dependent on man, and are badly treated by him. The position is little better in other civilised lands, with the strange exception of Russia, where women are socially more free than in any other part of Europe. In France, the women of the upper middle class are more unhappily situated than in England. Those of the lower middle and working-classes are better off than either in England or Germany. But two consecutive paragraphs in the *Code Civil*, 340 and 341, show that injustice to women is not only Teutonic. *La recherche de la paternité est interdité* and *La recherche de la maternité est admise.*

Every one who refuses to blink facts knows that Demosthenes words of the Athenians are true of our English middle and upper classes today, "We marry in order to obtain legitimate children and a faithful warder of the house; we keep concubines as servants for our daily attendance, but we seek the Hetairai for love's delight." The wife is still the child-bearer, the housewarder. The husband lives and loves according to his own bad pleasure. Even those who admit this will possibly join issue with us when we suggest as another wrong to women the rigorous social rule that from man only must come the first proffer of affection, the proposal for marriage. This may be on the principle of compensation. After marriage the proffers come generally from the woman, and the reserve is the man's. That this is no natural law our Shakespeare has shown. Miranda, untrammelled by society, tenders herself to Ferdinand. "I am your wife if you will marry me: if not I'll die your maid;" and Helena, in *All's Well that Ends Well*, with her love for Bertram, that carries her from Rousillon to Paris and Florence, is, as Coleridge has it, *Shakespeare's loveliest character.*

We have said that marriage is based upon commercialism. It is a barter transaction in many cases, and in all, under the condition of things today, the question of ways and means plays of necessity a large part. Among the upper classes the business is carried on quite unblushingly. The Sir Gorgius Midas pictures in *Punch* testify to this. The nature of the periodical in which they appear reminds us that all the horrors they reveal are only regarded as foibles, not as sins. In the lower middle class many a man denies himself the joy of home life until he grows out of the longing for it; many a woman closes the book of her life at its fairest page for ever, because of the dread *rerum angustarum domi* [*of the narrow confines of domestic life*]. . . .

All this tells far more on the women than on the men. Society provides, recognises, legalises for the latter the means of gratifying the sex instinct. In the eyes of that same society an unmarried woman who acts after the fashion habitual to her unmarried brothers and the men that dance with her at balls, or work with her in the shop, is a pariah. And even with the working classes who marry at the normal time, the life of the woman under the present system is the more arduous and irksome of the two. The old promise of the legend, *in sorrow shalt thou bring forth children,* is not only realised, but extended. She has to bring them up through long years, unrelieved by rest, unbrightened by hope, in the same atmosphere of perennial labour and sorrow. The man, worn out as he may be by labour, has the evening in which to do nothing. The woman is occupied until bedtime comes. Often with young children her toil goes far into, or all through, the night.

When marriage has taken place all is in favour of the one and is adverse to the other. Some wonder that John Stuart Mill wrote, *Marriage is at the present day the only actual form of serfdom recognised by law.* The wonder to us is that he never saw this serfdom as a question, not of sentiment, but of economics, the result of our capitalistic system. After marriage, as before, the woman is under restraint, and the man is not. Adultery in her is a crime, in him a venial offence. He can obtain a divorce, she cannot, on the ground of adultery. She must prove that *cruelty* (i. e. of a physical kind) has been shown. Marriages thus arranged, thus carried out, with such an attendant train of circumstances and of consequences, seem to us – let us say it with all deliberation – worse than prostitution. To call them sacred or moral is a desecration . . . .

Many advanced thinkers plead for greater facility of divorce now. They contend that divorce ought to be made at least as easy as marriage; that an engagement entered into by people who have had little or no opportunity of knowing one another ought not to be irrevocably, or even stringently binding; that incompatibility of temper, non-realisation of deep-rooted hopes, actual dislike, should be sufficient grounds for separation; finally, and most important of all, that the conditions of divorce should be the same for the two sexes. All this is excellent, and would be not only feasible but just, if – but mark the if – the economic positions of the two sexes were the same. They are not the same. Hence, whilst agreeing with every one of these ideas theoretically, we believe that they would, practically applied under our present system, result, in the majority of cases, in yet further injustice to women. The man would be able to take advantage of them; the woman would not, except in the rare instances where she had private property or some means of livelihood. The annulling of the union would be to him freedom; to her, starvation for herself and her children.

We may be asked, will these same principles of divorce hold under the socialistic regime? Our answer is this-the union between men and women, to be explained in the sequel, will be seen to be of such a nature as wholly to obviate the necessity of divorce . . . .

With the false shame and false secrecy, against which we protest, goes the unhealthy separation of the sexes that begins as children quit the nursery, and only ends when the dead men and women are laid in the common earth. In the *Story of an African Farm*, the girl Lyndall cries out, "We were equals once, when we lay new-born babies on our nurses' knees. We shall be equals again when they tie up our jaws for the last sleep." In the schools this separation is carried out, and even in some churches the system, with all its suggestiveness, is in vogue. Its worst form is, of course, in the non-human institutions called monasteries and nunneries. But all the less virulent forms of the same evil are, only in less degree, non-human.

In ordinary society even, the restrictions laid upon the intercourse of the sexes are, like repressive measures with school-boys, the source of much mischief. These restrictions are especially dangerous in regard to conversational subjects. Every man sees the consequence of this, though he may not know it as a consequence, in the kind of talk that goes on in the smoking-rooms of middle and upper class society. Only when men and women pure-minded, or, at least, striving after purity, discuss the sexual question in all its bearings, as free human beings, looking frankly into each other's faces, will there be any hope of its solution. With this, as we are constantly iterating, must go the understanding that the basis of the whole matter is economic. Mary Wollstonecraft, in the *Rights of Woman*, taught, in part, this commingling of the sexes, instead of the separation of them throughout life. She demanded that women should have equal educational advantages, should be educated in the same schools and colleges with men; that from infancy to adult age the two should be trained side by side . . . .

It is time for men and women to recognise that the slaying of sex is always followed by disaster. Extreme passion is ill. But the opposite extreme of the sacrifice of healthy natural instinct is as ill. *They that are in extremity of either are abominable fellows*, is as true in this connection as of melancholy and over-mirth when Rosalind railed at them in the Forest of Arden. And yet thousands of women pass, through what hell-fires they only know, to the Moloch of our social system; thousands of women are defrauded, month after month, year after year, of *their unreturning Maytime*. Hence we – and with us, in this, at all events, most Socialists – contend that chastity is unhealthy and unholy. Always understanding by chastity the entire suppression of all instincts connected with the begetting of children, we regard chastity as a crime. As with all crimes, the criminal is not the individual sufferer, but the society that forces her to sin and to suffer. Here we are at one with Shelley. In his Notes to *Queen Mab* we have the following passage: – "Chastity is a monkish and evangelical superstition, a greater foe to natural temperance even than unintellectual sensuality; for it strikes at the root of all domestic happiness, and consigns more than half of the human race to misery, that some few may monopolise according to law." Finally, in this most important connexion, we call to mind the accumulated medical testimony to the fact that women suffer more than men under these restraints.

Our other point, before we pass to the concluding portion of this article, is that necessary result of our today system – prostitution. This evil is, as we have said, recognised, and it is legalised, in some European countries. All that we need add here is the truism that its chief supporters are of the middle class. The aristocracy are not, of course, excepted; but the mainstay of the hideous system is the respectable, well-to-do, most *seeming-virtuous* capitalist. This is not due only to the great accumulation of wealth and the consequent habits of luxury. The significant fact is that in a society based upon capital, whose centre is therefore the capitalistic middle class, prostitution, one of the worst outcomes of that society, is supported chiefly by that very class. This points clearly the moral that once again, under a new form, we urge. That which might be said on the special cases which the *Pall Mall Gazette* has made familiar to us applies to prostitution generally. To get rid of prostitution, we must get rid of the social conditions that are its parent. Midnight meetings, refuges for the distressed, all the well-meant attempts to grapple with this awful problem are, as their initiators despairingly admit, futile. And futile they will remain as long as the system of production lasts which, creating a surplus labour-population, creates with this, criminal men, and women that are very literally and sadly *abandoned*. Get rid of this, the capitalistic system of production, say the Socialists, and prostitution will pass away.

This leads us to our last point. What is it that we as Socialists desire? What is it that we expect? What is that of whose coming we feel as assured as of the rising of tomorrow's sun? What are the evolution changes in society that we believe are already close at hand? And what are the changes in the condition of woman that we anticipate as consequence of these? Let us disclaim all intention of the prophetic. He that, reasoning on a series of observed phenomena, sees the inevitable event to which they lead is no prophet. A man cannot prophesy any more than he has a right to wager, about a certainty. To us it seems clear that as in England the Germanic society, whose basis was the free landholder, gave way to the feudal system, and this to the capitalistic, so this last, no more eternal than its predecessors, will give way to the Socialistic system; that as slavery passed into serfdom, and serfdom into the wage-slavery Of today, so this last will pass into the condition where all the means of production will belong neither to slave-owner, nor to serf's lord, nor to the wage-slave's master, the capitalist, but to the community as a whole. At the risk of raising the habitual smile and sneer, we confess that into every detail of that Socialistic working of society we are no more prepared to enter than were the first capitalists to enter into the details of the system that they founded. Nothing is more common, nothing is more unjust, nothing is more indicative of meagre understanding, than the vulgar clamour for exact details of things under the social condition towards which we believe the world is moving. No expounder of any new great truth, no one of his followers, can hope to work out all the truth into its ultimate ramifications. That would have been thought of those who rejected the gravitation discovery of Newton because he had not, by application of it, found out Neptune? Or of those who rejected the Darwinian theory of Natural Selection because instinct presented certain difficulties? Yet this is precisely what the average opponents of Socialism do; always with a vacuous calmness, ignoring the fact that for every difficulty or misery they suppose will arise from the socialisation of the means of production a score worse are actually existent in the putrescent society of today.

What is it that we feel certain is coming? We have wandered so far from Bebel along our own lines of thought, at the entrance of whose ways his suggestive work has generally placed us, that for the answer to this question we return gladly and gratefully to him, "A society in which all the means of production are the property of the community, a society which recognises the full equality of all without distinction of sex, which provides for the application of every kind of technical and scientific improvement or discovery, which enrolls as workers all those who are at present unproductive, or whose activity assumes an injurious shape, the idlers and the drones, and which, while it minimises the period of labour necessary for its support, raises the mental and physical condition of all its members to the highest attainable pitch."

We disguise neither from ourselves nor from our antagonists that the first step to this is the expropriation of all private property in land and in all other means of production. With this would happen the abolition of the State as it now is. No confusion as to our aims is more common than that which leads woolly thinking people to imagine that the changes we desire can be brought about, and the conditions subsequent upon them can exist, under a State regime such as that of today. The State is now a force-organisation for the maintenance of the present conditions of property and of social rule. Its representatives are a few middle and upper class men contending for places yielding abnormal salaries. The State under Socialism, if indeed a word of such ugly historical associations is retained will be the organised capacity of a community of workers. Its officials will be no better and no worse off than their fellows. The divorce between art and labour, the antagonism between head and hand work, that grieves the souls of artists, without their knowing in most cases the economic cause of their grief, will vanish.

And now comes the question as to how the future position of woman, and therefore of the race, will be affected by all this. Of one or two things we may be very sure. Others the evolution of society alone will decide positively, though every one of us may have his own idea upon each particular point. Clearly there will be equality for all, without distinction of sex. Thus, woman will be independent: her education and all other opportunities as those of man. Like him, she, if sound in mind and body (and how the number of women thus will grow!) will have to give her one, two, or three hours of social labour to supply the wants of the community, and therefore of herself. Thereafter she will be free for art or science, or teaching or writing, or amusement in any form. Prostitution will have vanished with the economic conditions that made it, and make it at this hour, a necessity.

Whether monogamy or polygamy will obtain in the Socialistic state is a detail on which one can only speak as an individual. The question is too large to be solved within the mists and miasmata of the capitalistic system. Personally, we believe that monogamy will gain the day. There are approximately equal numbers of men and women, and the highest ideal seems to be the complete, harmonious, lasting blending of two human lives. Such an ideal, almost never attainable today, needs at least four things. These are love, respect, intellectual likeness, and command of the necessities of life. Each of these four is far more possible under the system towards which we move than under that in which we now *have our being*. The last is absolutely ensured to all. As Ibsen makes Helmer say to Nora, "Home life ceases to be free and beautiful directly its foundations are borrowing and debts." But borrowing and debts, when one is a member of community, and not an isolated man fighting for his own hand, can never come. Intellectual likeness. The same education for men and women; the bringing up of these twain side by side, until they join hands at last, will ensure a greater degree of this. That objectionable product of capitalism, Tennyson's *In Memoriam* young woman, with her "I cannot understand, I love," will be a myth. Every one will have learnt that there can be no love without understanding. And the love and respect that are wanting, or are lost today, because of sins and shortcomings, the product of the commercial system of society, will be more easily forthcoming, and vanish almost never. The contract between man and woman will be of a purely private nature, without the intervention of any public functionary. The woman will no longer be the man's slave, but his equal. For divorce there will be no need.

And whether we are right or not in regarding monogamy as the best form of society, we may be sure that the best form will be chosen, and that by wisdoms riper and richer than ours. We may be equally sure that the choice will not be the barter-marriages, with its one-sided polygamy, of our own sad time. Above all, we may be sure, that two great curses that help, with others, to ruin the relations between man and woman will have passed. Those curses are the treatment of men and women as different beings, and the want of truth. There will no longer be one law for the woman and one for the man. If the coming society, like European society today, regards it as right for man to have mistresses as well as wife, we may be certain that the like freedom will be extended to women. Nor will there be the hideous disguise, the constant lying that makes the domestic life of almost all our English homes an organised hypocrisy. Whatever the matured and deliberate opinion of the community finds best will be carried out fairly, openly. Husband and wife will be able to do that which but few can do now-look clear through one another's eyes into one another's hearts. For ourselves, we believe that the cleaving of one man to one woman will be best for all, and that these will find each in the heart of the other, that which is in the eyes, their own image.

6

"THE ECONOMIC POSITION OF EDUCATED WORKING WOMEN," *EDUCATED WORKING WOMEN: ESSAYS ON THE ECONOMIC POSITION OF WOMEN WORKERS IN THE MIDDLE CLASSES*

Clara E. Collet

Source: Clara E. Collet, 'The Economic Position of Educated Working Women' (February 1890), in *Educated Working Women: Essays on the Economic Position of Women Workers in the Middle Classes* (London, P.S. King & Son, 1902), pp. 1–26

"*Because, precisely, I'm an artist, sir,*
And woman, if another sate in sight,
I'd whisper, – Soft, my sister! not a word!
By speaking we prove only we can speak,
Which he, the man here, never doubted. What
He doubts is, whether we can DO *the thing*
With decent grace, we've not yet done at all.
Now, do it; bring your statue, – you have room!
He'll see it even by the starlight here;
And if' tis e'er so little like the god
Who looks out from the marble silently
Along the track of his own shining dart
Through the dusk of ages, there's no need to speak;
The universe shall henceforth speak for you,
And witness, 'She who did this thing, was born
To do it, – claims her license in her work.'
And so with more works. Whoso cures the plague,
Though twice a woman, shall be called a leech:
Who rights a land's finances is excused
For touching copper, though her hands be white, –

 DOI: 10.4324/9780429321078-7

But we, we talk!"
"It is the age's mood"
He said; "we boast, and do not."

E. B. BROWNING. – "Aurora Leigh," Book viii

MRS. BROWNING's advice to women, much needed as it is at the present time, was somewhat harsh and unpractical at the time she gave it, more than thirty years ago. At that time it would not have been possible for a woman "to prove herself a leech and cure the plague"; for on the one hand she was debarred from obtaining the necessary qualifications, and on the other she was prohibited from practising without them. The hospitals and lecture rooms were closed to her by prejudice, and practice was therefore forbidden her by Act of Parliament. Even had she obtained admittance to the dissecting room and hospital by quiet perseverance and tried ability, she could not have hoped by such means alone to remove the obstacles which were placed in her path by legislation. The charters necessary to empower the Universities to confer degrees on women could never have been obtained, except through determined agitation; and if the agitators themselves did not seem competent to exercise the powers which they wished conferred on women, they performed the work for which they *were* most competent and made the path clear for those who could not have removed the obstacles themselves. The poet and the novelist had no such difficulties to contend with. Such women had no greater hardships to endure than men. If men disbelieved that a woman could write a powerful novel, she had only to do it to convince them of the contrary. But, generally speaking, women were prohibited from doing what they could, on the ground that they could not if they would. It was not universally so; in many cases girls who showed mathematical or logical power, for instance, were discouraged from exercising it, because reasoning power was considered undesirable in women and likely to hinder their chances of marriage. But, on the whole, women's incapacity for intellectual work was put forward as a reason for forbidding them to attempt it. The futility of forbidding women to do what they were incapable of doing was never perceived by the opponents of the movement for the higher education of women, who based their opposition on this ground. Nor did it avail much to point this out. Behind this asserted disbelief in the power of the educated woman to compete even with the average schoolboy, lay a real conviction, that if she could do so successfully, the more desirable it was to prevent her having the chance of proving it. It is on record that in the days of King Ahasuerus, more than 2,000 years ago, great terror was excited lest "the deed of Vashti should come abroad unto all women, so that they should despise their husbands in their eyes, when it should be reported that the King Ahasuerus commanded Vashti, the queen, to be brought in before him, but she came not. And in order that all wives should give to their husbands honour, both to great and small, Ahasuerus sent letters into all the King's provinces, that every man should bear rule in his own house." As in the days of King Ahasuerus, so thirty years ago it was felt that humility in women should be cultivated at all costs, and if they became aware that all men were not necessarily their intellectual superiors they would break out into open revolt. Women had been told that they should obey their husbands because the latter knew best. If that were denied, the claim to obedience would have to rest on the possession of might instead of right.

This reiterated assertion of their inferiority has rankled in women's hearts. For the last forty years it has been the source of most of the bitterness expressed openly on the platform, and the cause of invidious comparisons leading to mutual and undignified recriminations. It has affected the direction towards which the efforts of educational enthusiasts have been turned. Their one aim and object has been to show that capacities supposed to be essentially masculine are possessed by women also; to make it possible for women to compete on equal terms with men and to prove that they are not always the last in the race.

That the question of equality or inferiority was a wholly irrelevant one was not their fault; they had to answer the arguments of those who held the keys, and they were not to blame if these arguments were foolish. We owe much to the women who, at the risk of great unpopularity and much social loss, fought the battles by which the doors were opened, through which others passed without one effort of their own. It is because their work has been successful, not from any depreciation of its value, that I maintain that it is time to review the outcome of the last ten or twelve years, during which women have been free to compete with men in the College and the University, and to take a new departure. London and Cambridge have admitted them to examinations on equal terms, although the latter still refuses them the hall-mark of the degree. Newnham and Girton have had to extend their premises; Lady Margaret and Somerville have been established and have obtained some concessions from Oxford; University College, London, Mason's College, Birmingham, the Welsh Colleges, and other men's colleges, admit women to their class rooms on equal terms with men. London, Ireland, and Edinburgh admit them to their medical degrees; the Women's School of Medicine is prosperous, and they have admission to a few hospitals. At London and Cambridge they have done themselves credit in every branch. So far as receptive power is concerned, it is now at least admitted that the rather-above-the-average woman is quite on a level with the average man. So far, so good. But although our self-respect may be considerably increased, what is our economic position? There are not yet 800 women graduates of London and Cambridge. Of these the majority are assistant mistresses in public or private schools, visiting teachers, lecturers, or head mistresses. There were in 1881, according to the census of that year, 123,000 women teachers, and over 4,000,000 girls between the ages of five years and twenty; and yet already this little handful of graduates is told that it is in excess of the demand and that it must take lower salaries in consequence. In our public high schools not one in four teachers is a graduate; in private schools the proportion is much smaller. I do not propose to discuss this question, and will only make two remarks on it. The first, that after an expensive college course, which is only less expensive than that of a man because a woman is less extravagant in her personal expenditure, a Girton or Newnham student who has taken a good degree may hope for an initial salary of £105 to £120 non-resident, rising by very slow degrees to about £140 to £150 a year. Secondly, that every graduate should remember that when she accepts a lower rate still, she is making it easier to lower the salaries of the great majority below her. If all women graduates, and they are not many, agreed to a minimum, less than which they would not accept, the mass of teachers, already underpaid, could not be told as they are at present, that graduates could easily be obtained for the sum they ask. The teacher with a higher local certificate could hold out for her £90 a year, little enough in all conscience, because she would know that no graduate would take less than £100.

But the head mistress engages so few graduates, not merely because of the higher salary demanded, but because she is quite content, or rather because the British parent is quite content, that his daughter should be taught by less competent persons. If we look for the cause of this indifference, we shall find that he does not attach the slightest value to the education which she is receiving. For some unknown reason girls seem to think it absolutely necessary to learn Latin; he does not wish his daughter to be at any disadvantage with other girls; therefore he lets her learn Latin. If other girls are taught well, his daughter must be taught well; but if other girls are taught badly, he is quite content that his daughter should be so also. He perhaps learned Latin himself for some similar reason at school, and so far as he knows he derived no benefit from it, and he is quite certain he derived no enjoyment from it. The mass of parents do not wish their daughters to be teachers; and they pertinently ask, what good are classics and the higher mathematics and advanced natural science to girls unless they intend to teach? A few can answer honestly, "We enjoy the study. It is delight to us. Plato, Sophocles, Æschylus speak to us with a more living voice than any of our modern thinkers. Mathematics is not merely a discipline to us but an absorbing occupation, taking us completely out of ourselves for the time being. A natural science is to us not a mere mass of ascertained facts unrelated to each other, but a system of interdependent laws giving a new meaning to life; its very incompleteness is a charm, for it gives us the opportunity of being ourselves discoverers." A few can say this honestly; several, under the influence of a teacher whom they adore with that schoolgirl devotion so common in our high schools, persuade themselves that they feel some of the enjoyment that a properly-constituted mind would feel. What they really enjoy is the teacher's enjoyment, which is infectious. There is no subject so dry or so useless that a living, healthy, human teacher cannot persuade girls to think it interesting for the time being. But the majority of girls – and boys too for that matter – are Philistines and care for none of these things. They do their work conscientiously enough, because it is their work. They derive benefit from it as from a kind of mental gymnastics, and so far as their school days are concerned no harm is done, and they have benefited by the mental discipline.

When a girl or boy is about seventeen, the future career is considered. In the case of a son, the father to some extent takes into account the boy's natural bent, and also the chances of obtaining a post for him. Thenceforth his education takes a definite direction. If intended for one of the professions, the course is easily mapped out. In other cases the boy may be sent to the University, not so much for an academic as for a social training; very frequently he leaves school and at once begins his training for business or mercantile pursuits. If his father is a merchant, or large employer of labour, he will perhaps be sent elsewhere to learn all parts of his business, and then take some responsible post in his father's firm. If this is impossible, relatives or friends or business connections may be able to offer him a post, and no stone is left unturned. There is no question either of his being content to have a low salary because he can live at home. Nor does he, if he has any sense, deliberately choose to enter an overstocked market, merely because the men who succeed in it are admitted to be men of high intelligence. If he has a high opinion of his own talents, or if he prefers shining by reflected light to earning an income, he does perhaps become a barrister or a doctor, without much fitness for the profession. But at least those who take up business prefer to enter a labour market where there are comparatively few men of ability yet to be found, and where the supply of them is not so great as the demand.

The girl of seventeen is never helped in the same way, in many cases because it has never occurred to men that girls could be so assisted. There are many other reasons, which I do not propose to dwell on here. I am not addressing myself to those who do not wish women to earn their living, but to those who, having accepted the fact that many girls must work for a living, would be glad to help them in any way that might be suggested; and I am also speaking to those women who prefer, no matter what their private resources may be, to be trained for some occupation which will call for the exercise of mental powers which they know they possess. I am also confining my remarks to working women educated for their work in life, and am not referring to the large numbers of women who take up work without any other training than the general education acquired at school. If the woman, who from seventeen to twenty-two has been trained for her profession, cannot obtain the salary which, as Mr. Pollard has shown, is necessary to keep her in good health and provide for her old age, there is no need to say that the untrained schoolgirl enters the labour market at a greater disadvantage. Now, on what principles is a girl's career determined? In a large number of cases the parents take it for granted that she will be married in a few years, and they feel they can support her at home in comfort until then. Fortunately the girl herself does not always take this view; she thinks it quite possible that she never will be married, and she also sees that in that case she may in middle life be left with an income quite inadequate and necessitating a total change in her habits of living. If she has any public spirit, she will not undersell her poorer competitors, and will see no reason why she should not be paid the full worth of her services; she will be glad to know that her services are really worth her living. But all that she sees before her, unless she has exceptional talent, is teaching. It is the same with girls who *have* to earn their living and whose parents can only afford to give them an expensive training in the hope that a remunerative income may afterwards be obtained. They also must be teachers; it is the only brain-work offered them, and badly paid as it is, it is better paid than any other work done by women. The result is that we see girls following the stream and entering the teaching profession; after a few years, growing weary and sick of it, tired of training intellects, and doubtful about the practical value of the training, or altogether careless of it; discontented with a life for which they are naturally unsuited, and seeing no other career before them. We see others, who have a strong practical bent, giving themselves up to purely intellectual studies, because they are the only ones possible to them; and, on the other hand, clever girls, who have no scholastic ambitions, are left to fritter away their talents or exercise them with no aid but rule-of-thumb principles to guide them. The prizes, the exhibitions, the glory are all given to encourage scholarship. Brain-power is worshipped, and as people with brains are not encouraged to exercise them in a practical direction, the possession of brain-power is not ascribed to those who do not display capacity or liking for classics or mathematics or the abstract sciences. And the whole tendency is to compete with men where men are strongest. And here, socially, morally, and economically, we are making a great mistake. We are narrowing women to one kind of education, which would cut off the majority of them from sympathy with the men in their own class; they imbibe a false idea that culture means the possession of useless knowledge; and because men in the commercial world have a knowledge which enables them to perform services for which others are willing to pay, they are regarded as necessarily uncultured and mercenary. The leisured and professional classes take the precedence in the girl-graduate's eyes as being better educated and having less sordid aims. But, fortunately for England, the majority of men are neither leisured nor professional, and the organisation of industry and the extension of commerce give scope for the exercise of the highest powers. Socially, therefore, the educated woman at present is isolated from her class and suffers in consequence Morally she suffers, for she is not developing her natural powers. A woman's emotional nature is different from a man's, her inherited experience is different, her tastes are different, and – greatest heresy of all nowadays – her intellect is different. It is a common thing to say that there is no sex in intellect. If the upholders of this theory mean that from two given premisses the same conclusion must be drawn by men and women whenever they think rightly, of course no one can deny it. But this purely deductive work can be done by machinery. The real work of intelligence is the induction which supplies the premisses, the selection of premisses suitable to the purpose in view and the application of the conclusion. The working of intelligence is prompted, strengthened, and directed by interest and emotion; and here it is that men and women differ, and always will differ, a woman inheriting as she does, with a woman's nervous organisation, a woman's emotional nature. It is on this difference between men and women, amidst much which is common to both, that I build my hopes of women's success in the future. I do not urge women to compete with men because they can do what men can, but because I believe they can do what men cannot; and I believe that those branches in which men have attained the highest pitch of excellence are those in which women are least likely to find pleasure or excel. Creditable as have been their performances in the Mathematical Tripos, I am glad to see that their success in the Natural Science Tripos is much greater. Instead of glorying in having once in a score of years a Senior Classic, I take pride in the fact that in the four years since the Mediæval and Modern Language Tripos was instituted, women have always been in the front rank, and I notice with fear and trembling that, although during the first three years there was always a woman in the first class, and no men, last year, although there was no deterioration in the women's work, they did not have the first class all to themselves. I look forward to the day, but I hope it will be long before it comes, when the men's colleges shall rejoice because they have a man in the first class without a woman to share the honours. There are many things which men are doing alone, which could be done infinitely better if educated women helped them; and nowhere is this more obvious to me, although probably not to them, than in business. While there is much that can be done well by the human being, indifferently, whether man or woman, there is much that can only be done well by the male human being, much that can only be done well by the female human being, and much that can only be done well by the two in conjunction. And if men in business only considered their daughters' future in the same light as that of their sons, they would find many branches of business in which they could be most useful, and earn a good income. Girls inherit, to some extent, their intellectual capacities from their fathers, just as boys do from their mothers. And many a bright, clever, lazy girl would suddenly develop a most unexpected taste for study, if she had before her the prospect of doing practical, and to her most interesting work, as one of her father's managers, or as foreign correspondence clerk, or as chemist or artistic designer in a large manufactory; or as assistant steward on her father's property, or as a farmer on her own freehold, if (rents having gone down) he is unable to leave her an income. For all these a course of hard mental training is necessary or at least desirable; and the girl would be receiving culture on the one hand, and would have a chance of developing her natural gifts on the other. Many a girl, accustomed to a country life, would much prefer the occupations and life of a farmer to that of a teacher, provided she is allowed to have the college life and the free intercourse with other girls which is the main attraction of Girton and Newnham. The work would be far more interesting to her if she came to it with the enthusiasm of a scientist with theories to be tested. What is drudgery to an uneducated person may often be pleasurable to an educated one.

No one can study the organisation of industry at the present time without noticing that there is great room for improvement. Good organisers are extremely rare; and even in the internal management of a factory, perhaps the least important part of the work of a great manufacturer, much could be done which is rarely done at present. The admittance of educated women to a share in factory management should really be regarded in the light of co-operation with men, not competition with them. A man and a woman looking at a work-room are struck by different features, and each can be suggestive to the other. This is especially the case wherever women are employed.

The question of capacity is a more difficult one for me to answer, but an easier one for the individual girl, if she is not afraid of ridicule. And it is at this point that I would reiterate Mrs. Browning's advice. To any really clever girl who asked me for advice as to her future work I should say, "What do you think you could do best if it were possible for you to do it? Whatever that is, do your very best to get training in it, to show by capacity at one stage that you could master the next if you had the chance. If you do this, you will find that the men who laughed at women for thinking of doing such work will frequently be the very ones to make an exception in your favour and to help you over the next difficulty. If you wish to be a farmer, and to study every department of your work and be thoroughly grounded in agricultural science, make the best of your opportunities where you are, attend classes if possible in the technological department of a good college; and if the agricultural colleges are closed to women, when you have done everything you can without them, get one of them to make an exception in your favour. Whatever it may be that you wish to do, prepare yourself for it, and, instead of bemoaning the ill-treatment of women in general, persuade those in authority of your fitness in particular. And when you have gained your end help every girl you can who shows similar capacities."

One effect on the economic position of educated working women of such an extension of employment would be to enable them to measure their value. Teachers are paid out of fixed income, and their salaries are almost entirely determined by standard of living. If employed in business they would be employed for profit, and if they increased profits their value would rise, and could be measured; they would be paid according to their worth and not according to their standard of living. Education would be better adapted to practical needs, and teachers would be held in higher honour accordingly. Large numbers of clever girls would be spurred to exertion, whose intellectual powers have hitherto lain in abeyance, because no education was offered them corresponding to their needs. There are other arts, which women already practise, which it would be well for them to study on a scientific basis. Not only the future wife, mother, and housekeeper needs a knowledge of physiology, the laws of health, and domestic economy, but to a still greater extent the future Poor Law guardian, Board School manager, factory and workshop inspector, and sanitary officer; and both household manager and public officer should study the relation between domestic and national economics. Nor can any man do a greater injury to women in this respect than by placing a woman in a responsible post for which she has not been proved competent. The incapacity of a man is referred to the man himself; that of a woman is credited to the sex. But although a man may foolishly vote for a woman to be placed on the School Board or Board of Guardians merely because she is a woman, without knowing anything about her, I am not afraid that he will ever give her a well-paid post in his own business unless she is fit for it. Women who give their services for nothing are rarely told the truth; it will be a good thing for them when they receive, instead of flattery and thanks, criticism and payment.

I can only touch on one point more. I may be told that the effect of encouraging all girls, who display strength of character or intellectual power above the average, to make themselves pecuniarily independent, and to devote their energies to some special and definite occupation which will call forth their powers, will be to make them too absorbed or unwilling to enter upon marriage, and that the next generation must suffer from the strongest and most intellectual women holding aloof from wifehood and motherhood. Others, on the other hand, may say that their work will suffer, because the expectation of marriage will hinder them from doing their best. The latter objection will not, I think, be supported by those who are acquainted with the work of women graduates. There is much truth in the former one. Women who have been trained for a special work, and who like their work, either do not marry at all or marry comparatively late in life, and it may at first sight seem injurious to the race that this should be so. But I think this is a mistake. The men and women of the most marked individuality do not make the best husbands and wives, especially if they marry before they have become aware of their own character. Although a theory prevails to the contrary, I believe that women come to intellectual maturity later than men. They have a magnificent power of self-deception, of persuading themselves that they think and believe the things which those they care for think and believe – they are so little encouraged to think for themselves that many a woman, married when but a girl, has later on discovered that she has a character of her own, hitherto unrevealed to herself and unsuspected by her husband. Marriage, as George Eliot has said, must be a relation of sympathy or of conquest. But such women, if sympathy has not really existed between them and their husbands, are never conquered; they may be slaves or rebels, but never loyal subjects; and history is full of records of the disastrous early marriages of clever women. On the other hand, Hannah More, Jane Austen, Maria Edgeworth, Joanna Baillie, Caroline Herschell, Harriet Martineau, all women of brilliant intellect, have left their mark on history as good and happy women; and we can all of us give a long list of such bright and contented lives from the unmarried women of our own acquaintance who have found their vocation. If they have missed the best in life, they have always been true to themselves. The economic independence of women is as necessary to men's happiness as to women's. Their true interests can never be opposed or antagonistic, however much those of an individual man and woman may be. There is no hardship to women in working for a living; the hardship lies in not getting a living when they work for it. And the great temptation from which all women should most earnestly strive to be freed is that which presents itself to so many at one time or another – the temptation to accept marriage as a means of livelihood and an escape from poverty. And if men would escape the degradation of being accepted by a woman in such a spirit, they should be anxious to do all in their power to make women free, to remove all obstructions raised by prejudice; and when a woman can do anything worth doing, "to give her of the fruit of her hands and to let her own works praise her in the gates."

7

"WHAT ARE WE WORTH?" *A VOICE FROM THE SOUTH*

Anna Julia Cooper

Source: Anna Julia Cooper, 'What Are We Worth?', *A Voice from the South* (Xenia, Ohio: Aldine Printing House, 1892), pp. 175–86

One often hears in the North an earnest plea from some lecturer for "our working girls" (of course this means white working girls). And recently I listened to one who went into pious agonies at the thought of the future mothers of Americans having to stand all day at shop counters; and then advertised with applause a philanthropic firm who were giving their girls a trip to Europe for rest and recreation! I am always glad to hear of the establishment of reading rooms and social entertainments to brighten the lot of any women who are toiling for bread – whether they are white women or black women. But how many have ever given a thought to the pinched and down-trodden colored women bending over wash-tubs and ironing boards – with children to feed and house rent to pay, wood to buy, soap and starch to furnish – lugging home weekly great baskets of clothes for families who pay them for a month's laundrying barely enough to purchase a substantial pair of shoes!

Will you call it narrowness and selfishness, then, that I find it impossible to catch the fire of sympathy and enthusiasm for most of these labor movements at the North?

I hear these foreigners, who would boycott an employer if he hired a colored workman, complain of wrong and oppression, of low wages and long hours, clamoring for eight-hour systems and insisting on their right to have sixteen of the twenty-four hours for rest and self-culture, for recreation and social intercourse with families and friends – ah, come with me, I feel like saying, I can show you workingmen's wrong and workingmen's toil which, could it speak, would send up a wail that might be heard from the Potomac to the Rio Grande; and *should it unite and act*, would shake this country from Carolina to California.

But no man careth for their souls. The labor interests of the colored man in this country are as yet dumb and limp. The unorganized mass has found neither tongue nor nerve. In the free and liberal North, thanks to the amalgamated associations and

 DOI: 10.4324/9780429321078-8

labor unions of immigrant laborers, who cannot even speak English, —the colored man is relegated to the occupations of water and barber, unless he has a taste for school teaching or politics. . . . In the South, on the other hand, where the colored man virtually holds the labor market, he is too uncertain and unorganized to demand anything like a fair share of the products of his toil. And yet the man who thinks, must see that our labor interests lie at the foundation of our material prosperity . . . .

Stung by such imputations as that of Calhoun that if a Negro could prove his ability to master the Greek subjunctive he might vindicate his title to manhood, the newly liberated race first shot forward along this line with an energy and success which astonished its most sanguine friends.

This may not have been most wise. It certainly was quite natural; and the result is we find ourselves in almost as ludicrous a plight as the African in the story, who, after a sermon from his missionary pleading for the habiliments of civilization, complacently donned a Gladstone hat leaving the rest of his body in its primitive simplicity of attire. Like him we began at the wrong end. Wealth must pave the way for learning. Intellect, whether of races or individuals, cannot soar to the consummation of those sublime products which immortalize genius, while the general mind is assaulted and burdened with "what shall we eat, what shall we drink, and wherewithal shall we be clothed." Work must first create wealth, and wealth leisure, before the untrammeled intellect of the Negro, or any other race, can truly vindicate its capabilities. Something has been done intellectually we all know. That one black man has written a Greek grammar is enough to answer Calhoun's sneer; but it is leisure, the natural outgrowth of work and wealth, which must furnish room, opportunity, possibility for the highest endeavor and most brilliant achievement. Labor must be the solid foundation stone – the *sine qua non* of our material value; and the only effective preparation for success in this, as it seems to me, lies in the establishment of industrial and technical schools for teaching our colored youth trades. This necessity is obvious for several reasons. First, a colored child, in most cases, can secure a trade in no other way. We had master mechanics while the Negro was a chattel, and the ingenuity of brain and hand served to enrich the coffers of his owner. But to-day skilled labor is steadily drifting into the hands of white workmen – mostly foreigners. Here it is cornered. The white engineer holds a tight monopoly both of the labor market and of the science of his craft. Nothing would induce him to take a colored apprentice or even to work beside a colored workman. Unless then trades are to fall among the lost arts for us as a people, they must be engrafted on those benevolent institutions for Negro training established throughout the land. The youth must be taught to use his trigonometry in surveying his own and his neighbor's farm; to employ his geology and chemistry in finding out the nature of the soil, the constituents drafted from it by each year's crop and the best way to meet the demand by the use of suitable renewers; to apply his mechanics and physics to the construction and handling of machinery – to the intelligent management of iron works and water works and steam works and electric works. One mind in a family or in a town may show a penchant for art, for literature, for the learned professions, or more bookish lore.

You will know it when it is there. No need to probe for it. It is a light that cannot be hid under a bushel – and I would try to enable that mind to go the full length of its desires. Let it follow its bent and develop its talent as far as possible: and the whole community might well be glad to contribute its labor and money for the sustenance and cultivation of this brain. Just as earth gives its raw material, its carbons, hydrogen, and oxygen, for the tree which is to elaborate them into foliage, flower and fruit, so the baser elements, bread and money furnished the true brain worker come back to us with compound interest in the rich thought, the invention, the poem, the painting, the statue. Only let us recognize our assignment and not squander our portion in over fond experiments. James Russell Lowell says, "As we cannot make a silk purse out of a sow's ear, no more can we perform the opposite experiment without having a fine lot of spoiled silk on our hands."

With most of us, however, the material, such as it is, has been already delivered. The working of it up is also well under way. The gold, the silver, the wood, the hay, the stubble, whatever there was at hand has all gone in. Now can the world use it? Is there a demand for it, does it perform the function for which it was made, and is its usefulness greater than the cost of its production? Does it pay expenses and have anything over.

The world in putting these crucial questions to men and women, or to races and nations, classifies them under two heads – as consumers or producers. The man who consumes as much as he produces is simply *nil*. It is no matter to the world economically speaking whether he is in it or out of it. He is merely one more to count in taking the census. The man who consumes more than he produces is a destroyer of the world's wealth and should be estimated precisely as the housekeeper estimates moths and mice. These are the world's parasites, the shirks, the lazy lubbers who hang around rum shops and enter into mutual relationships with lamp posts to bear each the other's burdens, moralizing all the while (wondrous moralists and orators they often are!) and insisting that the world owes them a living! To be sure the world owes them nothing of the kind. The world would consider it a happy riddance from bad rubbish if they would pay up their debt and move over to Mars. Every day they live their unproductive bodies sink and destroy a regular portion of the world's values. At the very lowest estimate, a boy who has reached the age of twenty, has already burned up between three and four thousand dollars of the world's possessions. This is on the very closest and most economical count; I charge him nothing for fuel or lights, allowing him to have warmed by fires that would have burned for others and estimating the cost simply of what he has eaten and worn, *i.e.* the amount which he has actually sunk of the world's wealth. I put his board at the moderate sum of ten dollars per month, and charge him the phenomenally small amount of thirty dollars a year for clothing and incidentals. This in twenty years gives him a debt of three thousand dollars, which no honest man should be willing to leave the world without settling. The world does not owe them a living then – the world only waits for them to square up and change their residence. It is only they who produce more than they consume, that the world owes, or even acknowledges as having any practical value.

Now to which class do we belong? The question must in the first place be an individual one for every man of whatever race: Am I giving to the world an equivalent of what it has given and is giving me? Have I a margin on the outside of consumption for surplus production? We owe it to the world to give out at least as much as we have taken in, but if we aim to be accounted a positive value we must leave it a little richer than we found it. The boy who dies at twenty leaving three thousand dollars in bank to help another, has just paid expenses. If he lives longer it increases his debit and should be balanced by a corresponding increase on the credit side. The life that serves to develop another, the mother who toils to educate her boy, the father who invests his stored-up capital in education, giving to the world the energies and usefulness of his children trained into a well disciplined manhood and womanhood has paid his debt in the very richest coin, – a coin which is always legal tender, a priceless gift, the most precious payment we can make for what we have received. And we may be sure, if we can give no more than a symmetric life, an inspiring thought, a spark caught from a noble endeavor, its value will not be lost.

Previous to 1793 America was able to produce unlimited quantities of cotton, but unable to free the fibre from the seeds. Eli Whitney came to the rescue of the strangled industry and perfected a machine which did the work needed. The deliverance which he wrought was complete. The following year America's exports of cotton to England were increased from not one pound in previous years to 1,600,000 pounds. He gave dollars.

Just before the battle of Quebec Wolf[e] repeated and enjoyed Gray's "Elegy" saying he valued that gem more highly than the capture of the city before which he was encamped. The next day the city was taken and Wolf[e] was laid to rest. But the world is in debt to both the poet and the soldier – a boundless debt, to the one for an eternal thought-gem, to the other for immortal heroism and devoted patriotism.

Once there lived among men One whom sorrowing millions for centuries since have joyed to call friend – One whose "come unto me ye that are heavy laden" has given solace and comfort to myriads of the human race. *He gave a life.*

We must as individuals compare our cost with what we are able to give. The worth of a race or a nation can be but the aggregate worth of its men and women. While we need not indulge in offensive boasting, it may not be out of place in a land where there is some adverse criticism and not a little unreasonable prejudice, quietly to take account of stock and see if we really represent a value in this great American commonwealth. The average American is never too prejudiced, I think, to have a keen appreciation for the utilities; and he is certainly not behind the rest of the world in his clear perception of the purchasing power of a dollar. Beginning here, then, I find that, exclusive of the billions of wealth *given* by them to enrich another race prior to the passage of the Thirteenth Amendment, the colored people of America to-day hold in their own right $264,000,000 of taxable property; and this is over and above the $50,000,000 which collapsed in the Freedman's Savings Bank when that gigantic iniquity paralyzed the hope and shocked the faith of an inexperienced and unfinancial people.

One would like to be able to give reliable statistics of the agricultural and mechanical products of the colored laborer, but so far I have not been able to obtain them. It is a modest estimate, I am sure, to ascribe fully two-thirds of the 6,940,000 bales of cotton produced in 1888 to Negro cultivation. The reports give estimates only in bulk as to the products of a state or county. Our efficient and capable census enumerators never draw the color line on labor products. You have no trouble in turning to the page that shows exactly what percentage of colored people are illiterate, or just how many have been condemned by the courts; no use taking the trouble to specify whether it was for the larceny of a ginger cake, or for robbing a bank of a cool half million and skipping off to Canada: it's all crime of course, and crime statistics and illiteracy statistics must be accurately detailed – and colored.

Similar commendable handling meets the colored producer from the managers of our Big American Show at Chicago which we are all so nervously anxious shall put the best foot foremost in bowing to the crowned heads and the gracious lords and ladies from over the waters. To allow any invention or mechanism, art or farm product to be accredited [to] a black man would be drawing the color line! And our immaculate American would never be guilty of anything so vile as drawing a color line!!!

I am unable to say accurately, then, just how many bales of cotton, pounds of tobacco, barrels of molasses and bushels of corn and wheat are given to the world through Negro industry. The same difficulty is met in securing authentic information concerning their inventions and patents. The records of the Patent Office at Washington do not show whether a patentee is white or colored. And all inventions and original suggestions made by a colored man before emancipation were necessarily accredited to some white individual, a slave not being able to take the oath administered to the applicant for a patent. Prof. Wright, however, by simply collecting through personal inquiry the number of colored patentees which could be remembered and identified by examiners and attorneys practicing before the Patent Office authorities, published upwards of fifty in the *A.M.E. Review* for April, 1886. Doubtless this number was far within the truth, and many new patents have been taken out since his count was made. Almost daily in my walk I pass an ordinary looking black man, who, I am told, is considering an offer of $30,000 for his patent rights on a corn planter, which, by the way, has been chosen as part of the Ohio exhibit for the Columbian Exposition. He has secured as many as half a dozen patents within a few years and is carrying around a "new machine" in his head every day.

Granville Wood, of Cincinnati, has given valuable returns to the world as an electrician; and there is no estimating the money in the outright gift of this people through unremunerated toil. The Negro does not always show a margin over and above consumption; but this does not necessarily in his case prove that he is not a producer. During the agitations for adverse legislation against the Chinese, the charge was alleged that they spent nothing in the country. They hoarded their earnings, lived on nothing, and finally returned to China to live in luxury and to circulate the wealth amassed in this country. A similar complaint can never be lodged against the Negro. Poor fellow, he generally lives pretty well up to his income. He labors for little and spends it all. He has never yet gained the full consent of his mind to "take his gruel a little thinner" till his little pile has grown a bit. He does not like to seem short. And had he the wage of a thousand a year his big-heartedness would immediately put him under the painful necessity of having it do the entertainment of five thousand. He must eat, and is miserable if he can't dress; and seems on the whole internally fitted every way to the style and pattern of a millionaire, rather than to the plain, plodding, stingy old path of common sense and economy. This is a flaw in the *material* of the creature. The grain just naturally runs that way. If our basal question of economics were put to him: "*What do you give – are you adding something every year to the world's stored up capital?*" His ingenuous answer would be, as the ghost of a smile flits across his mobile lips – "Yea, Lord; I give back *all*. I am even now living on the prospects of next year's income. I give my labor at accommodation rates, and forthwith reconvert my wages into the general circulation. Funds, somehow, don't seem to stick to me. I have no talents, or smaller coins either, hid in a napkin." It will be well for him to learn, however, that it is not what we make but what we save that constitutes wealth. The hod-carrier who toils for $1.50 a day, spending the dollar and laying up the half, is richer than the congressman with an annual income of $5000 and annual duns of $8000. What he most urgently needs to learn is systematic saving. He works hard enough generally – but does not seem able to retrench expenses – to cut off the luxuries which people of greater income and larger foresight, seeing to be costly and unnecessary would deny themselves. He wants to set to work vigorously to widen the margin outside the expenditures. He cannot be too deeply impressed with the fact that tobacco and liquors – even leaving out their moral aspects – are too costly to be indulged in by any who are not living on the interest of capital ready in store. A man living on his earnings should eschew luxuries, if he wishes to produce wealth. But when those luxuries deteriorate manhood, they impoverish and destroy the most precious commodity we can offer the world.

For after all, the highest gifts are not measurable in dollars and cents. Beyond and above the class who run an account with the world and merely manage honestly to pay *in kind* for what they receive, there is a noble army – the Shakespeares and Miltons, the Newtons, Galileos and Darwins, – Watts, Morse, Howe, Lincoln, Garrison, John Brown – a part of the world's roll of honor – whose price of board and keep dwindles into nothingness when compared with what the world owes them; men who have taken of the world's bread and paid for it in immortal thoughts, invaluable inventions, new facilities, heroic deeds of loving self-sacrifice; men who dignify the world for their having lived in it and to whom the world will ever bow in grateful worship as its heroes and benefactors. It may not be ours to stamp our genius in enduring characters – but we can give what we are *at its best*.

Visiting the slave market in Boston one day in 1761, Mrs. John Wheatley was attracted by the modest demeanor and intelligent countenance of a delicate looking black girl just from the slave ship. She was quite nude save for a piece of coarse carpet she had tied about her loins, and the only picture she could give of her native home was that she remembered her mother in the early morning every day pouring out water before the rising sun. The benevolent Mrs. Wheatley expended some labor in polishing up this crude gem, and in 1773 the gifted Phillis gave to the world a small octavo volume of one hundred and twenty precious pages, published in London and dedicated to the Countess of Huntingdon. In 1776, for some lines she had sent him, she received from the greatest American the following tribute dated at Cambridge:

> Miss Phillis:
>
> . . . I thank you most sincerely for your polite notice of me in the elegant lines you enclosed; and however undeserving I may be of such encomium and panegyric, the style and manner exhibit a striking proof of your poetical talents; in honor of which and as a tribute justly due to you, I would have published the poem had I not been apprehensive that, while I only meant to give the world this new instance of your genius, I might have incurred the imputation of vanity. This and nothing else determined me not to give it place in the public prints. If you should ever come to Cambridge or near headquarters, I shall be happy to see a person so favored by the Muses, and to whom nature has been so liberal and beneficent in her dispensations. I am, with great respect,
>
> Your obedient humble servant,
> George Washington

That girl paid her debts *in song.*

In South Carolina there are two brothers, colored men, who own and conduct one of the most extensive and successful farms in this country for floriculture. Their system of irrigating and fertilizing is the most scientific in the state, and by their original and improved methods of grafting and cultivating they have produced a new and rich variety of the rose called *Loiseaux*, from their name. Their roses are famous throughout Europe and are specially prized by the French for striking and marvelous beauty. The Loiseaux brothers send out the incense of their grateful returns to the world in the *sweet fragrance of roses*.

Some years ago a poor and lowly orphan girl stood with strange emotions before a statue of Benjamin Franklin in Boston. Her bosom heaved and her eyes filled as she whispered between her clenched teeth, "Oh, how I would like to make a stone man?" Wm. Lloyd Garrison became her providence and enlarged her opportunity; *she paid for it* in giving to the world the *Madonna with the Christ and adoring Angels*, now in the collection of the Marquis of Bute. From her studio in Rome Edmonia Lewis, the colored sculptress, continues to increase the debt of the world to her by her graceful thoughts in the chaste marble.

On May 27, 1863, a mixed body of troops in blue stood eagerly expectant before a rebel stronghold. On the extreme right of the line, a post of honor and of danger, were stationed the Negro troops, the first and third regiments of the Louisiana Native Guards. On going into action, says an eye witness, they were 1080 strong, and formed into four lines, Lieut.-Colonel Bassett, 1st Louisiana, forming the first line, and Lieut.-Colonel Henry Finnegas the second. Before any impression had been made upon the earth works of the enemy, and in full face of the batteries belching forth their sixty-two pounders, the order to charge was given, – and the black regiment rushed forward to encounter grape, canister, shell and musketry, having no artillery but two small howitzers – which seemed mere popguns to their adversaries – and with no reserve whatever. The terrible fire from the rebel guns upon the unprotected masses mowed them down like grass. Colonel Bassett being driven back, Colonel Finnegas took his place, and his men being similarly cut to pieces, Bassett reformed and recommenced. And thus these brave fellows went on from 7 o'clock in the morning till 3:30 p.m., under the most hideous carnage that men ever had to withstand. During this time they rallied and were ordered to make six distinct charges, losing thirty-seven killed, one hundred and fifty-five wounded, and one hundred and sixteen missing, "the majority, if not all of these," adds a correspondent of the *New York Times*, who was an eye witness of the fight, "being in all probability now lying dead on the gory field without the rights of sepulture! *for when, by flag of truce our forces in other directions were permitted to reclaim their dead, the benefit, through some neglect, was not extended to these black regiments*."

"The deeds of heroism," he continues,

> performed by these colored men were such as the proudest white men might emulate. Their colors are torn to pieces by shot, and literally bespattered by blood and brains. The color-sergeant of the 1st La. on being mortally wounded, hugged the colors to his breast when a struggle ensued between the two color-corporals on each side of him as to who should bear the sacred standard – and during this generous contention one of the corporals was wounded. One black lieutenant mounted the enemy's works three or four times, and in one charge the assaulting party came within fifty paces of them. If only ordinarily supported by artillery and reserve, no one can convince us that they would not have opened a passage through the enemy's works. Captain Callioux, of the 1st La., a man so black that he prided himself on his blackness, died the death of a hero leading on his men in the thickest of the fight. One poor wounded fellow came along with his arm shattered by a shell, jauntily swinging it with the other, as he said to a friend of mine: "Massa, guess I can fight no more." I was with one of the captains looking after the wounded, when we met one limping along toward the front. Being asked where he was going, he said, "I been shot in de leg, cap'n, an' dey wants me to go to de hospital – but I reckon I c'n gib'em some mo' yit."

Says Major-General Banks in the report from Headquarters of the Army of the Gulf, before Port Hudson, May 30, 1863, writing to Major-General Halleck, General-in-Chief at Washington: "The position occupied by the Negro troops was one of importance and called for the utmost steadiness and bravery in those to whom it was confided. It gives me pleasure to report that they answered every expectation. Their conduct was heroic. No troops could be more determined or more daring."

"Charge!" Trump and drum awoke,
Onward the bondmen broke;
Bayonet and sabre-stroke
Vainly opposed their rush.
Through the wild battle's crush,
With but one thought aflush,
Driving their lords like chaff,
In the guns' mouths they laugh;
Or at the slippery brands
Leaping with open hands,
Down they bear man and horse,
Down in their awful course;
Trampling with bloody heel
Over the crashing steel,
All their eyes forward bent,
Rushed the black regiment.

"Freedom!" their battle-cry –
"Freedom! or leave to die!"
Ah! and they meant the word,
Not as with us 'tis heard,
Not a mere party-shout:
They gave their spirits out.
Trusted the end to God,
And on the gory sod
Rolled in triumphant blood!

And thus they paid *their debt*. "They gave – *their spirits out!*"

In the heart of what is known as the "Black Belt" of Alabama and within easy reach of the great cotton plantations of Georgia, Mississippi, and Florida, a devoted young colored man ten years ago started a school with about thirty Negro children assembled in a comical looking shanty at Tuskegee. His devotion was contagious and his work grew; an abandoned farm of 100 acres was secured and that gradually grew to 640 acres, largely wood-land, on which a busy and prosperous school is located; and besides a supply farm was added, of heavy rich land, 800 acres, from which grain and sugar cane are main products. Since 1881, 2,947 students have been taught here, of whom 102 have graduated, while 200 more have received enough training to fit them to do good work as teachers, intelligent farmers, and mechanics. The latest enrollment shows girls, 247; boys, 264. Of the 102 graduates, 70 per cent. are teachers, ministers and farmers. They usually combine teaching and farming. Three are printers (learned the trades at school), one is a tinner, one a blacksmith, one a wheel-wright, three are merchants, three are carpenters, others in the professions or filling miscellaneous positions.

That man is paying his debt by giving to this country *living, working, consecrated men and women*!

8

"COLORED WOMEN AS WAGE-EARNERS," *SOUTHERN WORKMAN AND HAMPTON SCHOOL RECORD*

Anna Julia Cooper

Source: Anna Julia Cooper, 'Colored Women as Wage-earners', *Southern Workman and Hampton School Record*, August 1899, pp. 295–98

I shall not take time to discuss ideal situations on the speculative side. There may be those who think that woman has no business to enter the struggle for existence as a wage-earner; who think that she should be as the lilies of the field, and should toil not except to spin and array herself in gorgeous raiment to delight the Solomons in all their glory.

The fact remains that a large percentage of the productive labor of the world is done by women; and also another fact, recently brought out through investigations under Atlanta University, that "of 1,137 colored families 650, or 57.17 percent, are supported wholly or in part by female heads." So that in comparison with white, female heads of families and others contributing to family support, there is, by a house to house enumeration, quite a large excess on the part of colored women.

Sentiment aside then, if men will not or cannot help the conditions which force women into the struggle for bread, we have a right to claim at least that she shall have fair play and all the rights of wage-earners in general, or, as Herbert Spencer puts it, "Justice demands that women, if they are not artificially advantaged, must not at any rate be artificially disadvantaged."

I shall have to ask first, therefore, careful attention to a few of the dry but fundamental principles of economics, to which science our subject properly belongs. Wage-earning is the complement or proper corollary to the human element in the creation of wealth. Land, labor, and capital are the factors in the production of wealth. The term land includes all natural opportunities or forces; the term labor, all human exertion; and the term capital, all wealth used to produce more wealth. The whole produce is distributed in returns to these three factors. That part which goes to land owners as payment for the use of natural opportunities is called rent;

DOI: 10.4324/9780429321078-9

the part which constitutes the reward of human exertion is wages; and the part which constitutes the return for the use of capital is called interest.

The income of an individual may be made up from any one, two, or three of these sources according to the nature of his contribution to the product. But the laborer is always worthy of his hire. Should the owner of the land and the capital have the power and the greed to disregard the claims of the man who contributed the labor, and pocket the entire product, he is manifestly a robber whether the jailors can catch him or not.

In many thousands of homes the indoor partner of the firm, who undertakes to discharge the domestic and maternal duties within, is just as truly a contributor to the product gained, as the outdoor manager who conducts the business and controls the wages. The woman in the home has a right to a definite share in the wealth she produces through relieving the man of certain indoor cares and enabling him to give thereby larger effort to his special trade of calling.

But, say you, the highest services can not be measured by dollars and cents. It is sordid to talk about paying mothers to be mothers, and giving a wage to wife to be wife! True, there is a class of services transcending all rewards; but because the wife of your bosom does not take you by the throat saying, "Pay me that thou owest!" should she be made to feel like a pensioner on your bounty every time she needs a pair of gloves?

The family tie is a sacred union – the most sacred on earth. It is full of mystery and God-appointed sanctity. But does it not at the same time recognize the existence of some very plain and practical rights founded on simple justice as between man and man? Two human beings have voluntarily contracted to unite their forces for mutual help and advantage. The fact that they pledged themselves to the partnership "Till death do us part" but adds solemnity to the duties and obligations on either side. That the partnership carries divine sanction makes all the more inviolable those duties and obligations. That the interests involved are the most precious to the state, – the building of homes and the rearing of its citizens, insures the guardianship of society over those duties and obligations.

Of this partnership, the one member goes forth in the morning, whether to dig ditches or to add figures. The world knows him as the bread winner for the firm. The silent partner toils in the home, whether to cook the dinners or direct little feet and hands. Her heart is in the work. Faithfulness and devotion are hers. At the end of her monotonous round of days' doings she prepares to welcome in the eventide the battle-scarred veteran of the outer life.

She opens the door with a smile. That smile is an important part of her program. She leads him to the dinner that she has prepared; he eats with a right good relish, for he likes to be fed. Yes, she eats of the dinner too, for she has her food and her shelter and her clothes whenever she asks for them.

But it never occurs to this "boarder" that his wife earns a definite part of the wage that he draws; and that, though she has never figured it out and presented the bill, his account is greatly in arrears for simple wages. On the other hand every right implies a duty, and woman on entering this partnership should see to it that she contributes a real increment to the stock of value.

When we pass from the home and enter the dusty arena of the world, we find women wage-earners shoulder to shoulder with men in the struggle in almost all the avenues of labor and here it may be well to repeat [that] this term labor with its correlate wage-earning, in the broad economic sense, includes all the capacities in man, intellectual as well as physical and moral, which have economic significance. Moral and intellectual qualities increase the productiveness of labor.

"Temperance, trustworthiness, skill, alertness, perception, a comprehensive mental grasp – all these," says an eminent writer on political economy, "and other good qualities belonging to the soul of man are of chief importance in man. The economic value of intellectual training," he continues "is generally not sufficiently appreciated. It has been ascertained that with no exceptions, the higher in any part of the United States the per capita expenditure for schools, the higher is the average of wages, and the larger, consequently, the production of wealth." This is a fact I would like specially to emphasize for those who intend training either girls or boys for self support as laborers or wealth producers. The broadest and fullest development of all powers, though it cost a greater outlay, pays the best interest in actual returns of dollars and cents.

It may be hard to do without your daughter's help while she studies a few more years in preparation for her labor, but the greater productiveness of that labor will more than repay your abstinence. And now let us apply what has been said to the special class of women mentioned in our subject. The colored woman as wage-earner must bring to her labor all the capacities, native or acquired, which are of value in the industrial equation. She must really be worth her wage and then claim it.

"Nature has made up her mind," says Emerson, "that what cannot defend itself shall not be defended," and if women enter the struggle for independent existence they should claim all the rights of advantage to men in the same positions. The world has a cold substratum of fair play and abstract justice, but it is so encrusted over with prejudices and favoritisms that the one who waits for its waters to bubble up spontaneously will die of thirst. No one deplores more than I do the "woman with elbows."

Aesthetically, she pains me. But every wage-earner, man or woman, owes it to the dignity of the labor he contributes, as well as to his own self-respect, to require the rights due to the quality of service he renders, and to the element of value he contributes to the world's wealth.

As colored wage-earners, we are today under a double disadvantage destined sorely to try our fitness to survive if it does not overwhelm us in the very day of its ostentation and self-satisfaction, we are "let go" to start from zero – nay, from a chasm infinitely below zero, to build up our fortunes.

As a consequence, the social wealth of the Negro is two hundred and fifty years behind that of the white American. You will understand what I mean by social wealth when you reflect on the many things owned by individuals which are really consumed by the society in which these individuals move. Take for example a child born in 1865 of emancipated parents. Leaving out hereditary drawbacks and losses, that child is born into a society without books, without pictures, without comforts, without homes. If he goes to school he has no dictionaries or cyclopedias to help him understand his lessons. His environment does not even furnish the language in which his books are written.

Now, suppose he struggles to accumulate, secures a home, puts in it a few comforts, some books and pictures, carpets and curtains, a piano perhaps, a dictionary certainly; or he goes further and acquires orchards and lawns, a country seat and carriages – these things are not for himself alone. All who associate with him are made the richer by such acquisitions of his, and would be to that extent impoverished should he, on dying, take them away from the society in which he had moved by bequeathing them to a white man.

Colored society is today in available social wealth in the position of a company of pioneers, or where the white American was when he conned his solitary book by the light of a pine knot, and contended with bears and Indians for the possession of his potato patch and his one-story cabin. But the white American at that stage of his social accumulation worshipped God in a log hut and his wife went to meeting in her linsey-woolsey gown and brogan shoes. The Black American, however, comes up on the stage when his white forerunner is becoming blasé with luxury and surfeiting. He takes the white man's standard of living just where he finds it, rears and tries to support churches as magnificent, gives presents as costly, maintains in his weddings and funerals a style as lavish and idiotic.

It is as if a little harpsichord with only middle and lower gamut were keyed up to a magnificent grand piano which stands with all its eight or more octaves already at concert pitch. A terrible strain results to all the strings of the little harpsichord. Its notes are but discordant shrieks and screams, ineffectual attempts to reach the easy ringing tones of the grand; and a miracle it is if you do not hear a snap, a pop – resulting in utter ruin to what might have been a very sweet instrument, had it only been allowed to keep its range.

Economically considered, the colored people in this country are a society of wage-earners, but their standards of living and their judgments of one another are as if they were a race of capitalists.

Perhaps the severest trial of all for the colored wage-earner is the impossible height to which the standard of life is raised among us. "Standard of life," in the economic sense, "is the number and character of the wants which a man considers more important than marriage and family."

Now I hold that not only does the strain from keying our life to the American pitch divert into the struggle to "keep up appearances" a large part of the wage which should go to physical comforts, such as sanitary housing and feeding and clothing our bodies, but worse yet, through this artificial and hopelessly high standard of living, many young men feel that they cannot support a wife and family;

and so we lose the impetus toward a higher civilization that good homes would give us.

Our children make their first bow before the public in a dazzling shimmer of costly roses and laces; and however many pinches and sweat pounds it has cost the wage-earner to afford it, we somehow feel that our child ought to appear as fine as the rest, and so it goes. Wage-earners will have to learn to discriminate between wages and interest if we are ever to bequeath to posterity a capital out of our wages.

Indeed, if we are ever to start homes and families at all that in the next generation our name be not blotted from the face of the earth, it will be necessary for us to have plain living and homely virtues in honest homes, built and banded by honest earnings. For it is here, as I conceive the matter and not, as Prof. Kelly Miller suggests in his review of Hoffman, in the "surplus" of women among us, that lies the real explanation of unnatural conditions in our large cities.

Certainly the removal of the tension that comes from our effort to reach an extravagant and unattainable standard of life, by a return to simplicity of manners and naturalness of living, is a more facile remedy for increasing the number of honorable marriages and pure homes than by killing off the surplus women, the only remedy apparent as Prof. Miller depicts the situation.

Surely the greatest sufferer from the strain and stress attendant upon the economic conditions noted among our people is the colored woman, and she is the one who must meet and conquer the conditions. She must be too wary to be lured on with the chaff of flattery. When her fine appearance or that of her daughter is commented upon, let that be a signal for retreat. Study economy. Utilize the margins.

Preach and practice plain living and high thinking. Let the wife come in as a sensible helper in building up the fortunes of the family. Let her prove that she can contribute something more than good looks and milliners' bills to the stock in trade. If her husband starts a business, let her study how she can be useful to him in it, and, shoulder to shoulder, let them plant and till, and then gather and garner the fruits of their united industry. So, by her foresight and wisdom, her calm insight and tact, her thrift and frugality, her fertility of resource and largeness of hope and faith, the colored woman can prove that a prudent marriage is the very best investment that the working man can make.

9

"THE PAY OF COLLEGE WOMEN," *THE NORTH AMERICAN REVIEW*

Frances M. Abbott

Source: Frances M. Abbott, 'The Pay of College Women', *The North American Review*, Vol. 163, No. 478, Sept. 1896, pp. 337–44

THE woman problem and the industrial problem are subjects of paramount interest to this generation. When the two are interwoven the interest of the combined problem is equalled only by the ignorance concerning it. The Association of Collegiate Alumnæ, numbering nearly 2,000 women who have received college degrees, has just issued a valuable compendium of statistics on the "Compensation in Certain Occupations of Women Who have received College or Other Special Training." Like all the publications of the A. C. A., this pamphlet is distinguished by admirable thoroughness of compilation and fairness of statement. It is my purpose to put the facts into such form that they may be readily assimilated by the general mind.

Before beginning, I wish to warn my readers not to repose too much confidence in these statistics, carefully prepared though they be. Anyone who has ever conducted a written examination in school knows something of the variety of answers that a question can evoke from the human mind. When the minds are mature and highly trained, and the answer depends upon original thought and not upon a previously learned lesson, it seems as if the permutations were infinite. One might almost say that no inquiry ever strikes two people exactly alike. Again, as every collator knows to his sorrow, no matter how intelligent and responsible are the persons to whom a list of inquiries is sent, half of the forms will not be returned, and of the other half a goodly number will have the blanks imperfectly filled out. The marking system as commonly practised in school and college seems to me not less fatuous than the minute fractions of *per cent.* that are elaborately worked out of necessarily imperfect *data*.

Having placed all statistical information in the limbo of uncertainty where it properly belongs, I wish expressly to say that the statements in this paper will

DOI: 10.4324/9780429321078-10

have no value five years, possibly two years, hence, for woman's opportunities, and, moreover, industrial conditions in general are changing as rapidly as scientific inventions are being patented.

The object of the A. C. A. in its recent investigation was to find out why, and to what extent an inequality of wages is paid to men and women performing the same kind of work. Circulars were sent out to members of the A. C. A. engaged chiefly in professional, mercantile, or technical pursuits; but the pamphlet says that the inquiries were not in all cases restricted to alumnae, but include in some instances women, not college-bred, engaged in occupations requiring special training. We are led to infer that the proportion of non-college women is small; but it is to be regretted that the exact figures have not been given, as it leads to confusion, both about the kind of work done by graduates and the compensation they receive.

The number of schedules returned in response to this investigation was 451. They represent all parts of the country – 90 from New York, 61 from California, 59 from Massachusetts, 55 from Minnesota, 44 from Connecticut, 40 from Rhode Island, 39 from Indiana, 14 from Illinois, and the remainder (153) scattered among other States. The total number of occupations given is 66, but many of these are very nearly allied. There are 169 teachers, the largest number in any single employment, 47 librarians and women engaged in library work, 28 stenographers, 22 nurses and superintendents of nursing, 19 journalists, including editors and reporters, and 19 clerks without specification as to the kind of service. To show the variety of occupations represented, it may be mentioned that there is an actress, advertising agent, assistant in the National Herbarium, assistant on dictionary, assistant in observatory, astronomer, car recorder, draughtswoman, insurance broker, insurance solicitor, writer of advertisements, reviser of patents, water analyst, beside several proofreaders, telegraph operators, bookkeepers, and artists.

In looking over this list one is at once struck by the absence of physicians. This is probably due to the fact that this investigation does not consider independent workers, but only those employed by some firm or institution. The earnings of independent workers depend so much upon individual qualities that it is little use to try to classify them.

It may be mentioned in passing, however, that the profession of medicine is probably the most lucrative, as it is certainly one of the most useful and honorable in which women can engage. It has always been a matter of surprise to me that more college women have not undertaken it. Out of a total of 1,945 members in the last register of the A. C. A., but 35, or less than two per cent. write M. D. after their names. So far as I can learn, the woman physician in general practice in the smaller cities receives precisely the same fee as a man. In fact, the fee for an ordinary office or house visit is usually fixed by custom, and the young physician receives the same pay as the older one. The charges of specialists are graded by their reputation; and in the large cities all doctors' fees depend upon the quarter of the town they live in. The income of an established physician (male or female) in any of our cities of 15,000 or more inhabitants cannot be less than several thousand dollars yearly, and though the living expenses (house and horses) must be considerable, the physician can probably make a better financial showing than almost any other woman worker. The profession requires a long and expensive preparatory training, but one would suppose there are plenty of college women who would not be daunted by that.

To return to our tables, we find that 338 of the total number of respondents have some other remunerative occupation besides their main work; 74 have no other, while 39 make no answer. This seems rather surprising, especially as we immediately learn that in 350 cases (about 78 per cent. of the whole) the wages derived from the main occupation are sufficient for the support of the worker. It is further interesting to know that 117, or nearly 26 per cent., report that they are occupied with domestic cares besides their main work. The compilers note that this diversification of industrial pursuits seems to indicate that the burden of the woman is probably heavier than that of her male fellow-worker.

The table most interesting to the general reader is that relating to salaries. There is some surprise that these are given by the monthly instead of the yearly rate. The latter estimate is more intelligible, and also more accurate, because some occupations, mainly teaching, engage one's time for only nine months of the year. In the absence of any information to the contrary, we may suppose that the teacher's yearly income is divided into twelve parts, in order to classify it with the salary of workers whose occupation continues all the year round.

By consulting the tables we find that 144 respondents, the largest number in any one class, are paid a salary between \$50 and \$75 a month, *i. e.*, from \$600 to \$900 a year. On either side of them we find two equal groups of 88 each. One of these groups receives between \$25 and \$50 a month (\$300 to \$600 a year) and the other receives between \$75 and \$100 a month (\$900 to \$1,200 a year). There are 73 who receive between \$100 and \$200 a month (\$1,200 to \$2,500 a year); two who are paid between \$200 and \$300 a month (\$2,400 to \$3,600 a year); and then comes the glorious news that two women receive over \$300 a month (\$3,600 a year).

This last fact ought to give a momentary gleam of happiness to every woman who reads these lines. There are two college women in this country whose services are adjudged by the firm or corporation which employs them as worth over \$3,600 a year. One of these women is classed as a teacher (she may be a college president), and one as an insurance solicitor. Under cover of their brilliant record we can slip in the fact that six women acknowledge that they receive less than \$25 a month (\$300 a year). This is such a manifestly inadequate sum that we are forced to conclude that the whole time of the workers is not paid for, either because they are learning the business or because the business does not require many hours a day. These six workers are classified as follows: Three in library employment, one typesetter, one stenographer, and one assistant postmaster.

To recapitulate: There are 238 who receive less than \$75 a month, and 165 who receive from \$75 to \$300 and over. Perhaps the profession of teaching deserves to be especially considered. Of the 161 teachers who reply to this question, 24 receive under $50 a month; 64 receive between $50 and $75; 42 receive between $75 and $100; 29 between $100 and $200; one between $200 and $300, and one over $300. There is but one other woman who receives between $200 and $300 a month, and she is an editor.

A salary of between $100 and $200 a month ought to support a single woman in comfort. Besides the 29 teachers there are 44 other women who receive this amount. Nine are engaged in library work, four as editors or reporters, four as nurses or superintendents of nursing, four as clerks, three as stenographers, four as typesetters (is not this unexpected?), and one each as artist, assistant in the National Herbarium, assistant curator, assistant on dictionary, assistant postmaster, astronomer, bookkeeper, bookkeeper and cashier, examiner of bonds, manager, telegraph manager, stenographer and bookkeeper, stenographer and typewriter, combination stenography, teaching and newspaper work, typewriter, writer of advertisements, reviser of patents. While about 38 per cent. of the whole number of respondents are teachers, about 40 per cent. of those earning over $100 a month are teachers.

It is often asked why the majority of self-supporting, educated women continue to enter the profession of teaching. There seems to be good financial reason for it, notwithstanding the enormous competition. Other reasons are that a college graduate can undertake teaching without special training and that it offers large vacations, which are particularly acceptable to women. I have sometimes been told by teachers that the only redeeming feature of their work is the vacation, also that every day of it has to be utilized to get strength enough to go through with the next term. Still, a vacation gives a certain amount of independence. With past social conditions any woman engaging in active work has been almost obliged to forego social life during her period of work. The hours of labor are not those of society. Perhaps for this reason more than any other have cultivated women hesitated to undertake regular employment. They may have liked the work; they may have needed the money; but they were unwilling to sacrifice so much of what makes life worth living. There are signs of coming change. Club life seems to be reforming society along new lines. The constantly increasing army of working women of culture and social ability is compelling readjustments in our ways of thinking and forms of living.

The investigation asked one question, to which for some reason four-ninths of the respondents failed to reply. This is: How does the pay of men performing the same grade of work differ from yours? Of the 250 women who make reply, 150 get less pay than men for the same work, 95 receive the same pay, and 5 women actually receive more pay. The only comment we can make on this is that the facts are not nearly so bad as we had feared. The cheering information that five women receive more pay than men for the same work deserves analysis. One is employed in a bureau of charities, one is an editor or journalist, one is a proof-reader, and two are actually teachers!

It is often said that men should receive more pay than women because they have families to support. A teacher said to me some years ago that she did not believe there was a woman over thirty years of age earning her own living who did not have some one dependent upon her. She added: "These family obligations are not a matter of choice with women as with men. Men usually incur them by their own marriage; women find families thrust upon them through the marriage of some one else, perhaps of their own parents, years before they were born." Of the 379 women who answer this question about family support, 157 or about 41 per cent. aid in supporting others, while 222 or over 58 per cent. do not. The number of unhampered workers would seem to indicate that many young women, or women of well-to-do parents, are engaged in gainful occupations.

The committee of the A. C. A. were evidently determined to leave no side of the problem of woman's work unturned. It is sometimes alleged that women do not remain continuously in one employment or remain long enough to gain proficiency. There were 333 replies on this subject. Of the whole number of respondents, 214, nearly two-thirds, had followed but one kind of employment since beginning work. They had been at work on an average 7 years and 8 months. There were 88 who had two kinds of work in which they had been engaged 5 years and 4 months each; 19 had had three kinds of work for an average period of 4 years and 8 months; 9 had had four kinds; 2 had had five kinds, while 1 confesses to the extraordinary versatility which enabled her to perform eight kinds of work in succession for an average period of 7 months each. So far as this evidence is worth anything, it shows that the majority of women, when they have once chosen a vocation, stick to it.

In order to throw all the light possible on the reason for the inequality of male and female wages a number of employers were asked for their opinion. Replies were received from 104 employers, 25 from Massachusetts, 25 from California, 15 from Rhode Island, 14 from New York and the remainder from other States. In their establishments 7,794 persons were employed, 4,697 men and 3,097 women. It must be borne in mind that a large part of the female help could not have been college-women, though it is to be supposed that firms employing college-women were consulted whenever possible.

Of the 90 employers who replied to the question on the comparative value of the services of men and women, 46 said that they were equally valuable, 29 said the services of women were less valuable, 7 made indefinite replies, while 8 answered, "On some work, yes; on other work, no." If this is not all that could be hoped for, it is probably a better showing than could have been made ten years ago. When asked for the reason why women, in general, receive less pay than men for the same work, 67 replied as follows: 29 attribute it to the effect of supply and demand; 21 to physical and mental differences or difference in general ability, while 17 allege custom as an excuse.

I imagine that many of my readers, if they have had interest enough to follow my statements thus far, have done so for the sake of getting a definite answer to the question: Does it pay to send a girl to college? Many a well-to-do father, whose family is living comfortably and spending all he earns, and many a hard-worked mother, who wishes her daughter to have some easier and more remunerative occupation than herself, are anxiously pondering this question. After many years of investigation and observation I can give but an oracular answer. If pecuniary return be the chief motive for sending a girl to college, I should say the venture is as risky as any other business investment.

The necessary expenses at a woman's college are about $500 a year. The charges for board and tuition at Vassar and Wellesley are $400 a year; at Smith and Bryn Mawr, where there is greater variety in the accommodations, the average price is about the same. One hundred dollars is a reasonable sum for books, class and club dues, and necessary incidentals. Clothes and travelling expenses depend upon the individual. I have been told by a woman of wide experience, and my own observation confirms it, that a college woman is doing well if, upon graduation, she can obtain a place to teach for $500 a year without board. A teacher is obliged to dress decently, to live in a respectable quarter of the town, to attend an occasional concert, lecture, or play, and she ought not to be prohibited from buying books now and then, or taking a trip during vacation. She must manage well if she can do all this, even in a small city, on $500 a year. Of course, unless she is a young woman in comfortable circumstances, boarding at home, she hopes for speedy promotion; but it does not always come. I know of women who have taken advanced degrees at American and foreign universities (and this class is small enough to make its services valuable), who are filling subordinate positions in schools at less than $1,000 a year, and are unable to get any farther. Still, let us always remember that there are two women in this country who are paid a salary of over $300 a month.

It is becoming the fashion to send girls to college. The institutions are filled to overflowing, and at least three of them turn away hundreds of applicants every year for lack of room. A professor of chemistry at a woman's college, asking for enlarged laboratory facilities, said recently: "I am not begging this for myself. The pressure comes from outside. What can we do when well-prepared students insist upon coming?" There is scarcely a man's institution of any importance in the length and breadth of our land that does not admit the feminine mind, singly or in numbers, to some form of co-education, though in many instances the trustees are shy about acknowledging it.

The question, "Ought Woman to Learn the Alphabet?" which Thomas Wentworth Higginson discussed so wittily a quarter of a century ago, is happily settled, at least in this country. It has been proven that the majority of maidens take the baccalaureate degree without injury to health or manners. It has even been proven that a diploma is not necessarily a bar to their matrimonial prospects. Socially, a college woman is almost sure to have opportunities open to her, though sometimes she may be so overworked as to be unable to take advantage of them. For a rich girl a college training offers delightful possibilities. Howells says that we are getting to that state when our women are almost the only class left who have any use for what was once considered the education of a gentleman. Let us hope that some time, and the signs point that way, they may be thought worthy to receive the wages of the workingman.

10

"A POUND A WEEK; WHY GIRLS SHOULD EARN IT," *THE GIRL'S OWN PAPER*

Margaret Bateson

Source: Margaret Bateson, 'A Pound a Week – Why Girls Should Earn It', *The Girl's Own Paper*. October 1896, pp. 14–5

CURIOUS, some may think it, curious and perhaps a little ludicrous as well, that the propriety of a young woman earning a certain wage should call for any serious defence. The payment of wages in exchange for services rendered (whether we distinguish those wages by the term Civil List, salary, rent, honorarium, fee or price) is so unquestionably a part of the constitution of a sound social system, that it may well seem ridiculous to speak of it at this time of day. But humanity, with its inveterate love of change, has lately tried to oust the principle that those who render services should receive a wage, and to substitute for it the illogical practice of paying wages to those who render no service, and of demanding services from those who receive no wage. Humanity cannot of course convert these practices into a principle under penalty of starvation: but it introduces them here and there among certain sections of the population. I need not observe that among those sections women are largely comprised.

But indifferent success can, in the nature of things, attend the effort to make women work without wage. An appeal to this effect meets, I admit, with noble response from women of the highest type who engage in public work. Women of a type less than the highest take out their wage in distinction, popularity and advertisement; or they give such poor work that nobody but themselves would call it work at all. But since asking even women to do work without wage is much like inviting water to climb up-hill, I need not long tarry over this part of my subject.

For it is to the converse side of our modem heresy that I think it more needful to draw attention: the theory that women should take a wage and do no work. The expression which I have just given to the heresy will not perhaps be recognisable

DOI: 10.4324/9780429321078-11

to the ears of some of its upholders; but I think it discloses the truth of the matter. For what many women are being asked to do is to accept board, lodging, and a dress allowance on condition either of remaining absolutely still, or of only making believe to be busy. And this request is put to women by persons of the most diverse views in all other matters.

There are the old-fashioned parents who say, "You should remember that you are a young lady, my dear. If you struggle to earn your living, vulgar people will forget that you are the daughter of gentlefolk." There arc the sentimental people who say, "A girl should always be sweet, and beautiful, and passive. Follow this prescription, and you will certainly find a man – father, brother, or the eventual husband to support you." If the girl should murmur a distaste for the "supported" condition, she is "unwomanly," and with that all disapproval is uttered. Laughter, however, is driving both the old-fashioned people and the sentimentalists out of existence; therefore we need scarcely trouble to send ridicule after the retreating figures. But younger heretics are coming into the field to take their place; heretics who assure us that they are ultra-modern and advanced. These come dressed, moreover, in a panoply of pseudo-science, and don the air of sage political economists; so that a simple girl with no arguments, save youth's instinctive craving for activity, can scarcely defend herself against their sophistries.

Everyone must be familiar with the usual line of attack. It takes the form of an appeal to a girl's generosity and to her fellow-feeling for other girls. The individual girl is reminded that if she remains living at home tranquilly and quietly (for movement is of itself expensive), she can just manage to subsist. Then why should she insist upon doing work for pay? It is sordid of her to wish it. Moreover – and it is at this point that our tender-hearted girl succumbs – she must infallibly deprive other girls of a wage who need it more. Some persons I have known to be so possessed by the force of this reasoning that they will gravely argue that a responsible post should be filled by the poorest candidate, regardless of all qualifications of efficiency; and I have also heard the argument pushed yet a point further in the assertion that a housewife should not hang up her own pictures or make her own jam, because, by so doing, she must be keeping some person out of employment.

The upholders of these preposterous views would have yet to go a few steps further to be absolutely consistent. They should choose for Premier a claimant for Poor-House relief; they should buy only the books of indigent writers, and should decline to take tickets to see the performance of a prosperous actress. They have not, however, to the best of my knowledge, yet gone so far, nor have I yet heard them express disapprobation at the conduct of any woman who earns an income that is exceptionally large, or who obtains fancy prices for her pictures or books. The argument, in short, is almost entirely reserved for the deterring of young women from entering the field of professional and industrial life. And since I believe that girls are far more often withheld by such an argument than by any indisposition of their own to wholesome, well-paid labour, I think space may not be thrown away in considering upon what foundation the argumental structure rests.

It rests, does it not, upon the assumption that the amount of work which can be done in the world is limited? As the population of the world increases, the amount of employment, we would be led to suppose, does not increase, but tends to diminish to a smaller and smaller allowance per head, like drinking-water in time of drought. Consequently the less each person can contrive to do the kinder he (and particularly she) will be to his neighbours. Yet each person who is born requires to be fed, clothed, educated, amused, and the rest; thereby adding to the stock of work that wants doing. The whole train of ideas sounds too absurd for human acceptance. We do it an injustice, however, if we do not bethink ourselves of the circumstance that has given it strength. The introduction of machinery has altered the conditions of some kinds of work, and has shifted employment from one set of persons to another.

But there is no proof that the general stock of work is growing less. It needs little imagination to foresee that manufactures may increase greatly, that trade can be indefinitely extended, and that a demand for many services is only waiting to be formulated when the services are supplied. Indeed what we term the "Woman's Movement" means, if we regard it from one point of view, the creation of many demands. Who is it, for instance, who employs the expert woman shorthand-writer? It is in many cases, the woman-lecturer, the woman of business, or the woman-doctor. Who requires the woman-accountant? The society for promoting some reform in which women are interested, or the governing body of a public girls' school. The employment of girls in the Civil Service leads to the engagement of a woman-doctor to attend them, and the factory girls whose labour machinery so largely utilises, need women-inspectors to safeguard their conditions of work. And though in London and our large towns we are slowly waking up to the fact that the capacities of women of the educated middle and upperclass are not wisely allowed to atrophy, the country at large still wastes much useful labour. In how many of our rural districts is there a trained nurse, much less a cottage hospital, with a nursing staff of women? In how many country places are educated women trying by their own practical exertions to unravel the farmers' and the labourers' problems; in how many are they idling through their days, or at best bicycling over the country to kill time – and simply because they believe paid labour to be wrong.

You will ask, seeing that I am so near the end of my exhortation, why I am especially appealing to girls to earn a pound a week? My chief reason is that I regard a pound a week as the average beginning salary of the middle-class girl. To the girl who in the factory or the workshop is earning less, and by very hard labour, I have no need to appeal. My only word to her is one of inducement, to try by superior training, by combination, by whatever fair means lie in her power, to win more adequate pay.

But the middle-class girl should begin with a pound a week; if possible, of course, with more; certainly not with less. And here I may say that the stories which I hear of girls who destroy each other's chances of salary, by offering to do work for board and lodging only, or for a salary less than that offered, I regard much as I should some exhibition of cannibalism. If the women who practice this industrial cannibalism are really well off, their conduct is wholly inexcusable. Generally inquiry reveals that these women are not really well off. They appear to be in comfortable circumstances, but actually they are at their last gasp to obtain a livelihood. And the last gasp assumes the shape of this monstrous and cut-throat underselling.

Introduce into the labour market women with some capital of means and ability; you will not observe that underselling is the policy of such of these. On the contrary, the market, in trade parlance, will acquire tone; better salaries will be offered, better work be discovered that wants doing. It is only so long as women are withheld from earning a living until the moment when they are absolutely penniless, that the iniquities of underselling and under-paying can characterise women's employment. That is why I would beg girls not to wait to earn a living till the day of misfortune, poverty and helplessness comes, but now, while youth, energy, and independence are theirs, to take the Queen's shilling of the worker's world – a pound a week.

In my next article, the readers of THE GIRL'S OWN PAPER and I may take counsel together in what way that pound shall be earned.

11

"THE PROBLEM OF EMPLOYMENT FOR NEGRO WOMEN," *SOUTHERN WORKMAN*

Fannie Barrier Williams

Source: Fannie Barrier Williams, 'The Problem of Employment for Negro Women', *Southern Workman*, Vol. 32, September, pp. 432–471

It can be broadly said that colored women know how to work, and have done their full share of the paid and unpaid service rendered to the American people by the Negro race. This is a busy world; the world's work is large, complicated, and increasing. The demand for the competent in all kinds of work is never fully supplied. Woman is constantly receiving a larger share of the work to be done. The field for her skill, her endurance, her finer instincts and faithfulness is ever enlarging; and she has become impatient of limitations, except those imposed by her own physical condition. In this generalization, colored women, of course, are largely excepted. For reasons too well understood here to be repeated, ours is a narrow sphere. While the kinds and grades of occupation open to all women of white complexion are almost beyond enumeration, those open to our women are few in number and mostly menial in quality. The girl who is white and capable is in demand in a thousand places. The capable Negro girl is usually not in demand, This is one of the stubborn facts of to-day. Shall we waste our energy and soul in fretting over it, or shall we bravely say, "Well, what I would do, I cannot, so I will do that which I can in the best way I can." Thoreau said that "if people would spend half as much effort in trying to be happy with what they have, as they spend in wishing for what they haven't got, the world would be far happier." It seems to me that this bit of philosophy aptly applies to our case in this matter of employment.

In the face of this condition, then, what can we do? To answer this question there is required large-heartedness and much wisdom. This answer must be worked out, not by our women alone, but by the co-operation of the best minds and best hearts of all the people. In considering the present-day opportunities and lack of opportunities for colored women I shall not consider the teachers nor the

DOI: 10.4324/9780429321078-12

few women here and there who are in the professions. We need have no anxiety about the superior woman. She will make her way in the world in spite of restrictions. But it is with the average colored woman that we must reckon. We find her engaged in some one of the following occupations: domestic service, laundering, dressmaking, hair dressing, manicuring, and nursing. Here and there is a typewriter and stenographer, a book-keeper, or a government employee. In Southern communities colored women as a rule are not employed in factories, nor do they form part of the great army of clerks of all kinds.

In the city of Chicago domestic service is the one occupation in which the demand for colored women exceeds the supply. In one employment office during the past year there were 1,500 applications for colored women and only 1,000 of this number were supplied. Girls of other nationalities do not seem to compete with colored women as domestics. It is probably safe to say that every colored woman who is in any way competent can find good employment. Her wages for general housework range from four to seven dollars per week, while a good cook receives from seven to ten dollars. Now what is the condition of this service? The two most important things are that the wages paid are higher than those given for the same grade of intelligence in any other calling, and that colored women can command almost a monopoly of this employment.

It might be safe to presume that since our women are so much in demand for this service they give perfect satisfaction. In considering this it is important to bear in mind that there are two kinds of colored women who perform domestic service. First, there are those who take to the work naturally and whose training and habits make them perfectly satisfied with it; and second, those who have had more or less education and who are ambitious to do something in the line of "polite occupations." The women of the latter class do not take to domestic service very kindly. They do not enter the service with any pride. They feel compelled to do this work because they can find nothing else to do. They are always sensitive as to how they may be regarded by their associates and friends and shrink from the term servant as something degrading "per se." There is a general complaint among housekeepers that the younger and more intelligent colored women are unreliable as domestics. They say that as soon as a young woman has earned enough money to buy a fine dress she leaves her place, that she demands a holiday every time there is a picnic or a funeral and wears herself out in social dissipations of all kinds. These are some of the complaints that may be heard concerning the present generation of young women who "work out." I am sorry to say that there is a great deal of truth in them. Women who take up any kind of work with a fixed dislike and shame for it are not apt to win the good will of their employers.

But of course there is another side to this story. It must be remembered that the ordinary mistress of a house is far from being an angel. Although I am a woman and a housekeeper, I must admit that the average housewife is apt to be a petty tyrant, and while she has smiles, graciousness, and gentleness for the parlor, [she is likely] to show all kinds of meanness and harshness in the kitchen. She seldom assumes that there is a higher nature in her helpers that might sometimes be appealed to. Many mistresses cannot rid themselves of the idea that the woman whom she employs to do housework is inferior and servile by nature, and must receive the treatment accorded to inferiors. The woman who understands this haughtiness of spirit and exaggerated superiority is always resentful and on the defensive. If it were possible to change the disposition and heart of the average American housewife, and so to elevate the service that the cook or housemaid would not be looked down upon because she is a servant and as such not supposed to possess womanly instincts and aspirations, a better grade of helpers would gladly enter this field of employment.

It is of course an easy thing to condemn our young women who have been fairly educated and have had good home training, because they prefer idleness to domestic service, but I am rather inclined to think that we must share in that condemnation. If our girls work for wages in a nice home, rather than in a factory or over a counter, they are ruthlessly scorned by their friends and acquaintances. Our young men, whose own occupations by the way will not always bear scrutiny, will also give her the cut direct, so that between the scorn of her associates and the petty tyranny of the housewife, the colored girl who enters domestic service is compelled to have more than ordinary strength of character.

But after all is said, I believe that it is largely in the power of the young woman herself to change and elevate the character of domestic service. She certainly cannot improve it by taking into it ignorance, contempt, and inefficiency. There is no reason why a woman of character, graciousness, and skill should not make her work as a domestic as respectable and as highly regarded as the work of the girl behind the department-store counter. For example, if, by special training in domestic service, a girl can cook so well and do everything about a house so deftly and thoroughly that she will be called a real home helper and an invaluable assistant, it is in her power, with her intelligent grasp upon the possibilities of her position, to change the whole current of public opinion in its estimate of domestic service. These young women, as a general thing, belong to families that are too poor to keep them well dressed if they are idle, yet colored girls on the streets of Chicago and other cities are often better dressed than the girls of any other race in like circumstances. There is a strong suspicion prevalent that this fine dressing is at a cost that demoralizes the social life of the colored people. This is the most serious consequence of our restricted employment. The girl who is barred from the occupation she would like to follow, and has no taste, talent, or desire for what she must do, is apt to become discouraged and indifferent. If she finds that society on all sides is hostile to her ambitions, she will become in turn hostile to society and contemptuous of its ethics and code of morals.

What, then, shall we do for the young colored woman with refined instincts and fair education? She is ambitious to choose and follow the occupation for which she is best fitted by talents and inclination, but she is shut out from most of the employments open to other women, and does not realize that her refinement and training are as much needed and as well paid for in domestic service as in other occupations. We are afraid of the word "servant." In England the terms master and servant are not hateful to the thousands of self-respecting Englishmen who bear them. If we could in some way create a sentiment that the girl who can carry as much intelligence and graciousness of manner into the kitchen will be as much respected and will get married just as soon as her sisters in other occupations, much of the present-day false notions about domestic service would be changed. A young woman of character and intelligence, who is competent to do domestic work, can never be a servant in an offensive sense and will not be so regarded. To bring about this change so as to enable our girls to enter upon this occupation without loss of self-respect and without the danger of ostracism by so-called society is a problem worthy of the best thought and devotion of our men and women.

What is called the servant-girl problem is one of the most vexatious of the many social questions of the hour. The work of housekeeping is neither a trade nor a profession; it is without discipline or organization and is largely irresponsible and uncertain. It is usually a case of a good mistress and a bad servant or a bad mistress and a good servant. Thousands of housekeepers attempt to manage their help who have never learned to manage themselves. The housekeeper's manner to the butcher, the baker, the milkman, the shoemaker, the dressmaker, and the milliner and to every other person upon whom she is more or less dependent, is often more respectful than it is to the woman upon whom she is dependent every hour of the day for ease and comfort, health and happiness. Many of the leading women of the country have begun to study this problem for the purpose of elevating the service. The first thing to be done is to bring it strongly to our consciousness that domestic service is not necessarily degrading. In the city of Chicago, schools of domestic science are as eagerly patronized as schools in which book-keeping and typewriting are taught. They are slowly teaching the all-important fact that the thing we call domestic service has in it the elements of high art and much science. It is an occupation that intelligence elevates, that character adorns and ennobles, and that even now brings a higher salary to women than almost any other kind of employment.

When domestic service becomes a profession, as it surely will, by the proper training of those who shall follow it, what will be the condition of colored girls who would participate in its benefits? It is now time to prepare ourselves to answer this question. In my opinion, the training for this new profession should be elevated to the dignity and importance of the training in mathematics and grammar and other academic studies. Our girls must be made to feel that there is no stepping down when they become professional housekeepers. The relative dignity, respectability, and honor of this profession should first be taught in our schools. As it is now, the young woman in school or college knows that if she enters domestic service, she loses the relationships that she has formed. But schools of domestic science cannot do it all. The every-day man and woman who make society must change their foolish notions as to what is the polite thing for a young woman to do. The kind of stupidity that calls industrial education drudgery is the same kind of stupidity that looks upon the kitchen as a place for drudges. We must learn that the girl who cooks our meals and keeps our houses sweet and beautiful deserves just as high a place in our social economy as the girl who makes our gowns and hats, or the one who teaches our children. In what I have said on this particular phase of our industrial life, I do not wish to be understood as advocating the restriction of colored girls to house service, even when that service is elevated to the rank of a profession. My only plea is that we shall protect and respect our girls who honestly and intelligently enter this service, either from preference or necessity.

It seems to me that we lose a great opportunity if we fail to take hold of this problem in a thoroughly broad and philosophic way and work out its solution. If we wish to contribute something substantial to the social betterment of American living, we have the opportunity in helping to solve this servant-girl problem. Vexation of spirit, waste, indigestion, and general demoralization cry out from the American home for relief from its domestic miseries. We have it in our power to assist in answering this Macedonian cry. It would help to give our race a standing if we could count several of our men and women as the best thinkers and most effective workers in the solution of this problem. Shall we lead or shall we follow in this movement? Shall we, in this as in many other things, beg for an opportunity further on instead of helping to create opportunities now?

There is still another consideration which suggests the importance to the colored people of taking the lead in helping to improve and elevate this service. Race prejudice is kept up and increased in thousands of instances by the incompetent and characterless women who are engaged in this work. While there are thousands of worthy and really noble women in domestic service who enjoy the confidence and affection of their employers, there is a large percentage of colored women who, by their general unworthiness, help to give the Negro race a bad name. For white people North and South are very apt to estimate the entire race from the standpoint of their own servant girls. When intelligence takes the place of ignorance, and good manners, efficiency, and self-respect take the place of shiftlessness and irresponsibility in American homes, one of the chief causes of race prejudice will be removed.

It should also be borne in mind that the colored girl who is trained in the arts of housekeeping is better qualified for the high duties of wifehood and motherhood.

Let me say by way of summary that I have dwelt mostly upon the opportunities of domestic service for the following reasons:

1. It is the one field in which colored women meet with almost no opposition. It is ours almost by birthright.

2. The compensation for this service, in Northern communities at least, is higher than that paid for average clerkships in stores and offices.

3. The service is susceptible of almost unlimited improvement and elevation.

4. The nature of the work is largely what we make it.

5. White women of courage and large intelligence are lifting domestic service to a point where it will have the dignity of a profession, and colored women are

in danger, through lack of foresight, of being relegated to the positions of scrub women and dishwashers.

6. The colored girl who has no taste or talent for school teaching, dressmaking, or manicuring is in danger of being wasted in idleness, unless we can make domestic service worthy of her ambition and pride.

7. There can be no feature of our race problem more important than the saving of our young women; we can, perhaps, excuse their vanities, but idleness is the mildew on the garment of character.

8. Education has no value to human society, unless it can add importance and respectability to the things we find to do.

9. Though all the factories and offices close their doors at our approach, this will be no calamity if we are strong enough to so transform the work that we must do that it shall become an object of envy and emulation to those who now deny us their industrial fellowship.

12

"HARRIET MARTINEAU AND THE EMPLOYMENT OF WOMEN IN 1836," *JOURNAL OF POLITICAL ECONOMY*[1]

Edith Abbott

Source: Edith Abbott, 'Harriet Martineau and the Employment of Women in 1836', *Journal of Political Economy*, Vol. 14, No. 10, Dec. 1906, pp. 614–626

It is essential to any profitable discussion of women's work that the gainful employment of middle-class women be distinguished from the gainful employment of women of the working-classes. This is not so much an insistence on "class distinctions" in discussions of the woman question as it is a recognition of the fact that, while the problems which these two classes of women have been obliged to face may have a certain fundamental identity, they are as practical problems quite different. And a failure to see important points of unlikeness has led at times to confusion in theory and to unfortunate practical results. It is, for example, a part of the history of the struggle for factory legislation in England that an unwillingness to grant that the working-woman had peculiar grievances delayed the progress of very necessary reforms,[2] and it has followed from the resulting theoretical confusion that, in attempts to formulate the achievements of the long efforts of the last century to enlarge the opportunities and activities of women – efforts which to the German economist assume the importance of a *Bewegung*[3] – such progress as has been made is assumed to have been a progress without "class distinctions" in which working-women and professional women have shared alike. In the following brief study – a study in economic history and not in present conditions – an attempt is made to present a more detailed account than has been given before of the industrial opportunities open to women seventy years ago. No list of the industries in which women were then engaged that can lay the smallest claim to completeness has been heretofore accessible, and it has been easy to be misled into believing that we are estopped from obtaining any such information for a period earlier than 1860.[4]

DOI: 10.4324/9780429321078-13

The most convenient and definite statement regarding the early employment of women is one made on the authority of Harriet Martineau, to the effect that, when she visited America in 1836, but seven occupations were open to women:[5] teaching, needlework, keeping boarders, work in cotton-mills, typesetting, bookbinding, and domestic service. Of these only four – work in cotton-mills, typesetting, needlework, and bookbinding – come within the present discussion of industrial occupations. It should be said at the outset, in fairness to Miss Martineau, that, although this is taken from a chapter[6] on the "Occupations of Women," it is a casual and not a carefully prepared enumeration. She does not herself even include domestic service, though she often refers to it; and she also mentions that in Lynn many of the women were engaged in binding and trimming shoes;[7] yet this occupation though a vastly more important one than bookbinding or typesetting, is not included in the list. It should be added, too, that she used the more general term "mills"[8] instead of "cotton-mills," which is used in the list as commonly quoted, and she may well have had in mind other textile factories in operation at that time.

Miss Martineau's casual statement[9] of the meager opportunities of employment for working-women in 1836 lends convenient color to vague and comforting generalizations regarding the multiplication of industrial openings for women that has come with our years of progress. No attempt will be made here to contradict these generalizations or to offer new ones. It is only hoped that more exact information regarding the earlier period may be useful as a trustworthy basis for future discussions.

Fortunately, valuable data for this early period are by no means so unobtainable as has been represented. There are three important sources of information for 1836 and the fifteen years preceding. . . .

It appears from these reports that prior to 1837 women were employed in more than one hundred different industrial occupations. In the *Documents* of 1832 the New Hampshire returns show that they were employed in the manufacture of brushes, bobbins, books, batting, cigars and snuff, gum, garden seeds, glass bottles, fur and wool hats,[10] leather and morocco leather, musical instruments, paper,[11] starch, straw hats, roots and herbs, tin-plating, wire, wheel-heads, whips; as well as in printing, tailoring, and cloth-dressing, and of course in cotton- and woolen-mills and in "boots and shoes."

The Connecticut investigation found women also employed[12] in brass foundries, in silversmith work, in the manufacture of buttons and combs,[13] cabinet-ware, coaches and wagons, caps, clocks, cotton-webbing and cotton-wicks, iron nails, jewelry,[14] line twine, metal-clasps,[15] razor strops, stone-ware, suspenders,[16] and pocket-books.

Putting together the returns in the census of 1837 and those in the *Documents* for Massachusetts, the list of industries is extended to include the manufacture of boxes, bed-cords and clothes-lines, blacking, children's carriages, cards, chocolate, cordage and twine, candles and soap, cork-cutters, cigars[17] and tobacco, chairs,[18] chair stuff, crackers, carpets, curtains, cheese, and butter, copperas, furs, furniture, flax, flint glass, fishing-nets, gimlets, hair cloth and hair beds, hosiery, hooks and eyes, india-rubber, lead, lead pencils, lace,[19] letter-boxes, locks, looking-glasses, paper hangings, pails, rakes, stocks, tacks, types, thread and sewing silk, umbrellas, window blinds; and they were also engaged in millinery,[20] tailoring and mantua-making, making of instruments, wool-pulling, gold-beating, silk- and wool-dyeing, lithographing, bed-binding, and upholstering; and women were employed as silversmiths and in publishing houses.[21]

Returns from other states were not detailed enough to add any other industries to this list, which would have been greatly extended if returns from New York had even approached in completeness those from Massachusetts. The *Digest* of 1822, while not so complete for any one section as that of 1832 was for Massachusetts, covers the whole country more evenly, and therefore increases the variety of industries which had women employees during this period. The list[22] for 1822 shows that women were employed in the manufacture of *anchors, beer, brass nails*, books, *barrels, boats, button-molds*, buttons, brushes, *bar-iron, bagging (hemp)*, bakery products, *beds*, boots and shoes, candles and soap, coaches, cheese, combs, cigars, cotton cloths, cordage and twine, chairs, clocks, cards, *cooper's ware*, clothing, *carts, earthen-ware*, furniture, *flour, floor-cloth, gloves, gold-leaf, gunpowder, gunstocks*, fur and wool hats, *hardware, iron castings, iron work, iron (bar), iron (pig), iron (rolled)*, leather, lace, *lumber, machinery, maple sugar*, morocco leather, *medicines, millstones, oil (flaxseed)*, paper, *plow-line* and ropes, *salt*, saddles, *saddletrees, stoves*, straw hats, *shovels*, silver- and gold-ware, *saltpeter*, tin-ware, tobacco and snuff, types, woolen goods, yarn, whips, *whiskey and gin.*

The exact number of industries in these lists would be hard to estimate fairly, as some of the expressions used are clearly redundant. Other industries, it has been found, might have been added if the newspapers of the time had also been used as sources of information. It seemed better, however, for many reasons, to confine the discussion within the limits of the three official reports. Using these, all that seems to be possible in the way of a fair summary is to repeat what has already been said – that more than one hundred industrial occupations were open to women at this time. Of all these, needlework or tailoring, binding shoes, making straw hats, and work in the cotton- and woolen-mills were by far the most important.[23]. . . The sewing trades, whether in ready-made or custom work, seem to have been seventy-five years ago, as they are today, numerically the most important occupation, as well as the last hope and degradation of the woman wage-earner.

In concluding this fragmentary study, it should be emphasized that its purpose has not been to describe the condition of the working-woman in the thirties, or to compare her situation then with that of today. It has not even been attempted to compare the field of employment then and now. But it should, perhaps, be said that, while a large proportion of the enumerated occupations employed only a very few women and were relatively unimportant, the same comment may be made upon the long list of women's occupations today. The last census, for example, showed that women were carpenters, masons, miners, blacksmiths, "quarrymen," and the like, which obviously means little when the real field of employment is considered. There is, moreover, great need that this field should have been widened. The female population over ten years of age has increased from 234,654 in 1830 to 1,343,905 in 1900 – nearly fivefold. No positive statement can be made as to whether the number of women who are competing for industrial employment, out of every one hundred of this population, has increased or not. But even had there been no change – which is, of course, highly improbable – the need of new occupations would still exist, unless the old ones had become five times as important; and there are good reasons for supposing that this has not been the case.[24]

Any attempt to present the conditions or the statistics of women's employment in 1836 must be disclaimed. The purpose of the present note has been merely to call attention to the fact that the field of employment for women in industry was broader at that time than is generally supposed; so much broader, in fact, that one is bound to question whether the world has changed as much for the working-class woman in the last seventy-five years as it has, for example, for women in educational or professional work. Miss Martineau wrote then, in the *Society in America:*

> One consequence, mournful and injurious, of the "chivalrous" taste and temper of a country with regard to its women is that it is difficult where it is not impossible for women to earn their bread. Where it is a boast that women do not labor the encouragement and rewards of labor are not provided. It is so in America. In some parts there are now so many women dependent on their exertions that the evil will give way before the force of circumstances. In the meantime the lot of the poor women is sad.

How far Miss Martineau's comments were true then, and how far they are still true, would be perhaps a matter of opinion. But one could not go far wrong in saying that the lot of the poor woman is still sad. Opportunity of employment is scarce now as it was then.[25] The sewing trades are still demoralized, and women's wages are still low. Now as then working-women are unorganized and exploited, and they still live, as they always have lived, in "ways known only to the poor."

NOTES

1 The writer is under obligations to the Department of Economics of the Carnegie Institution of Washington for the opportunity of making the investigation of which this is one of the results.

2 In an interesting chapter on "The Woman's Rights Opposition," Miss Hutchins and Miss Harrison point out (*History of Factory Legislation*, pp. 183, 184) the difference between the "social and customary disabilities which have been placed on women's work in the professions . . . . and the restraints placed by law on the over-work of women in industry. Not exclusion but exploitation is the trouble here . . . . [working-women] are not denied the opportunity of exercising their muscles as their better-off sisters were or are of exercising their brains."

3 E. g., Conrad, *Handwörterbuch der Staatswissenschaft*, Vol. III, pp. 564, 565.

4 In Campbell's *Women Wage-Earners,* a prize monograph of the American Economic Association in 1891, it is said: "Defeat and discouragement attend well-nigh every step

of the attempt to reach any conclusions regarding women workers in the early years of the century. . . . . It is to the United States Census of 1860 that we must look for the first really definite statement as to the occupations of women and children" (pp. 95, 96). For a similar statement see Willett, *Women in the Clothing Trades*, p. 24.

5 See, for example, Levasseur's *L'ouvrier américain,* Adams' Translation, p. 337, and Wright's *Industrial Evolution of the United States,* p. 202.

6 Harriet Martineau, *Society in America* (London, 1837), Vol. II, pp. 131–51.

7 In a chapter on "Manufacturing Labor," *ibid.,* Vol. II, pp. 249, 250.

8 *Ibid.,* p. 148.

9 Another casual statement easy to "quote" is found in the same chapter: "Wifely and motherly occupations may be called the sole business of woman there. . . . . The only alternative . . . . is making an occupation of either religion or dissipation." (*Ibid.,* Vol. II. p. 245.)

10 This was a very important industry at that time and an old one for this country. In 1831 it was estimated that 3,000 women were employed in the manufacture in various parts of the country. See the "Reports of Committees" in the *Address and Proceedings of the Friends of Domestic Industry at the New York Convention, October 26, 1831* (Baltimore, 1831), p. 39.

11 The manufacture of paper had long furnished an occupation for women. Before 1789, women and girls were employed in paper-mills, and more than a thousand women and children were shown to have been employed in 1822 (*Digest of 1822,* and Bishop's *History of Manufactures*, Vol. II, p. 207). About 1825, paper began to be made by the use of the Fourdernier machine, and the most extensive manufactory was said to have been at Springfield, Mass., "employing twelve engines, more than 100 females besides the usual number of male hands" (Bishop, *op. cit*., p. 303). The "census" of 1837 showed 605 women in the paper-mills of Massachusetts.

12 Industries that were on the New Hampshire list are of course not repeated.

13 An important industry in Connecticut and Massachusetts, employing nearly a thousand women.

14 The manufacture of jewelry was more important in Rhode Island, where 122 women were employed.

15 A New Britain industry, which employed 157 women.

16 The manufacture of stocks and suspenders in the two states of Connecticut and Massachusetts gave employment to more than 700 women.

17 The *Documents* showed 230 women in cigar-making for Massachusetts, but undoubtedly a complete investigation would have showed many more in the industry.

18 According to the returns, *ibid*., 219 women were employed in chair factories.

19 Lace-making was an important "woman's industry" at this time. The *Documents* returned more than 500 women engaged in it in Massachusetts; and it was said to be extensively carried on elsewhere, employing 600 women in Newport, R. I. (See the *Report of the Harrisburg Convention in the Interests of Domestic Industry,* a pamphlet published in 1827.)

20 It was estimated that 60 milliners employed 420 women at $0.75 a day in Boston (*Documents,* Vol. I, p. 451). The enumerator commented in a rather caustic vein: "This class of manufacturers it has been found difficult to estimate as women are not generally accountants and therefore it is not easy for them to answer the questions proposed. Many of them decline giving any answer apparently from the apprehension that their statements may be considered absurd. Others refuse for the usual woman's reason *because*. The estimate is believed to be rather within the actual amount than to exceed it."

21 More than 300 women in Boston were engaged in bookbinding or in other work for "booksellers and publishers."

22 The complete list is given here, and all industries which have not already been enumerated are italicized.

23 Work in paper-mills, and the manufacture of fur and wool hats, perhaps belong here. It has already been noted *supra* that both occupations were very important. It is significant, too, that two of the four occupations enumerated by Miss Martineau – viz., bookbinding and typesetting – are not included.

24 For a discussion of this point see the October, 1906, number of this *Journal*, on the "History of the Industrial Employment of Women, etc."

25 Among the replies from manufacturers in the *Documents* of 1831 is a letter from Smith Wilkinson, who is remembered because of his early association with Samuel Slater. An extract from this letter, written as he said, out of his twenty-five years' experience is worth quoting, not as a typical but as an interesting statement: "Our greatest difficulty at present is a want of females – women and children – and from the great number of factories now building, have my fears that we shall not be able to operate all our machinery another year."

13

"THE ECONOMIC FOUNDATIONS OF THE WOMEN'S MOVEMENT"

Mabel Atkinson

Source: Mabel Atkinson, 'The Economic Foundations of the Women's Movement', Fabian Women's Group Series, no. 4 Fabian Tract, no. 175 (London: Fabian Society, 1914).

The spiritual aspect of the women's movement

PURELY economic causes are never sufficient to account entirely for any great revolt of the human spirit. Behind every revolution there lies a spiritual striving, a grasping after an ideal felt rather than seen. Most emphatically is it true that there is a social impulse independent of economic conditions, which has over and over again asserted itself in the demand for the emancipation of women. All the greatest seers and prophets have insisted on the equal value of men and women, and on the right of women to control their own lives. Four centuries before Christ, Plato claimed that in the life of the State women, as well as men, should take their place; and in all the records of Christ's conversations, which the Gospels have handed down to us, there is not one hint that he advocated that subordination of women on which his disciples later on insisted. In Rome also, at the Renaissance, and at the time of the French Revolution, powerful voices were raised in denunciation of the subjection of women.

These demands were, however, only sporadic. At most they affected a small class. It was not until the nineteenth century that the demand of women for political, economic, and educational freedom was heard among any considerable mass of the people. This extension of the demand for emancipation was due to economic changes, to those alterations in human control over environment which are associated with the substitution of mechanical power for human energy in the making of commodities, and with the development of powerful and smoothly working machines in place of human hands and simple tools.

DOI: 10.4324/9780429321078-14

THE EFFECT OF THE INDUSTRIAL REVOLUTION

Probably when Hargreaves invented his spinning jenny, and when Arkwright established his first cotton mill, in which the power of water took the place of the easily wearied arms of humanity, they had no conception of the fact that they were preparing the way for the greatest revolution in human society which has ever taken place since man learnt the use of fire. Yet nothing less was the truth, for then first men learnt how to utilize for their service the energies of the universe without previously absorbing them into their own bodies or into the bodies of domesticated animals in the form of food. Before the end of the eighteenth century man did indeed use water power on a small scale for grinding corn, and the capricious force of the wind for the same end and for propelling sailing vessels. But the energies of steam and electricity and petrol were lying dormant or running to waste all around him, while he sweated at the forge or the loom, and was hauled slowly over badly made roads by the straining sinews of horses. Now throughout human society inanimate forces are at work, harnessed at last successfully to the service of man, shaping iron and steel plates, setting to work looms and printing presses, propelling enormous trains of waggons, urging leviathan ships across the ocean.

Before this mighty revolution, whatever alterations man wanted made in his world must be made through his own physical exertions; now he sets to work the energies of his environment to remould that environment according to his needs. From himself there is demanded merely the brain work of planning and directing and the nervous strain of tendence on the marvellous machines. It is true that in our badly arranged social system (all of whose concepts of property, contract, wages, and labor are still adjusted to the pre-machine era) the increased control over nature has brought but little advantage to the mass of the workers. But the full effects of the substitution of inanimate for human energy have not yet been seen, and will ultimately work themselves out into conditions of life vastly different from those which we know at present.

WOMEN BEFORE THE INDUSTRIAL REVOLUTION

Of all the changes introduced by the industrial revolution there is none greater than the alteration brought about in the position of women. Many people believe that it was only in the nineteenth century that women began, on a large scale, to work for their living. There could be no greater mistake. All the evidence goes to show that before the eighteenth century women, with few exceptions, worked as hard and as long as men did. In the sixteenth century women not only helped their husbands in farm work, but they toiled at spinning and carding of flax and wool as a by-industry of their own. Few nineteenth century women could work harder than the wife of a sixteenth century husbandman, whose duties are thus described by Fitzherbert, writing in 1534:

"First swepe thy house, dresse up thy dysshe bord, and sette all thynges in good order within thy house. Milk thy kye, suckle thy calves, sye up thy mylke, take uppe thy children and array them, and provide for thy husband's brekefaste, dinner, souper, and thy children and servants, and take thy part with them. And to ordayne corne and malt to the myll, and bake and brue withal whanne nede is. And meet it to the mill and fro the mill, and se that thou have thy measure again beside the toll, or else the miller dealeth not truly with the or els thy corn is not drye as it should be. Thou must make butter and cheese when thou maist, serve thy swyne both morning and evening and give thy poleyn [i.e., poultry] meat in the morning; and when tyme of the year cometh thou must take hede how thy hennes, duckes, and geese do ley, and to gather up their eggs, and when they wax broodie to set them there as no beasts, swyne, or other vermin hurt them . . . . And when they brought forth their birds to see that they be well kept from the gleyd, kites, crowe, polecats, fullymarts, and other vermin. And in the beginning of March or a little before is tyme for a wife to make her garden, and to gette as many good seedes and herbes as she canne, and specially such as be good for the pott and to eat. And also in March is tyme to sowe flax and hemp . . . but how it should be sown, weded, pulled, rippled, watered, washen, dryed, beaten, braked, tawed, heckled, spon, wounded, wrapped, and woven, it needeth not for me to show, for they be wise enough. And thereof may they make shetes, bordclothes, towels, sherts, smocks, and such other necessaries; and therefore let thy distaff be always ready for a pastime, that thou be not idle . . . . May fortune sometime that thou shalt have so many things to do that thou shalt not well know where is best to begin . . . . It is convenient for a husband to have shepe of his owne for many causes, and then maye his wife have part of the wool to make her husband and herself some clothes. And at the least way she may have the locks of the sheep either to make clothes or blankets and coverlets, or both. And if she have no wool of her own, she may take wool to spyn of clothmakers, and by that means she may have a convenient living and many tymes to do other works. It is a wife's occupation to wynowe all manner of corns, and make malt, to wasshe and wrynge, to make haye, shere corn, and in tyme of nede to helpe her husband fyll the muckwain or dungcart, drive the plough, to load hay, corn, and such other. And to go or ride to the market to sell butter, cheese, milk, eggs, chekyns, capons, henns, pigs, geese, and all manner of corns. And also to bye all manner of necessary things belonging to the household, and to make a trewe reckoning and account to her husband what she hath paid. And if the husband go to the market to bye or sell, as they oft do, he then to show his wife in like manner."[1]

About two hundred years later a realistic Scotch novelist makes his hero write thus of his second marriage:

"I had placed my affections, with due consideration, on Miss Lizy Kibbock, the well brought up daughter of Mr. Joseph Kibbock, of the Gorbyholm . . . whose cheeses were of such excellent quality that they have, under the name of Delap cheese, spread far and wide over the civilized world . . . . The second Mrs. Balquhidder that was had a genius for management . . . for she was the bee that made my honey. There was such a buying of wool to make blankets, with a booming of the meikle wheel to spin the same, and such birring of the little wheel for sheets and napery, that the manse was for many a day like an organ kist. Then we had milk cows and the calves to bring up and a kirning of butter and a making of cheese. In short, I was almost by myself with the jangle and din . . . and I for a time thought of the peaceful and kindly nature of the first Mrs. Balquhidder with a sigh; but the outcoming was soon manifest. The second Mrs. Balquhidder sent her butter on the market days to Irville, and her cheese from time to time to Glasgow to Mrs. Firlot, that kept the huxtry in the Salt Market; and they were both so well made that our dairy was just a coining of money, insomuch that after the first year we had the whole lot of my stipend to put untouched into the bank."[2]

THE FAMILY AS THE ECONOMIC UNIT; MARRIAGE AN INDUSTRIAL PARTNERSHIP

These extracts – and many like them could be quoted[3] – show clearly that before the industrial revolution women took a full share in industrial work. The basis of their work, however, was quite different from what it is to-day. Speaking generally, before the industrial revolution the economic unit was the family, and not the individual. So much was this the case, that in the censuses of 1811, 1821, and 1831 it was assumed that all the members of the family would practise the same occupation. Much of the work done by women in the family was of a domestic nature for the immediate service of their husbands and children, and not for profit. In technical language it was the production of use values, and not of exchange values. This can be illustrated from the inventory of the furniture of a middle class house at Brook, near Wingham, in 1760, which is preserved in an auctioneer's catalogue in the British Museum. The equipment of the establishment included a bolting room, where were kept "one large neading trough, one meal tub and sieve, and one quilting frame"; a bottle house, which contained, among other things, "one brine tub, one syder stock and beater, one pickling trough"; a milk house, where were kept "milk keelers, churns, a butter board, and a butter printer." In the "larder" were "pickling pans and stilling tubs"; in the brew house "a mash tub, five brewing keelers, and one bucking tub" (whatever that may have been).

But it would be a mistake to assume that women never worked for profit. The second Mrs. Balquhidder obviously did. It is common to find a woman carrying on the farm or shop of her husband after his death, and the farmer's wife, who has been already described, was her husband's working partner in his business enterprise as well as his housekeeper and servant. In fact, before the nineteenth century marriage was an industrial partnership as well as a relation of affection. The women worked, and worked hard, contributing much to the wealth of England, which was sold in her markets. This situation must have served to modify considerably the harshness of the common law, which decreed the husband's entire control of his wife's property. Fitzherbert's husbandman, depending as he did on his wife's energy in poultry yard, garden, and spinning room, would not be likely to insist upon his legal rights to take absolute possession of her earnings. And in one way the law recognized the wife's partnership. A husband could not leave his property entirely away from his wife. The widow's ancient right to one third of her husband's property was only abolished in England by the Reform Parliament,[4] that Parliament which was called together on the basis of the Franchise Act, which for the first time introduced the word "male" into the qualifications of the parliamentary elector.

THE ALTERATION OF THE ECONOMIC BASIS OF THE FAMILY

Before the industrial revolution, then, the household was, as a general rule, the unit of industry, and women worked in it as members of the family for the production of exchange as well as of use values. Now what was the effect of the industrial revolution on the position of women in relation to these economic activities of the family? Briefly, the answer is that the introduction of machinery, by taking work out of the home and establishing the factory, the railway, and the mine as the organs of industry, broke up the family as an economic unit and diminished the amount of production for use carried on within the home. Brewing, baking, butter-making, spinning, weaving, even – to a large extent – the making of clothes, have ceased to be activities of the family; and increasingly house-wives are finding that it is cheaper and more convenient to hand over jam making, laundry work, even window cleaning and floor polishing, to agencies that exist independently of the home. This is an inevitable development. Modern machinery and the use of artificial sources of power immensely cheapen production, but they can only be used by organizations bigger than the family group. So that the economic basis of the family has altered more within the last hundred years than in the whole course of Christian civilization preceding that time.

Inevitably this has reacted on the position of women, whose relation to the family was always closer than that of men; and the changes in the nature and aspirations of women, which have developed in the nineteenth century, are very largely, though not entirely, due to these altered economic conditions.

THE CHANGED POSITION OF WOMEN

But different classes of women were affected very differently. Among the wealthier people attempts were made to preserve the subordination of women to the family unit, although the economic justification for that dependence had ceased. Among the poor the necessity for the women's contribution to the family income was so strong that they were drafted into the new forms of industrial life without any consideration of their powers or capacities. To put it shortly, parasitism became the fate of the middle class women, ruthless exploitation that of the working class women. The latter were absorbed in large numbers by the new factories, as were also the children, who equally had worked as parts of the family unit; and the first stage of machine production saw the women and children workers cruelly and shamelessly sacrificed to the demands of profit.

THE EXPLOITATION OF THE WORKING WOMEN

There is no need to repeat this oft told story, but it may be pointed out that the previous close relation of the women and children to the family unit had rendered them incapable of asserting themselves against the powers of capital and competition. And the low wages which they received made them dangerous rivals of the men and no longer co-operators with them. No one during the first agitation for the Factory Acts seems to have realized that the general labor of women and children pulled down the wages of men. The conditions became so bad that dead in the face of a public opinion more strongly individualistic than has ever been the case either before or since, the State was forced to constitute itself the established guardian of the women and children, and to bring into existence all the machinery of the Factory Acts, by which, first in the textile industries and in mining, later on in in all branches of machine production, and still later in practically the whole field of industry, an attempt was made to preserve women and children from the degradation and suffering due to over long hours and work in unsanitary conditions. The problem is, of course, not yet fully solved. In the industrial world the cheap labor of women is continually threatening new industries. Since these women believe themselves inferior to men, and since most of them expect to marry early and regard their occupation only as a makeshift, they are naturally willing to work more cheaply than men, and so constitute a perpetual menace to the masculine standard of life, while they themselves are subjected to conditions unfit for human beings. It cannot be wondered at that under these circumstances many social reformers regard the work of women outside the home as an evil development. For women in the industrial world are frequently forced to be blacklegs. Moreover, the conditions of modern large scale industry are determined not by the needs of the human beings who work in it, but by the demands of the machinery, and are therefore often unsuitable for women (equally so, in all probability, for men). In the early days of the movement for State regulation of industry, that innovation on the doctrine of *laissez faire* which then prevailed was justified on the ground that women were not free agents. Men, it was asserted, could and should stand out for themselves against the power of their employers. The State ought never to interfere in the wages contracts formed by its citizens among themselves, but women and children were not citizens. They were weak, ignorant, easily exploited. Further, they represented in a special way the human capital of the nation. The men might be used from generation to generation and the life of the race would still continue, but a nation which lived upon the labor of its women and children was doomed to degeneration.

THE PARASITISM OF THE MIDDLE CLASS WOMEN

In this view there is, of course, a truth which must never be forgotten. But it ignores another part of the problem, that which confronted the other class of women. The middle class women had so awful and so bitter an experience that for a time they were quite unable to appreciate the need of State protection for women. The result for them of the introduction of machinery was altogether opposite to the effect produced upon the industrial women. As the economic functions of the family diminished, the daughters of lawyers, doctors, wealthy shopkeepers, and manufacturers did not work out new forms of activity for themselves. It would have been against the dignity of their fathers and brothers to permit them to do so. Moreover, it would have diminished their chances of marriage, and would have involved a breach with the people who were nearest and dearest to them. They remained within the family group, occupied in the insignificant domestic duties that still remained and in the futilities of an extraordinarily conventional social intercourse. Dusting, arranging the flowers, and paying calls were the important duties of their existence. The married middle class woman had indeed, as wife and mother, a definite place and important responsibility, though the decay of household activities and the growing habit of living in suburbs, quite apart from the man's business, lessened at every point her contact with the social world and cut even her off more than had ever been the case previously from intercourse with the spheres of industry and commerce. But the unmarried woman, forbidden during her years of greatest vitality and strongest desire for new scenes and fresh interest to find any channels for her energies, save those of "helping mamma" and "visiting the poor," suffered intensely from the inactive parasitism forced upon her. Exploitation brings great suffering; but suffering as acute, though more obscure, is experienced by those whose growing powers and growing need for human contacts are dammed within them by an incomprehensible social fiat, resting really on conditions that had passed away a generation earlier. The only escape from this enforced inactivity and dependence was through marriage. The middle class woman, in fact, was regarded solely from the standpoint of sex. There was no way by which she might satisfy her natural wish to use the welling energies within her other than by becoming the mistress of a household. Naturally, therefore, she often regarded "to be settled" as an end to be aimed at, quite apart from the personality of the man who offered to make her his wife. And the irony of the situation was that to the finer spirits who refused to acquiesce in this degradation of love to the economic plane, there was no other alternative than an existence which became "that useless, blank, pale, slow-trailing thing" of which one of Charlotte Bronte's heroines so bitterly complains.

THE SURPLUS OF WOMEN

As the nineteenth century wore on other tendencies came into play which further increased the hardships of middle class women. The presence of a surplus of women in the middle classes made itself more and more apparent. Probably the cause of this is the emigration of young men, rendered necessary by our enormous colonial development; but it may be that some other and more subtle cause is at work. Exact statistics are difficult to give, as our statistics are not based on class distinctions. But certain conclusions can be drawn, as Miss Clara Collet first pointed out, from the distribution of unmarried males and females over certain ages in different boroughs of London, which to some extent are peopled by different classes of the community . . . the surplus of females tends to accumulate in the better off districts. Some have urged that these surplus females are really domestic servants. But the number of female unmarried domestic servants over thirty-five is comparatively small.

ECONOMIC INDEPENDENCE

Few men understand what importance the modern middle class woman attaches to her economic independence. To men the right to earn a livelihood does not present itself as a hardly won and cherished privilege, but as a tiresome necessity. They may have earned an income with difficulty, but, at least, when they earned it it was theirs to spend as they would. But many women, even wealthy women, dressed in gorgeous raiment, with servants and horses and carriages at their command, never know what it is to be able to spend a guinea on the gratification simply of their own tastes. The money that they receive comes from father or husband, and must be spent as father or husband approve. Workers in the feminist movement are perfectly familiar with the well-dressed and prosperous-looking woman who declares, "Yes, I quite agree with you. I have often thought these things myself, and I wish I could help, but my husband does not approve of Women's Suffrage, and I have no money except what I get from him."[5] The life of the professional woman is often toilsome and often lonely, but the power of self-direction and self-activity which economic independence brings with it counts for much, and few women who have realized what sex-parasitism means, and have succeeded in emerging from it will ever willingly return to it.

THE TWO SECTIONS OF THE WOMEN'S MOVEMENT

So, at the present time there are two main sections in the modern women's movement – the movement of the middle class women who are revolting against their exclusion from human activity and insisting, firstly, on their right to education, which is now practically conceded on all sides; secondly, on their right to earn a livelihood for themselves, which is rapidly being won; and, thirdly, on their right to share in the control of Government, the point round which the fight is now most fiercely raging. These women are primarily rebelling against the sex-exclusiveness of men, and regard independence and the right to work as the most valuable privilege to be striven for.

On the other hand, there are the women of the working classes, who have been faced with a totally different problem, and who naturally react in a different way. Parasitism has never been forced on them. Even when the working class woman does not earn her own living in the world of industry – though practically all the unmarried girls of the working classes do so – her activities at home are so unending, and she subconsciously feels so important and so valuable, that she has never conceived of herself as useless and shut out from human interests, as was the parasitic middle class woman. What the woman of the proletariat feels as her grievance is that her work is too long and too monotonous, the burden laid upon her too heavy. Moreover, in her case that burden is due to the power of capitalistic exploitation resulting from the injustice of our social system. It is not due, or not, at least, to any considerable extent, to the fact that the men of her class shut her out from gainful occupations. Therefore, among the working women there is less sex consciousness. Evolving social enthusiasm tends to run rather into the channel of the labor revolt in general than into a specific revolution against the conditions alleged to be due to sex differences. The working woman feels her solidarity with the men of her class rather than their antagonism to her. The reforms that she demands are not independence and the right to work, but rather protection against the unending burden of toil which has been laid upon her. A speaker at a working women's congress said once, "It is not work we want, but more love, more leisure to enjoy life, and more beauty." These facts explain the relative lukewarmness of working class women in the distinctively feminist movement, and one of the possible dangers of the future is that the working class women in their right and natural desire to be protected against that exploitation which the first development of machinery brought with it, should allow themselves to drift without observing it into the parasitism which was the lot of middle class women. If the exclusion of married women from all paid work were carried out; if the unmarried women were at the same time prevented from following all those occupations which reactionary male hygienists choose, without adequate investigation, to assume to be bad for women; if at the same time the growth of the public supply of schools and other agencies for the care of children were to go on and the number of children in each family were to continue to diminish; if the home, by reason of the development of machinery and large scale production, were to lose all those remaining economic activities which are carried on within it, then working women might come to live through the same experience as the middle class women have already known.

SEX-CONSCIOUSNESS AMONG WORKING WOMEN

But changes are proceeding in this situation. The consciousness of their rights and wrongs as a sex is arising among the working class women. They are beginning to see the possibility that even in the fight against capitalist exploitation, on which the men of their class are now entering, their specific interests may be overlooked. The shocking disregard of the needs of women by the Insurance Act has given them a clear proof of this. The great calamity against which the working class woman needs insurance is the death of her husband and bread winner; yet it is commonly stated that in the bargain with the big insurance societies the Government simply threw overboard the plans for a form of insurance which would make more secure the position of widows and orphans. Again, the home-staying working class woman finds that the Government cares little for her health, and makes practically no provision for her care should she fall ill, save in the one case of maternity benefit, and that, by curious irony, was originally to be paid to the husband and not to herself, save where the woman was herself a wage earner. Moreover, the development of social legislation is throwing heavier burdens on the working woman, and is yet making scant provision for her special needs. There are clubs, lectures, holidays provided for men, for boys, for young girls; but for the married working woman how little is done? A few schools for mothers, still mainly supported by private charity, in the poorest districts is about the sum total; yet all the while it is she who bears the burden of the insurance paid by her husband, for it comes in nine cases out of ten out of her housekeeping money. It is she who has to send the children to school clean and tidy and has to keep the great appetites of growing boys satisfied; it is she who is regarded as responsible for buying inflammable flannelette, for not providing fireguards or separate cradles for the babies, and whatever else a Government of men may choose to impose on her. So that there is appearing also among the working women an understanding of the fact that their interests are not altogether safe in the hands of men, though the working class women will never probably arrive at the intense consciousness of sex antagonism which characterizes some sections of the middle class feminists, and is due to men's callous disregard of their claims as human beings.

CHANGED VIEWS AMONG THE MIDDLE CLASS WOMEN

At the same time among the middle class women, too, the situation is altering. Many of them are realizing that to earn their own living is not always the joy it had appeared at first, for the living may be so meagre as to provide, at the cost of perpetual toil, only the merest food and shelter. Although the number of girls among the middle classes who are working for their living is steadily increasing, every now and then one comes across a young woman who finds the rigor of her work and the fierce competition too much for her, and hastens back gladly to the parasitic shelter of her relatives' roof. The lower sections of professional women, in short, are coming to understand the possibilities of exploitation, and are dimly beginning to feel rather than to comprehend the fact that work may be so monotonous and so ill-paid that even their human qualities, and much more their feminine attractiveness, will be beaten out of them in the process of earning their living.

And among the whole community the growth of collectivist feeling is bringing us to realize that State regulation of the conditions of labor is a necessity, and therefore we seldom find now among the feminists that embittered opposition to factory legislation which caused so many difficulties in the seventies and eighties. It is realized on all hands that the position of women in industry is not an exceptional one; that men, too, need protection against over-long hours of work, low wages, and insanitary conditions; and that, therefore, women are not accepting an inferior position in demanding the intervention of the State to secure for them suitable conditions of work.

THEY WANT BOTH WORK AND MARRIAGE

An even more momentous change is occurring in the attitude towards marriage. The first generation of feminists did not so much oppose marriage as ignore it; but there is now coming into existence a second generation of advanced women, few at present, but destined to increase. Most of them know nothing at first hand of the old struggles. They have gone to high schools and colleges, and education has come to them as naturally as to their brothers. Many under the care of feminist relatives have been carefully trained to win the economic independence for which their mothers and aunts agonized in vain. And now these younger women find themselves face to face with a new set of problems. The fierceness and bitterness of the old struggles caused the first set of feminists to put the question of marriage and the supposed special disabilities of their sex altogether on one side. To-day many of these elder women, looking at their young relatives in receipt of independent incomes, doing work that is of real value to the world, and enjoying in such matters as foreign travel, theatre and concert going, and the cultivation of friendships a degree of freedom which they had longed for as unattainable, wonder what difficulties the young women of to-day can possibly have to contend with. But there are fundamental human instincts which can be disregarded only for a time. The problem of the modern professional woman is that she is forced to reconcile two needs of her nature which the present constitution of society make irreconcilable. She wants work, she wants the control of her own financial position, she wants education and the right to take part in the human activities of the State, but at the same time she is no longer willing to be shut out from marriage and motherhood. And the present organization of society means that for most women the two are alternatives. In almost all occupations the public acknowledgement of marriage means for a woman dismissal from her post and diminished economic resources. This is the case in practically all the Government posts: women civil servants, including even factory inspectors and school inspectors, are compelled to resign on marriage. Even the women school medical officers of the L.C.C. are now forced to sign a contract stating that they will retire on marriage,[6] and although the same rule is not so strict in private business, there, too, it is rare for married women to be employed. Most women, that is to say, can only continue to preserve that economic independence, so keenly appreciated and won by such fierce struggles, on condition of compulsory celibacy and, what to many women is far worse, compulsory childlessness. Against this state of things a revolt is beginning which so far is barely articulate, but which is bound to make itself heard in public before long. What women who have fully thought out the position want, is not this forced alternative between activity in the human world and control of their own economic position on the one hand and marriage and children on the other, *but both*. The normal woman, like the normal man, desires a mate and a child, but she does not therefore desire nothing else. Least of all does she desire to sink back into a state of economic dependence and sex parasitism. Women do not want either love *or* work, but both; and the full meaning of the feminist movement will not develop until this demand becomes conscious and articulate among the rank and file of the movement.

CAN CHILD-BEARING WOMEN EARN THEIR LIVING?

Now there can be no denying the fact that this demand will raise many difficulties. Some writers, chief of whom is that extraordinarily suggestive and interesting American, Charlotte Perkins Gilman, assume that with improved conditions of household management and the development of large scale housekeeping and publicly managed crèches and nursery schools it will be possible even for child-bearing women to continue to earn their own living in such a way that they will be able not only to keep themselves during this period, but to contribute their share towards the bringing up of children, and this without any injury to the children. To the writer this seems a very optimistic attitude. It may, perhaps, be practicable for a few exceptional women, who possess sufficient ability to earn large incomes and have sufficient energy to endure, without breaking down, the twofold strain of working for a living and bringing children into the world. But it is obvious that for the vast majority of women regular work on exactly the same terms as those which men now submit to in office or factory is most undesirable for women during at least six months of the pre-natal and post-natal life of each child. If the child is to be nursed by its mother, as it should be, probably in most cases an even longer period of rest should be taken. The common sense of mankind knows well that just as increasing civilization leads to an increasing protection of children, so, too, it should mean more care for young mothers. During the child-bearing years the welfare of the child should have the precedence over all other considerations. But this does not mean that the woman need be incapacitated for earning her own living during her whole married life. It is not marriage that prevents a woman from working. On the contrary, the married woman who is leading a normal and healthy life is likely to do better work and be a more satisfactory person than the spinster. The real hindrance is not marriage, but motherhood. Most people assume that the two are identical; but should absorption in maternal duties extend over the whole of married life? The days have gone past (one hopes never to return) when the married woman had a child every one or two years during the whole of the fertile period of life. The modern family, it seems probable, will not consist in the future of more than three or four children, and even if one made the assumption[7] that the woman should devote herself entirely to the care of the children until the youngest reached school age, there would still remain many years of her life during which she would be strong and fit for work. Indeed, one of the most pathetic sights of to-day is the middle aged woman whose children have ceased to afford her complete occupation. They are absorbed in school life and in the training for their future occupations. The husband, too, gives up his time to his work and his sport, and the woman of forty or fifty, still at the height of her maturity, stronger perhaps, and certainly wiser, than she was in her youth, is left stranded by the current of life, with no interests outside her family; whilst by the family the necessary task of being "company to mother" is resented and evaded.[8] How much happier would such women be if, when their children no longer needed all their time, they could return to activities outside the household; and how much richer would humanity be if it could avail itself of the services of such women. A type might come into existence, of which only one or two instances have yet appeared, of mature women who, as girls, had worked for themselves and known what human life, as opposed to sex life, meant; who then had lived through the normal feminine experiences of being sought in marriage, loved, and made mothers of children; and who, ripened and enriched by these experiences, returned in middle age to the activities of the world, knowing – because they have lived through – both sides of life. How enormously valuable such women would be in education and in the medical profession, where, indeed, even now a few of them may be found.

THE PROBLEM OF THE FUTURE

So, then, the problem before the future is to secure for women freedom and independence, the right to control their own destinies, and yet to make it possible for the same women to be wives and mothers. The solution of this problem will not be easy. It cannot be attained through the methods advocated by either of the schools of thought that now hold the field; neither by the feminists of the more old fashioned sort, on the one hand, who simply demand for women the same rights as men possess, ignoring all the inevitable differences of sex; nor, on the other hand, by those who believe that sex is the only characteristic of women that matters, and disregard in her the human nature that she shares with man. Neither independence alone nor protection alone will meet the case. The whole problem is still so new that it is perhaps best to be cautious in dealing with it, and to avoid committing oneself too soon to any specific solution.

SOCIALISM AND FEMINISM

It will be seen that these changes in the status of women cannot come about in our present individualistic society. In the first place, under the existing state of competition in business a woman who drops out for the childbearing period can hardly expect to be reinstated, and the world will probably honestly have to face the fact that certain readjustments, not otherwise desirable, must be made in order that the mother may not be penalized in her later economic life by reason of her motherhood. Even among elementary school teachers to-day a married teacher who frequently demands leave of absence because of her approaching confinement finds herself at a serious disadvantage. The absence and subsequent return of the married women to their work will no doubt be inconvenient, but the inconvenience must be faced, and the women as far as possible be placed at no disadvantage, if we are to put a stop to our present practice of the deliberate sterilization of the ablest and most independent women.[9]

Such a system could be deliberately and consciously introduced into the public services; it could be imposed on private enterprise by factory legislation, though with much greater difficulty. But it is the development of Socialism, and that alone, which can make it possible throughout the whole fabric of society for the normal woman to attain her twin demands, independent work and motherhood. It is only Socialism which can make the endowment of the women during the maternal years a possibility, that endowment being one of the first charges on the surplus value or economic rent which the State will absorb; and until the State has made itself master of the land and the capital of this country, it will not have an income big enough to enable it to provide adequate endowments for the child-bearing women. Therefore it becomes clear that the only path to the ultimate and most deep lying ends of the feminist movement is through Socialism, and every wise feminist will find herself more and more compelled to adopt the principles of Socialism. But the wise Socialists must also be feminists. The public spirit of willingness to serve the community which will be necessary if the Socialist principles are to work must be inculcated into children from their earliest days. Can they be so inculcated by women who know nothing of the activities of the world beyond the four walls of their homes? Women, too, must be citizens and fully conscious of the privileges and duties of their citizenship if Socialism is to be attained. Not least among the duties of that citizenship should be what Plato long ago demanded of his women guardians: – that they should bear children for the service of the State.

NOTES

1 Fitzherbert's "Book of Husbandry." English Dialect Society. 1882.

2 Galt. "Annals of the Parish," Chapter VI. Pages 38–9 of edition in Routledge's Universal Library.

3 "The staff consisted of the general manager. John Dalton; a collier, who prepared the charcoal from the brushwood of the neighboring forest; a 'blomesmyth,' or 'smythman,' in charge of the 'blomeharth'; and a 'faber,' working at the stryng hearth . . . . The employment of the wives of the foreman and smith lends an air of domesticity to the little settlement. The wife of John Gyll, the 'blomesmyth,' seems to have been a general factotum, sometimes helping her husband or the laborers, then working at the bellows. At first her employment was intermittent and her payment irregular, but later she seems

to have settled down to fixed employment at a regular rate of a halfpenny a blome, i.e., a weight of fifteen stones of thirteen pounds each." "Durham County History," Vol. II., p. 279, quoting Account Roll of John Dalton, first Durham ironmaster (about 1410).

4 Dower Act, 3 & 4 Will. IV., c. 105.

5 The personal experience of the writer will illustrate this point. She was once staying with the wife of a millionaire, and was going on after her visit for a walking tour with a friend in the Lake district. Mrs. D., when she heard of the plan, said: "Are you two going off by yourselves just where you like? That must be delightful. All my life I have never been able to do that kind of thing. Before my marriage I had to go where mamma said, and now, of course. Mr. D. always decides about our holiday." Many a wealthy lady is as much subservient to the whims of her husband as though she were one of his upper servants, which, indeed, in many cases, she is, with the difference that they have holidays and she has none.

6 As these pages pass through the press, the desirability of requiring women doctors to retire on marriage is again being raised on the L.C.C.

7 The writer is not prepared to admit that this assumption is true in every case, or indeed in many cases. Many women who can *bear* splendid children are not necessarily fit to care for all the details of their health and rearing, and in many cases it would be well that the mother should return to her normal occupation as soon as ever the child no longer required to be nursed every two or three hours, and should use her earnings to pay for the skilled care given in crèche or nursery, resuming charge of the child in the non-working hours. But that this is possible cannot yet be considered as established beyond a doubt.

8 See the serial story "Won Over," which appeared in Mrs. Gilman's magazine *The Forerunner* during 1913.

9 Cf. Shaw, "Man and Superman," p. 220. "Mr. Graham Wallas has already ventured to suggest, as Chairman of the School Management Committee of the London School Board, that the accepted policy of the sterilization of the school mistress, however administratively convenient, is open to criticism from the national, stockbreeding point of view."

SHORT BIBLIOGRAPHY

BEBEL, AUGUST. Woman in the Past, Present, and Future. Reeves. 1893. 1s. net.

BONDFIELD, MARGARET. The National Care of Maternity. Women's Co-operative Guild. 1d.

BRAUN, LILY. Die Frauenfrage; ihre geschichtliche Entwicklung und wirtschaftliche Seite. Leipzig: Hirzel. 1910.

Bronte, Charlotte. Shirley.

BROWNLOW, J. M. E. Women in Local Government in England and Wales. Nutt. 1911. 2s. 6d. net.

GILMAN, MRS. CHARLOTTE PERKINS. Women and Economics. Cheap edition. Putnams. 1910. 1s. net.

GALT. Annals of the Parish. Routledge. Universal Library. 1s. net.

GISSING, GEORGE. The Odd Women. Cheap edition. 7d.

HUTCHINS, B. L., and HARRISON, A. History of Factory Legislation. Second edition. King. 1911. 6s. net.

HUTCHINS, B. L. Conflicting Ideals: Two Sides of the Woman's Question. Murby. 1913. 1s. 6d. net.

JAMES, EMILY. The Lady: Studies of Certain Significant Phases of Her History. Putnams. 1910. 10s. 6d. net.

KEY, ELLEN. The Woman Movement. Putnams. 1913. 6s.

MARTIN, ANNA. The Married Working Woman. N.U.W.S.S. 1911. 2d.

MEISEL-HESS, GRETA. Die Sexuelle Krise unserer Zeit: Eine sozial-psycholische Untersuchung. Jena: Eugen Diederich. 1909.

MILL, JOHN STUART. The Subjection of Women. Popular edition. Longmans. 6d. net.

MORLEY, EDITH J. (Editor). Women in Seven Professions. Issued by the Studies Committee of the Fabian Women's Group. Routledge & Sons. 6s.

SCHREINER, OLIVE. Women and Labor. Unwin. 1911. 8s. 6d. net.

VILLIERS, BROUGHAM. The Case for Woman's Suffrage. Unwin. 1907. 2s. 6d. net.

WOOD, G. H. The Woman Wage Earner. Church League for Woman Suffrage. 1910. 2d.

Part 3

DOMESTIC ECONOMICS

Editorial Headnote

Domestic Economics

One of classical political economy's distinguishing characteristics was its move away from the œconomics that preceded it. While political economy focused on the economics of the state and the public sphere, œconomics included a broader range of subjects, including household management. As scholars have long noted, classical political economy helped to usher in the separate spheres ideology, a gendered framework for understanding the world, wherein men occupied the public sphere and women occupied the private sphere. The implications of such thinking are significant, especially when it comes to women's perceived relationships to economics. Most political economists give very little attention to the economics of marriage, family, and the household. Even T. R. Malthus, whose central economic theory is an argument about reproduction, spends very little time discussing the economic management of a household. And yet, as the readings in this section demonstrate, the economics of the home was a vital component of the economic landscape of the period.

The selection from Lydia Marie Frances Child's *The American Frugal Housewife* offers an example of the popular genre of household manuals that instructed women on how to run a fiscally responsible household. Catherine Selden's article "The Tyranny of the Kitchen" provides a conservative take on household management, arguing that it is difficult for the middle-class woman to run her household because of the inferior work of household servants. For many female writers, the economic stakes of women's domestic lives were most acutely felt in courtship and marriage. With its emphasis on the domestic sphere, the nineteenth-century novel offered space for female writers to imagine how economic circumstances shaped the lives of individual characters. The excerpt from Maria Edgeworth's *Castle Rackrent* is an example of such depictions; the centrality of economics to the novel's plot is made clear in the first chapter, excerpted here, which delineates the protagonist's family's economic history and introduces the reader to the decaying Rackrent estate.

DOI: 10.4324/9780429321078-15

Selections by Cecily Hamilton and Marie Corelli demonstrate how female writers deployed economic metaphors – such as "Marriage as Trade" – to illuminate the material conditions of women's married lives. In *The Modern Marriage Market*, for example, Marie Corelli, Lady Jeune, Flora Annie Steel, and Susan, Countess of Malmesbury, debate whether marriage is a market corrupted by materialism and the desire for luxuries. Similarly, selections by Mary Ann Radcliffe, Ada Heather-Bigg, Jane Addams, and Kate Sheppard focus on the economic disempowerment of married women and argue for increasing their independence. Such arguments are fundamentally a critique of coverture, the common-law doctrine that declared a husband and wife to be one person, and that person was the husband. Coverture stripped married women of a legal identity, thus preventing them from having control over their earnings, from making contracts, and from inheriting property. Many of the writers in this section argue that the economic conditions of marriage are inherently flawed and have potentially devastating consequences, stripping women of their autonomy and making them vulnerable within their own homes. Katherine Anthony focuses specifically on the economics of mothering, offering statistical evidence for why women work and an analysis of the conditions of their labor. Olive Malvery's critique of children employed in home industries reveals how, for many, the home was not a sanctuary from the public sphere, but rather another manifestation of it.

Many of the female writers featured in this section combined economic discourse with the domestic discourse that characterized women's writing, more broadly, in the nineteenth century. With their emphasis on women and the domestic sphere, their writing makes legible something that political economy does not: the economic stakes of women's lives and of the domestic sphere.

14

"THE STORY OF FIDELIA," *THE FEMALE ADVOCATE, OR AN ATTEMPT TO RECOVER THE RIGHTS OF WOMEN FROM MALE USURPATION*

Mary Ann Radcliffe

Source: Mary Ann Radcliffe, 'The Story of Fidelia', in *The Female Advocate, or an Attempt to Recover the Rights of Women from Male Usurpation* (London, Vernor and Hood, 1799), pp. 97–127

TO THE READER

The subject of the following pages is an attempt to delineate the situation of those poor, helpless, females whose sufferings, from a variety of causes, are too grievous to be borne; the sources and dire consequences of which the exalted in life cannot form the least conception, unless they condescend to examine for themselves, when, it is to be hoped, their grievances will be sought into and redressed. The munificence of the people of Great Britain, which is ever ready and adequate to the support, aid, and comfort, of the afflicted, when their troubles are fully investigated; and the great number of unfortunate women, who, doubtless, would rejoice to become virtuous and useful members of society, in some lawful employment, have encouraged the author to offer this feeble representation. Nor can she despair of eventual success to the cause she has engaged in, if she is but so happy as to excite the attention of those whose souls are enlarged with the exalted ideas of Christian charity.

THE STORY OF *FIDELIA*

SAYS FIDELIA I shall make no apology for the trouble I am about to give you, since I am sure the motives that induce me to give it will have as much weight with you as they have with me; I shall, therefore, without farther preface, relate to you the events of a life, which, however insignificant and unentertaining, affords a lesson of the highest importance; a lesson, the value of which I have experienced, and may therefore recommend.

DOI: 10.4324/9780429321078-16

I am the daughter of a gentleman of good family, who, as he was a younger brother, purchased, with the portion that was allotted him, a genteel post under government. My mother died when I was but twelve years old, and my father, who was excessively fond of me, determined to be himself my preceptor, and to take care that my natural genius, which his partiality made him think above the common rank, should not want the improvements of a liberal education.

He was a man of sense, with a tolerable share of learning. In his youth he had been a free liver, and, perhaps, for that reason took some pains to become a free thinker. But whatever fashionable frailties he might formerly have allowed in himself, he was now in advanced life, and had, at least, worldly wisdom enough to know, that it was necessary his daughter should be restrained from those liberties, which he had looked upon as trifling errors in his own conduct. He therefore laboured with great application to inculcate in me the love of order, the beauty of moral rectitude, and the happiness and self-reward of virtue; but, at the same time, professed it his design to free my mind from vulgar prejudices and superstition, for so he called revealed religion. As I was urged to chuse virtue and reject vice, from motives which had no necessary connection with immortality. I was not led to consider a future state either with hope or fear. My father, indeed, when I urged him upon that subject, always intimated that the doctrine of immortality, whether true or false, ought not at all to influence my conduct, or interrupt my peace, because the virtue which secured happiness in the present state, would also secure it in a future state: a future state, therefore, I wholly disregarded, and, to confess the truth, disbelieved: for I thought I could plainly discover, that it was disbelieved by my father, though he had not thought fit explicitly to declare his sentiments. As I had no very turbulent passions, a ductile and good disposition, and the highest reverence for his understanding, as well as the tenderest affection for him, he found it an easy talk to make me adopt every sentiment and opinion which he proposed to me, as his own, especially as he took care to support his principles by the authority and arguments of the best writers against Christianity.

At the age of twenty, I was called upon to make use of all the philosophy I had been taught, by his death; which not only deprived me of a parent I most ardently loved, but with him of all the ease and affluence to which I had been accustomed. His income was only for life, and he had rather lived beyond than within it; consequently, there was nothing left for me, but the pride and helplessness of genteel life, a taste for every thing elegant, and a delicacy and sensibility that has doubled my sufferings. In this distress, a brother of my mother's, who was grown rich in trade, received me into his house, and declared he would take the same care of me as if I had been his own. When the first transports of my grief were abated, I found myself in an easy situation, and from the natural cheerfulness of my temper, I was beginning once more to taste of happiness. My uncle, who was a man of narrow understanding and illiberal education, was a little disgusted with me for employing so much of my time in reading; but still more so, when happening to examine my books, he found, by the titles, that some of them were what he called blasphemy, and tended, as he imagined, to make me me an atheist. I endeavoured to explain my principles, which I thought beneath the dignity of virtue to disguise or disavow; but as I never could make him conceive any difference between a deist and an atheist, my arguments only served to confirm him in the opinion, that I was a wicked wretch, who, in his own phrase, believed neither God nor devil, As he was really a good man, and heartily zealous for the established faith, though more from habit and prejudice than reason, my errors gave him great affliction. I perceived it with the utmost concern; I perceived too, that he looked upon me with a degree of abhorrence mixed with pity, and that I was wholly indebted to his good nature for that protection, which I had flattered myself I should owe to his love. I comforted myself, however, with my own integrity, and even felt a conscious pride, in suffering this persecution from ignorance and folly, only because I was superior to vulgar errors and popular superstition. And that Christianity deserved these appellations, I was not more convinced by my father's arguments, than my uncle's conduct, who, as his zeal was not according to knowledge, was by no means qualified to "adorn the doctrine which he professed to believe."

I had lived a few months under the painful sensibility of receiving continual benefits from a person whose esteem and affection I had lost, when my uncle one day come into my chamber, and after preparing me for some unexpected good fortune, told me, he had just had a proposal of marriage for me, from a man to whom I could not possibly have any objection. He then named a merchant with whom I had often been in company at his table. As the man was neither old nor ugly, had a large fortune, and a fair character, my uncle thought himself sufficiently authorised to pronounce as he did, that I could not possibly have any objection to him. An objection, however, I had, which I told my uncle was to me insuperable; it was, that the person whom he proposed to me as the companion, the guide, and director of my whole life, to whom I was to vow, not only obedience, but love, had nothing in him that could ever engage my affection: his understanding was low, his sentiments mean and indelicate, and his manner unpolite and unpleasing. "What stuff is all this?" interrupted my uncle, "sentiments indelicate, unpolite, his understanding forsooth, not equal to your own! Ah! child, if you had less romance, conceit, and arrogance, and more true discretion and prudence, it would do you more good than all the fine books you have confounded your poor head with, and, what is worse, perhaps, ruined your poor soul. I own it went a little against my conscience to accept my honest friend's kind offer, and give him such a pagan for a wife. But I know not, whether the believing husband may not convert the unbelieving wife? As to your slighty objections, they are such nonsense, that I wonder you can suppose me fool enough to be deceived by them. No, child, wife as you are, you cannot impose upon a man who has lived as many years in the world as I have. I see your motive; you have some infidel libertine rake in your eye, with whom you would go headlong to perdition. But I shall take care to have your soul to answer for, as well as your person. Either I shall dispose of you to an honest man that may convert you, or you shall dispose of yourself how you please for me; for I disclaim all farther care or trouble about you. So I leave you to consider, whether or no the kindness I have shewn you, entitles me to some little influence over you, and whether you chuse to seek protection where you can find it, or accept of the happy lot Providence has cut out for you."

He left me at the close of this fine harangue, and I seriously set myself to consider, as he bade me, which of the two states he had set before me, I ought to chuse. – To submit to a legal sort of prostitution, with the additional weight of perjury on my conscience, or to expose myself to all the distress of friendless poverty and unprotected youth. After some hours of deliberation, I determined on the latter, and that more from principle than inclination; for, though my delicacy would have suffered extremely in accepting a husband, at least indifferent to me, yet as my heart was perfectly disengaged, and my temper naturally easy, I thought I could have been less unhappy in following my uncle's advice than I might probably be by rejecting it. But then I must have submitted to an action I could not think justifiable, in order to avoid mere external distresses. This would not have been philosophical. I had always been taught, that virtue was of itself sufficient to happiness; and that those things which are generally esteemed evils, could have no power to disturb the felicity of a mind governed by the eternal rule of right, and truly enamoured of the charms of moral beauty, I resolved, therefore, to run all risques, rather than depart from this glorious principle. I felt myself raised by the trial, and exulted in the opportunity of shewing my contempt of the smiles or frowns of fortune, and of proving the power of virtue to sustain the soul under all accidental circumstances of distress.

I communicated my resolution to my uncle, assuring him at the same time of my everlasting gratitude and respect, and that nothing should have induced me to offend or disobey him, but his requiring me to do what my reason and conscience disapproved; that supposing the advantages of riches to be really as great as he believed, yet still those of virtue were greater, and I could not resolve to purchase the one by a violation of the other; that a false vow was certainly criminal; and that it would be doing an act of the highest injustice, to enter into so solemn an engagement without the power of fulfilling it; that my affections did not depend on my own will; and that no man should possess my person, who could not obtain the first place in my heart.

I was surprised that my uncle's impatience had permitted me to go on thus far; but looking in his face, I perceived that passion had kept him silent. At length the gathering storm burst over my head in a torrent of reproaches; my reasons were condemned as romantic absurdities, which I could not myself believe. I was accused of designing to deceive, and to throw myself away on some worthless fellow, whose principles were as bad as my own. It was in vain for me to assert, that I had no such design, nor any inclination to marry at all. My uncle could sooner have believed the grossest contradiction, than that a young woman could so strenuously refuse one man, without being prepossessed in favour of another. As I thought myself injured by his accusations and tyranny, I gave over the attempt to mitigate his anger. He appealed to Heaven for the justice of his resentment, and against my ingratitude and rebellion; and then giving me a note of fifty pounds, which he said would keep me from immediate indigence, he bade me leave his house, and see his face no more. I bowed in sign of obedience, and collecting all my dignity and resolution, I arose, thanked him for his past benefits, and, with a low curtsey, left the room.

In less than an hour, I departed, with my little wardrobe, to the house of a person who had formerly been my father's servant, and who now kept a shop and let lodgings. From thence I went the next day to visit my father's nephew, who was in possession of the family estate, and had lately married a lady of great fortune. He was a young gentleman of good parts, his principles the same as my father's, though his practice had not been quite agreeable to the strict rules of morality. However, setting aside a few of those vices which are looked upon as genteel accomplishments in young fellows of fortune, I thought him a good sort of man; and, as we had always lived in great kindness, I doubted not that I should find him my friend, and meet with approbation and encouragement, at least, if not assistance, from him. I told him my story, and the reasons that had determined me to the refusal that had incurred my uncle's displeasure; but how was I disappointed, when, instead of the applause I expected for my heroic virtue and unmerited persecutions, I perceived a smile of contempt on his face, when he interrupted me in the following manner:

"And what in the devil's name, my dear cousin, could make a woman of your sense behave so like an ideot? What! forfeit all your hopes from your uncle, refuse an excellent match, and reduce yourself to beggary because, truly, you were not in love? Surely one might have expected better from you even at fifteen. Who is it, pray, that marries the person of their choice? For my own part, who have rather a better title to please myself, with a good fifteen hundred a year, than you who have not a shilling, I found it would not do; and that there was something more to be sought after in a wife, than a pretty face or a genius. Do you think I cared three farthings for the woman I married? – No, faith; but her thirty thousand pounds were worth having; with that I can purchase a seraglio of beauties, and indulge my taste in every kind of pleasure. And, pray, what is it to me, whether my wife has beauty, or wit, or elegance, when her money will supply me with all that in others? You, cousin, had an opportunity of being as happy as I am. The men, believe me, would not like you a bit the worse for being married; on the contrary, you would find, that for one who took notice of you as a single woman, twenty would be your admirers and humble servants, when there was no danger of being taken in: thus you might have gratified all your passions, made an elegant figure in life, and have chosen out some gentle swain, as romantic and poetical as you pleased, for your cecisbeo. The good John Trot husband would have been easily managed."

My indignation could be contained no longer, and I was leaving the room in disdain, when he caught me by the hand. "Nay, prithee, my dear cousin, none of these violent airs: I thought you and I had known one another better. Let the poor souls who are taught by the priests and their nurses to be afraid of hell-fire, and to think they shall go to the devil for following nature, and making life agreeable, be as outrageously virtuous as they please, you have too much sense to be frightened at bugbears. You know that the term of our existence is but short, and it is highly reasonable to make it as pleasant as possible."

I was too angry to attempt confusing his arguments; but, bursting from his hold, told him, I would take care not to give him a second opportunity of insulting my distress, and affronting my understanding; and so left his house with a resolution never to enter it again.

I went home mortified and disappointed; my spirits sunk into a dejection which took from me, for many days, all inclination to stir out of my lodging, or to see a human face. At length I resolved to try whether indigence and friendship were really incompatible, and whether I should meet with the same treatment from a female friend, whose affection had been the principal pleasure of my youth. Surely, thought I, the gentle Amanda, whose heart seems capable of every tender and generous sentiment, will do justice to the innocence and integrity of her unfortunate friend; her tenderness will encourage my virtue, and animate my fortitude; her praises and endearments will compensate all my hardships. Amanda was a single woman, of a moderate independent fortune, which I heard she was going to bestow on a young officer, who had little or nothing besides his commission. I had no doubt of her approbation of my refusing a mercenary match, since she herself had chosen from motives so opposite to those which are called prudent. She had been in the country some months, so that my misfortunes had not reached her ear, till I myself related them to her.

She heard me with great attention, and answered with politeness enough, but with a coldness that chilled my very heart.

"You are sensible, my dear Fidelia," said she, "that I never pretended to set my understanding in competition with yours. I know my own inferiority, and though many of your notions and opinions appeared to me very strange and particular, I never attempted to dispute them with you. To be sure, you know best: but it seems to me a very odd conduct, for one in your situation to give offence to so good an uncle; first, by maintaining doctrines which may be very true for ought I know, but which are very contrary to the received opinions we are brought up in, and therefore are apt to shock a common understanding; and secondly, to renounce his protection, and throw yourself into the wide world, rather than marry the man he chose for you; to whom, after all, I do not find you had any real objection, nor any antipathy for his person."

"Antipathy, my dear," said I, "are there not many degrees between loving and honouring a man preferably to all others, and beholding him with abhorrence and aversion. The first is, in my opinion, the duty of a wife, a duty voluntarily taken upon herself, and engaged in under the most solemn contract. As to the difficulties that may attend my friendless, unprovided state, since they are the consequences of a virtuous action, they cannot really be evils, nor can they disturb that happiness which is the gift of virtue." – "I am heartily glad," answered she, "that you have found out the art of making yourself happy by the force of imagination. I wish your enthusiasm may continue, and that you may still be farther convinced, by your own experience, of the folly of mankind, in supposing poverty and disgrace to be evils."

I was cut to the soul by the unkind manner which accompanied this sarcasm, and was going to remonstrate against her unfriendly treatment, when her lover came in, with another gentleman, who, in spite of my full heart, engaged my attention, and, for a while, made me forget the stings of unkindness. The beauty and gracefulness of his person caught my eye, and the politeness of his address, and the elegance of his compliments, soon prejudiced me in favour of his understanding. He was introduced by the captain to Amanda as his most intimate friend, and seemed desirous to give credit to his friend's judgment, by making himself as agreeable as possible. He succeeded so well, that Amanda was wholly engrossed by the pleasure of his conversation, and the care of entertaining her lover and her new guest. Her face brightened and her good humour returned. When I arose to leave her, she pressed me so earnestly to stay dinner, that I could not, without discovering how much I resented her behaviour, refuse. This, however, I should probably have done, as I was naturally disposed to shew every sentiment of my heart, had not a secret wish arisen there to know a little more of this agreeable stranger. This inclined me to think it prudent to conceal my resentment, and to accept the civilities of Amanda. The conversation grew more and more pleasing; I took my share in it; and had more than my share of the charming stranger's notice and attention. As we all grew more and more unreserved, Amanda dropped hints in the course of the conversation relating to my story, my sentiments, and unhappy situation. Sir George Freelove, for that was the young gentleman's name, listened greedily to all that was said of me, and seemed to eye me with an earnest curiosity, as well as admiration. We did not part till it was late; and Sir George insisted on attending me to my lodgings. I strongly refused it, not without a sensation, which more properly belonged to the female than the philosopher, and which I condemned in myself, as arising from dishonest pride.

I could not, without pain, suffer the polite Sir George, upon so short an acquaintance, to discover the meanness of my abode. To avoid this, I sent for a chair, but was confused to find that Sir George and his servants prepared to attend it on foot, by way of guard. It was in vain to dispute: he himself walked before, and his servants followed it. I was covered with blushes, when, after all this parade, he handed me in at the little shop door, and took leave with as profound respect, as if he had guarded me into a palace. A thousand different thoughts kept me from closing my eyes that night. The behaviour of Amanda wounded me to the soul: I found that I must look on her as no more than a common acquaintance, and that the world did not contain one person whom I could call my friend. My heart felt desolate and forlorn. I knew not what course to take for my future subsistence. The pain which my pride had just given me, convinced me that I was far from having conquered the passions of humanity, and that I should feel too sensibly all the mortifications which attend on poverty. I determined, however, to subdue this pride, and call to my assistance the example of ancient sages and philosophers, who despised riches and honours, and felt no inconveniencies from the malice of fortune. I had almost reasoned myself into a contempt for the world, and fancied myself superior to its smiles or frowns, when the idea of Sir George Freelove rushed upon my mind, and destroyed, at once, the whole force of my reasoning. I found that, however I might disregard the rest of the world, I could not be indiffernt to his opinion; and the thought of being despised by him was insupportable. I recollected that my condition was extremely different from that of an old philosopher, whose rags, perhaps, were the means of gratifying his pride, by attracting the notice and respect of mankind: at least, the philosopher's schemes and wishes were very different from those which, at that time, were taking possession of my heart. The looks and behaviour of Sir George, left me no doubt, that I had made as deep an impression in his favour as he had done in mine. I could not bear to lose the ground I had gained, and to throw myself into a state below his notice. I scorned the thought of imposing on him with regard to my circumstances, in case he should really have had favourable intentions for me; yet to disgrace myself for ever in his eye, by submitting to servitude, or any low way of supporting myself, was what I could not bring myself to resolve on.

In the midst of these reflections. I was surprised, the next morning, by a visit from Sir George. He made respectful apologies for the liberty he took; told me he had learned from my friend, that the unkindness and tyranny of an uncle had cast me into uneasy circumstances; and that he could not know that so much beauty and merit were so unworthily treated by fortune, without earnestly wishing to be the instrument of doing me more justice. He entreated me to add dignity and value to his life, by making it conducive to the happiness of mine; and was going on with the most fervent offers of service, when I interrupted him, by saying that there was nothing in his power that I could with honour accept, by which my life could be made happier, but that respect which was due to me as a woman and a gentlewoman, and which ought to have prevented such offers of service from a stranger, as could only be justified by a long-experienced friendship; that I was not in a situation to receive visits, and must decline his acquaintance, which, nevertheless, in a happier part of my life would have given me pleasure.

He now had recourse to all the arts of his sex, imputing his too great freedom to the force of his passion, protesting the most inviolable respect, and imploring on his knees, and even with tears, that I would not punish him so severely, as to deny him the liberty of seeing me, and making himself more and more worthy of my esteem. My weak heart was but too much touched by his artifices, and I had only just fortitude enough to persevere in refusing his visits, and to insist on his leaving me, which at last he did; but with such a profusion of tenderness, prayers, and protestations, that it was some time before I could recal my reason enough to reflect on the whole of his behaviour, and on my own situation, which compared, left me but little doubt of his dishonourable views.

I determined never more to admit him to my presence, and accordingly gave orders to be denied, if he came again. My reason applauded, but my heart reproached me, and heavily repined at the rigid determination of prudence. I knew that I acted rightly, and I expected that that consciousness would make me happy; but I found it otherwise, I was wretched beyond what I had ever felt, or formed any idea of. I discovered that my heart was entangled in a passion which must for ever be combated, or indulged at the expence of virtue. I now considered riches as truly desirable, since they would have placed me above disgraceful attempts, and given me reasonable hopes of becoming the wife of Sir George Freelove. I was discontented and unhappy, but surprised and disappointed to find myself so, since hitherto I had no one criminal action to reproach myself with; on the contrary, my difficulties were all owing to my regard for virtue.

I resolved, however, to try still farther the power of virtue to confer happiness, to go on in my obedience to her laws, and patiently wait the good effects of it. But I had stronger difficulties to go through than any I had yet experienced: Sir George was too much practised in the arts of seduction to be discouraged by a first repulse, every day produced either some new attempt to see me, or a letter full of the most passionate protestations and entreaties for pardon and favour: it was in vain I gave orders that no more letters should be taken in from him: he had so many different contrivances to convey them, and directed them in hands so unlike, that I was surprised into reading them, contrary to my intentions. Every time I stirred out, he was sure to be in my way, and to employ the most artful tongue that ever ensnared the heart of woman, in blinding my reason and awakening my passions.

My virtue, however, did not yet give way, but my peace of mind was utterly destroyed. Whenever I was with him, I summoned all my fortitude, and constantly repeated my commands, that he should avoid me: his disobedience called for my resentment, and, in spite of my melting heart, I armed my eyes with anger, and treated him with as much disdain as I thought his unworthy designs deserved. But the moment he left me, all my resolution forsook me, I repined at my fate, I even murmured against the Sovereign Ruler of all things, for making me subject to passions I could not subdue, yet must not indulge. I compared my own situation with that of my libertine cousin, whose pernicious arguments I had heard with horror and detestation; who gave the reins to every desire; whose house was the seat of plenty, mirth, and delight; whose face was ever covered with smiles; and whose heart seemed free from sorrow and care. Is not this man, said I, happier than I am? and if so, where is the worth of virtue? Have I not sacrificed to her my fortune and my friends? Do I not daily sacrifice to her my darling inclination; yet, what is the compensation she offers me? What are my prospects in this world but poverty, mortification, disappointment, and grief? Every wish of my heart denied, every passion of humanity combated and hurt, though never conquered! Are these the blessings with which Heaven distinguishes it favourites? Can the King of Heaven want power or will to distinguish them? or does he leave his wretched creatures the sport of chance, the prey of wickedness and malice? Surely no. Yet is not the condition of the virtuous often more miserable than that of the vicious? I myself have experienced that it is. I am very unhappy, and see no likelihood of my being otherwise in this world – and all beyond the grave is eternal darkness. Yet why do I say that I have no prospect of happiness? does not the most engaging of men offer me all the joys that love and fortune can bestow? Will not he protect me from every insult of the proud world that scoffs at indigence? Will not his liberal hand pour forth the means of every pleasure, even of that highest and truest of all pleasure, the power of relieving the sufferings of my fellow-creatures, of changing the tears of distress into tears of joy and gratitude, of communicating my own happiness to all around me? Is not this a state far preferable to that in which virtue has placed me? But what is virtue? Is not happiness the laudable pursuit of reason? Is it not then laudable to pursue it by the most probable means? Have I not been accusing Providence of unkindness, whilst I myself only am in fault for rejecting its offered favours? Surely, I have mistaken the path of virtue: it must be that which leads to happiness. The path which I am in is full of thorns and briars, and terminates in impenetrable darkness; but I see another that is strewed with flowers, and bright with the sun shine of prosperity: this, surely, is the path of virtue and the road to happiness. Hither then let me turn my weary steps, nor let vain and idle prejudices fright me from felicity. It is surely impossible that I should offend God, by yielding to a temptation which he has given me no motive to resist. He has allotted me a short and precarious existence, and has placed before me good and evil. What is good but pleasure? What is evil but pain? Reason and nature direct me to chuse the first, and avoid the last. I sought for happiness in what is called virtue, but I found it not: shall I not try the other experiment, since I think I can hardly be more unhappy by following inclination, than I am by denying it?

Thus had my frail thoughts wandered into a wilderness of error, and thus had I almost reasoned myself out of every principle of morality, by pursuing, through all their consequences, the doctrines which had been taught me as rules of life and prescriptions for felicity, the talismans of truth, by which I should be secured in the storms of adversity, and listen without danger to the syrens of temptation; when, in the fatal hour of my presumption, sitting alone in my chamber, collecting arguments on the side of passion, almost distracted with doubts, and plunging deeper and deeper into falsehood, I saw Sir George Freelove at my feet, who had gained admittance, contrary to my orders, by corrupting my landlady. It is not necessary to describe to you his arts, or the weak effects of that virtue which had been graciously implanted in my heart, but which I had taken impious means to undermine by false reasoning, and which now tottered from the foundation: suffice it that I submitted to the humiliation I have so well deserved, and tell you, that, in the pride of human reason I dared to condemn, as the effect of weakness and prejudice, the still voice of conscience, which would yet have warned me from ruin; that my innocence, my honour was the sacrifice to passion and sophistry; that my boasted philosophy, and too much flattered understanding, preserved me not from the lowest depth of infamy, which the weakest of my sex with humility and religion would have avoided.

I now experienced a new kind of wretchedness: my vile seducer tried in vain to reconcile me to the shameful life to which he had reduced me, by loading me with finery, and lavishing his fortune in procuring me pleasures which I could not taste, and pomp which seemed an insult on my disgrace. In vain did I recollect the arguments which had convinced me of the lawfulness of accepting offered pleasures, and following the dictates of inclination. The light of my understanding was darkened, but the sense of guilt was not lost: my pride and my delicacy, if, criminal as I was, I may dare to call it so, suffered the most intolerable mortification and disgust every time I reflected on my infamous situation. Every eye seemed to upbraid me, even that of my triumphant seducer. O depth of misery! to be conscious of deserving the contempt of him I loved, and for whose sake I was become contemptible to myself.

This was the state of my mind during a year which I passed in Sir George's house: his fondness was unabated for eight months of the time; and as I had no other object to share my attention, neither friend nor relation to call off any part of my tenderness, all the love of a heart naturally affectionate centered in him. The first dawnings of unkindness were but too visible to my watchful eyes. I had now all the torments of jealousy to endure, till a cruel certainty put an end to them; I learnt, at length, that my false lover was on the brink of marriage with a lady of great fortune. I immediately resolved to leave him, but could not do it without first venting my full heart in complaints and reproaches. This provoked his rage, and drew on me insolence, which, though I had deserved, I had not learnt to bear. I returned with scorn, which no longer became me, all the wages of my sin, and the trappings of my shame, and left his house in the bitterest anguish of resentment and despair.

I returned to my old lodgings; but unable to bear a scene which recalled every circumstance of my undoing, ashamed to look in the face of any creature who had seen me innocent, wretched in myself, and hoping from change of place some abatement of my misery, I put myself into a post-chaise at two in the morning, with orders to the driver to carry me as far from town as he could before the return of night, leaving it to him to chuse the road.

My reason and my senses seemed benumbed and stupified during my journey. I made no reflections on what I was about, nor formed any design for my future life. When night came, my conductor would have stopped at a large town, but I bid him go on to the next village: there I alighted at a paltry inn, and dismissed my vehicle, without once considering what I was to do with myself, or why I chose that place for my abode. To say truth, I can give no account of my thoughts at this period of time: they were all confused and distracted. A short frenzy must have filled up those hours, of which my memory retains such imperfect traces. I remember only, that without having pulled off my clothes, I left the inn as soon as I saw the day, and wandered out of the village.

My unguided feet carried me to a range of willows by a river's side, where, after having walked some time, the freshness of the air revived my senses, and awakened my reason. My reason, my memory, my anguish, and despair returned together. Every circumstance of my past life was present to my mind; but most the idea of my faithless lover, and my criminal love tortured my imagination and rent my bleeding heart, which, in spite of all its guilt and all its wrongs, retained the tenderest and most ardent affection for its undoer. This unguarded affection, which was the effect of a gentle and kind nature, heightened the anguish of resentment, and compleated my misery. In vain did I call off my thoughts from this gloomy retrospect, and hope to find a gleam of comfort in my future prospects. They were still more dreadful: poverty, attended by infamy, and want groaning under the cruel hand of oppression, and the taunts of insolence were before my eyes. I, who had once been the darling and the pride of indulgent parents, who had once been beloved, respected, and admired, was now the outcast of human nature; despised and avoided by all who had ever loved me, by all whom I had most loved! hateful to myself, belonging to no one, exposed to wrongs and insults from all.

I tried to find out the cause of this dismal change, and how far I was myself the occasion of it. My conduct, with regard to Sir George, though I spontaneously condemned, yet, upon recollection, I thought the arguments which produced it would justify. But as my principles could not preserve me from vice, neither could they sustain me in adversity: conscience was not to be perverted by the sophistry which had beclouded my reason. And if any, by imputing my conduct to error, should acquit me of guilt, let them remember, it is yet true, that in this uttermost distress, I was neither sustained by the consciousness of innocence, the exultation of virtue, nor the hope of reward: whether I looked backward or forward, all was confusion and anguish, distraction and despair. I accused the Supreme Being of cruelty and injustice, who, though he gave me not sufficient encouragement to resist desire, yet punishes me with the consequences of indulgence. If there is a God, cried I, he must be either tyrannical and cruel, or regardless of her creatures. I will no longer endure a being which is undeservedly miserable, either from chance or design, but fly to that annihilation in which all my prospects terminate. Take back, said I, listing my eyes to Heaven, the hateful gift of existence, and let my dust no more be animated to suffering, and exalted to misery.

So saying, I ran to the brink of the river, and was going to plunge in, when the cry of some person very near me made me turn my eyes to see whence it came. I was accosted by an elderly gentleman, who, with looks of terror, pity, and benevolence, asked what I was about to do? At first I was sullen, and refused to answer him: but by degrees the compassion he shewed, and the tenderness with which he treated me, softened my heart, and gave vent to my tears.

"O, Madam!" said he, "these are gracious signs, and unlike those which first drew my attention, and made me watch you unobserved, fearing some fatal purpose in your mind. What must be the thoughts which could make a face like yours appear the picture of horror? I was taking my morning walk, and have seen you a considerable time: sometimes stopping and wringing your hands, sometimes quickening your pace, and sometimes walking slow, with your eyes fixed on the ground, till you raised them to Heaven, with looks not of supplication and piety, but rather of accusation and defiance. For pity tell me, how it is that you have quarrelled with yourself, with life, nay even with Heaven? Recal your reason and your hope, and let this seasonable prevention of your fatal purpose be an earnest to you of good things to come, of God's mercy not yet alienated from you, and stooping from his throne to save your soul from perdition?"

The tears which flowed in rivers from my eyes while he talked, gave me so much relief, that I found myself able to speak, and desirous to express my gratitude for the good man's concern for me. It was so long since I had known the joys of confidence, that I felt surprising pleasure and comfort from unburdening my heart, and telling my kind deliverer every circumstance of my story, and every thought of my distracted mind. He shuddered to hear me upbraid the Divine Providence, and stopping me short, told me he would lead me to one who should preach patience to me whilst she gave me the example of it.

As we talked he lead me to his own house, and there introduced me to his wife, a middle-aged woman, pale and emaciated, but of a cheerful placid countenance, who received me with the greatest tenderness and humanity. She saw I was distressed, and her compassion was before hand with my complaints. Her tears stood ready to accompany mine; her looks and her voice expressed the kindest concern; and her assiduous cares demonstrated that true politeness and hospitality, which is not the effect of art but of inward benevolence. While she obliged me to take some refreshment, her husband gave her a short account of my story, and of the state in which he found me. "This poor lady," said he, "from the fault of her education and principles, sees every thing through a gloomy medium. She accuses Providence, and hates her existence for those evils which are the common lot of mankind in this short state of trial. You, my dear, who are one of the greatest sufferers I have known, are best qualified to cure her of her faulty impatience, and to convince her, by your own example, that this world is not the place in which virtue is to find its reward. She thinks no one so unhappy as herself; but if she knew all that you have gone through, she would surely be sensible, that if you are happier than she, it is only because your principles are better."

"Indeed, my dear madam!" said she, "that is the only advantage that I have over you; but that indeed out weighs every thing else. It is now but ten days since I followed to the grave my only son, the survivor of eight children, who were all equally the objects of my fondest love: my heart is no less tender than your own, nor my affections less warm. For a whole year before the death of my last darling, I watched the fatal progress of his disease, and saw him suffer the most amazing pains. Nor was poverty, that dreaded evil, to which you could not submit, wanting to my trials: though my husband is, by his profession, a gentleman, his income is so small, that I and my children have often wanted necessaries: and though I had always a weakly constitution, I have helped to support my family by the labour of my own hands At this time I am consuming, by daily tortures, with a cancer, which must shortly be my death. My pains, perhaps, might be mitigated by proper assistance, though nothing could preserve my life; but I have not the means to obtain that assistance." O, hold! interrupted I, my soul is shocked at the enumeration of such intolerable sufferings: how is it that you support them? Why do I not see you, in despair like mine, renounce your existence, and put yourself out of the reach of torment? But, above all, tell me how it is possible for you to preserve, amidst such complicated misery, that appearance of cheerfulness and serene complacency which shines so remarkably in your countenance, and animates every look and motion.

"That cheerfulness and complacency," answered the good woman, "I feel in my heart. My mind is not only serene, but often experiences the highest emotions of joy and exultation, that the brightest hopes can give." And whence, said I, do you derive this astonishing art of extracting joy from misery, and of smiling amidst all the terrors of pain, sorrow, poverty, and death? She was silent for a moment, then stepping to her closet, reached a Bible, which she put into my hands: "See there," said she, "the volume in which I have learnt this art. Here I am taught, that everlasting glory is in store for all who will accept it upon the terms which Infinite Perfection has prescribed; here I am promised consolation, assistance, and support from the Lord of Life; and here I am assured, that my transient afflictions are only meant to fit me for eternal and unspeakable happiness. This happiness is at hand. The short remainder of my life seems but a point, beyond which opens the glorious prospect of immortality: thus encouraged, how should I be dejected? Thus supported, how should I sink? With such prospects, such assured hopes, how can I be otherways than happy?"

While she spoke, her eyes sparkled, and her whole face seemed animated with joy. I was struck with her manner, as well as her words. Every syllable she uttered seemed to sink into my soul, so that I never can forget it. I resolved to examine a religion, which was capable of producing such effects as I could not attribute either to chance or error. The good couple pressed me, with so much unaffected kindness, to make their little parsonage my asylum till I could better dispose of myself, that I accepted their offer. Here, with the assistance of the clergyman, who is a plain, sensible, and truly pious man, I have studied the Holy Scriptures, and the evidences of their authority. But after reading them with candour and attention, I found all the intrinsic arguments of their truth superfluous: the excellency of their precepts, the consistency of their doctrines, and the glorious motives and encouragements to virtue which they propose; together with the striking example I had before my eyes of their salutary effects, left me no doubt of their divine authority.

During the time of my abode here, I have been witness to the more than heroic, the joyful, the triumphant death of the dear good woman. With as much softness and tenderness as I ever saw in a female character, she shewed more dauntless intrepidity than the sternest philosopher, or the proudest hero. No torment could shake the constancy of her soul, or length of pain wear out the strength of her patience. Death was to her an object not of horror but of hope. When I heard her pour forth her last breath in thanksgiving, and saw the smile of extasy remain on her pale face when life was fled, I could not help crying out in the beautiful language I had lately learnt from the Sacred Writings, "O Death! where is thy sting? O Grave! where is thy victory?"

I am now preparing to leave my excellent benefactor, and get my bread in a service, to which he has recommended me in a neighbouring family. A state of servitude, to which once I could not resolve to yield, appears no longer dreadful to me; that pride, which would have made it galling, Christianity has subdued, though philosophy attempted it in vain. As a penitent, I should gratefully submit to mortification; but as a Christian, I find myself superior to every mortification, except the sense of guilt. This has humbled me to the dust: but the assurances that are given me by the Saviour of the world of the divine pardon and favour, upon sincere repentance, have calmed my troubled spirit, and filled my mind with peace and joy, which the world can neither give nor take away. Thus, without any change for the better in my outward circumstances, I find myself changed from a distracted, poor, despairing wretch, to a contented, happy, grateful being; thankful for, and pleased with my present state of existence; yet exulting in the hope of quitting it for endless glory and happiness.

O! Sir, tell the unthinking mortals, who will not take the pains of enquiring into those truths which most concern them, and who are led by fashion, and the pride of human reason, into a contempt for the sacred oracles of God, tell them this truth, which experience hath taught me, that though vice is constantly attended by misery, virtue itself cannot confer happiness in this world, except it is animated with the hopes of eternal bliss in the world to come.

15

CASTLE RACKRENT

Maria Edgeworth

Source: Maria Edgeworth, Excerpts from *Castle Rackrent* (London, J. Johnson, 1800) pp. 1–14

Monday Morning.

HAVING, out of friendship for the family, upon whose estate, praised be Heaven! I and mine have lived rent-free time out of mind, voluntarily undertaken to publish the MEMOIRS OF THE RACKRENT FAMILY, I think it my duty to say a few words, in the first place, concerning myself. My real name is Thady Quirk, though in the family I have always been known by no other than "Honest Thady," afterward, in the time of Sir Murtagh, deceased, I remember to hear them calling me "Old Thady," and now I've come to "Poor Thady"; for I wear a long greatcoat winter and summer, which is very handy, as I never put my arms into the sleeves; they are as good as new, though come Holantide next I've had it these seven years: it holds on by a single button round my neck, cloak fashion. To look at me, you would hardly think "Poor Thady" was the father of Attorney Quirk; he is a high gentleman, and never minds what poor Thady says, and having better than fifteen hundred a year, landed estate, looks down upon honest Thady; but I wash my hands of his doings, and as I have lived so will I die, true and loyal to the family. The family of the Rackrents is, I am proud to say, one of the most ancient in the kingdom. Everybody knows this is not the old family name, which was O'Shaughlin, related to the kings of Ireland – but that was before my time. My grandfather was driver to the great Sir Patrick O'Shaughlin, and I heard him, when I was a boy, telling how the Castle Rackrent estate came to Sir Patrick; Sir Tallyhoo Rackrent was cousin-german to him, and had a fine estate of his own, only never a gate upon it, it being his maxim that a car was the best gate. Poor gentleman! he lost a fine hunter and his life, at last, by it, all in one day's hunt. But I ought to bless that day, for the estate came straight into the family, upon one condition, which Sir Patrick O'Shaughlin at the time took sadly to heart, they say, but thought better of it afterwards, seeing how large a stake depended upon it: that he should, by Act of Parliament, take and bear the surname and arms of Rackrent.

 DOI: 10.4324/9780429321078-17

Now it was that the world was to see what was *in* Sir Patrick. On coming into the estate he gave the finest entertainment ever was heard of in the country; not a man could stand after supper but Sir Patrick himself, who could sit out the best man in Ireland, let alone the three kingdoms itself. He had his house, from one year's end to another, as full of company as ever it could hold, and fuller; for rather than be left out of the parties at Castle Rackrent, many gentlemen, and those men of the first consequence and landed estates in the country – such as the O'Neills of Ballynagrotty, and the Moneygawls of Mount Juliet's Town, and O'Shannons of New Town Tullyhog – made it their choice, often and often, when there was no room to be had for love nor money, in long winter nights, to sleep in the chicken-house, which Sir Patrick had fitted up for the purpose of accommodating his friends and the public in general, who honoured him with their company unexpectedly at Castle Rackrent; and this went on I can't tell you how long. The whole country rang with his praises! – Long life to him! I'm sure I love to look upon his picture, now opposite to me; though I never saw him, he must have been a portly gentleman – his neck something short, and remarkable for the largest pimple on his nose, which, by his particular desire, is still extant in his picture, said to be a striking likeness, though taken when young. He is said also to be the inventor of raspberry whisky, which is very likely, as nobody has ever appeared to dispute it with him, and as there still exists a broken punch-bowl at Castle Rackrent, in the garret, with an inscription to that effect – a great curiosity. A few days before his death he was very merry; it being his honour's birthday, he called my grandfather in – God bless him! – to drink the company's health, and filled a bumper himself, but could not carry it to his head, on account of the great shake in his hand; on this he cast his joke, saying, "What would my poor father say to me if he was to pop out of the grave, and see me now? I remember when I was a little boy, the first bumper of claret he gave me after dinner, how he praised me for carrying it so steady to my mouth. Here's my thanks to him – a bumper toast." Then he fell to singing the favourite song he learned from his father – for the last time, poor gentleman – he sung it that night as loud and as hearty as ever, with a chorus:

He that goes to bed, and goes to bed sober,
Falls as the leaves do, falls as the leaves do, and dies in October;
But he that goes to bed, and goes to bed mellow,
Lives as he ought to do, lives as he ought to do, and dies an honest fellow.

Sir Patrick died that night: just as the company rose to drink his health with three cheers, he fell down in a sort of fit, and was carried off; they sat it out, and were surprised, on inquiry in the morning, to find that it was all over with poor Sir Patrick. Never did any gentleman live and die more beloved in the country by rich and poor. His funeral was such a one as was never known before or since in the county! All the gentlemen in the three counties were at it; far and near, how they flocked! my great-grandfather said, that to see all the women, even in their red cloaks, you would have taken them for the army drawn out. Then such a fine whillaluh! you might have heard it to the farthest end of the county, and happy the man who could get but a sight of the hearse! But who'd have thought it? Just as all was going on right, through his own town they were passing, when the body was seized for debt – a rescue was apprehended from the mob; but the heir, who attended the funeral, was against that, for fear of consequences, seeing that those villains who came to serve acted under the disguise of the law: so, to be sure, the law must take its course, and little gain had the creditors for their pains. First and foremost, they had the curses of the country: and Sir Murtagh Rackrent, the new heir, in the next place, on account of this affront to the body, refused to pay a shilling of the debts, in which he was countenanced by all the best gentlemen of property, and others of his acquaintance; Sir Murtagh alleging in all companies that he all along meant to pay his father's debts of honour, but the moment the law was taken of him, there was an end of honour to be sure. It was whispered (but none but the enemies of the family believe it) that this was all a sham seizure to get quit of the debts which he had bound himself to pay in honour.

It's a long time ago, there's no saying how it was, but this for certain, the new man did not take at all after the old gentleman; the cellars were never filled after his death, and no open house, or anything as it used to be; the tenants even were sent away without their whisky. I was ashamed myself, and knew not what to say for the honour of the family; but I made the best of a bad case, and laid it all at my lady's door, for I did not like her anyhow, nor anybody else; she was of the family of the Skinflints, and a widow; it was a strange match for Sir Murtagh; the people in the country thought he demeaned himself greatly, but I said nothing: I knew how it was. Sir Murtagh was a great lawyer, and looked to the great Skinflint estate; there, however, he overshot himself; for though one of the co-heiresses, he was never the better for her, for she outlived him many's the long day – he could not see that to be sure when he married her. I must say for her, she made him the best of wives, being a very notable, stirring woman, and looking close to everything. But I always suspected she had Scotch blood in her veins; anything else I could have looked over in her, from a regard to the family. She was a strict observer, for self and servants, of Lent, and all fast-days, but not holidays. One of the maids having fainted three times the last day of Lent, to keep soul and body together, we put a morsel of roast beef into her mouth, which came from Sir Murtagh's dinner, who never fasted, not he; but somehow or other it unfortunately reached my lady's ears, and the priest of the parish had a complaint made of it the next day, and the poor girl was forced, as soon as she could walk, to do penance for it, before she could get any peace or absolution, in the house or out of it. However, my lady was very charitable in her own way. She had a charity school for poor children, where they were taught to read and write gratis, and where they were kept well to spinning gratis for my lady in return; for she had always heaps of duty yarn from the tenants, and got all her household linen out of the estate from first to last; for after the spinning, the weavers on the estate took it in hand for nothing, because of the looms my lady's interest could get from the

Linen Board to distribute gratis. Then there was a bleach-yard near us, and the tenant dare refuse my lady nothing, for fear of a lawsuit Sir Murtagh kept hanging over him about the watercourse. With these ways of managing,'tis surprising how cheap my lady got things done, and how proud she was of it. Her table the same way, kept for next to nothing; duty fowls, and duty turkeys, and duty geese, came as fast as we could eat 'em, for my lady kept a sharp look-out, and knew to a tub of butter everything the tenants had, all round. They knew her way, and what with fear of driving for rent and Sir Murtagh's lawsuits, they were kept in such good order, they never thought of coming near Castle Rackrent without a present of something or other – nothing too much or too little for my lady – eggs, honey, butter, meal, fish, game, grouse, and herrings, fresh or salt, all went for something. As for their young pigs, we had them, and the best bacon and hams they could make up, with all young chickens in spring; but they were a set of poor wretches, and we had nothing but misfortunes with them, always breaking and running away. This, Sir Murtagh and my lady said, was all their former landlord Sir Patrick's fault, who let 'em all get the half-year's rent into arrear; there was something in that to be sure. But Sir Murtagh was as much the contrary way; for let alone making English tenants of them, every soul, he was always driving and driving, and pounding and pounding, and canting and canting, and replevying and replevying, and he made a good living of trespassing cattle; there was always some tenant's pig, or horse, or cow, or calf, or goose, trespassing, which was so great a gain to Sir Murtagh, that he did not like to hear me talk of repairing fences. Then his heriots and duty-work brought him in something, his turf was cut, his potatoes set and dug, his hay brought home, and, in short, all the work about his house done for nothing; for in all our leases there were strict clauses heavy with penalties, which Sir Murtagh knew well how to enforce; so many days' duty-work of man and horse, from every tenant, he was to have, and had, every year; and when a man vexed him, why, the finest day he could pitch on, when the cratur was getting in his own harvest, or thatching his cabin, Sir Murtagh made it a principle to call upon him and his horse; so he taught 'em all, as he said, to know the law of landlord and tenant. As for law, I believe no man, dead or alive, ever loved it so well as Sir Murtagh. He had once sixteen suits pending at a time, and I never saw him so much himself: roads, lanes, bogs, wells, ponds, eel-wires, orchards, trees, tithes, vagrants, gravelpits, sandpits, dunghills, and nuisances, everything upon the face of the earth furnished him good matter for a suit. He used to boast that he had a lawsuit for every letter in the alphabet. How I used to wonder to see Sir Murtagh in the midst of the papers in his office! Why, he could hardly turn about for them. I made bold to shrug my shoulders once in his presence, and thanked my stars I was not born a gentleman to so much toil and trouble; but Sir Murtagh took me up short with his old proverb, "Learning is better than house or land." Out of forty-nine suits which he had, he never lost one but seventeen; the rest he gained with costs, double costs, treble costs sometimes; but even that did not pay. He was a very learned man in the law, and had the character of it; but how it was I can't tell, these suits that he carried cost him a power of money: in the end he sold some hundreds a year of the family estate; but he was a very learned man in the law, and I know nothing of the matter, except having a great regard for the family; and I could not help grieving when he sent me to post up notices of the sale of the fee simple of the lands and appurtenances of Timoleague.

"I know, honest Thady," says he, to comfort me, "what I'm about better than you do; I'm only selling to get the ready money wanting to carry on my suit with spirit with the Nugents of Carrickashaughlin."

He was very sanguine about that suit with the Nugents of Carrickashaughlin. He could have gained it, they say, for certain, had it pleased Heaven to have spared him to us, and it would have been at the least a plump two thousand a year in his way; but things were ordered otherwise – for the best to be sure. He dug up a fairy-mount against my advice, and had no luck afterwards. Though a learned man in the law, he was a little too incredulous in other matters. I warned him that I heard the very Banshee that my grandfather heard under Sir Patrick's window a few days before his death. But Sir Murtagh thought nothing of the Banshee, nor of his cough, with a spitting of blood, brought on, I understand, by catching cold in attending the courts, and overstraining his chest with making himself heard in one of his favourite causes. He was a great speaker with a powerful voice; but his last speech was not in the courts at all. He and my lady, though both of the same way of thinking in some things, and though she was as good a wife and great economist as you could see, and he the best of husbands, as to looking into his affairs, and making money for his family; yet I don't know how it was, they had a great deal of sparring and jarring between them. My lady had her privy purse; and she had her weed ashes, and her sealing money upon the signing of all the leases, with something to buy gloves besides; and, besides, again often took money from the tenants, if offered properly, to speak for them to Sir Murtagh about abatements and renewals. Now the weed ashes and the glove money he allowed her clear perquisites; though once when he saw her in a new gown saved out of the weed ashes, he told her to my face (for he could say a sharp thing) that she should not put on her weeds before her husband's death. But in a dispute about an abatement my lady would have the last word, and Sir Murtagh grew mad; I was within hearing of the door, and now I wish I had made bold to step in. He spoke so loud, the whole kitchen was out on the stairs. All on a sudden he stopped, and my lady too. Something has surely happened, thought I; and so it was, for Sir Murtagh in his passion broke a blood-vessel, and all the law in the land could do nothing in that case. My lady sent for five physicians, but Sir Murtagh died, and was buried. She had a fine jointure settled upon her, and took herself away, to the great joy of the tenantry. I never said anything one way or the other whilst she was part of the family, but got up to see her go at three o'clock in the morning.

"It's a fine morning, honest Thady," says she; "goodbye to ye." And into the carriage she stepped, without a word more, good or bad, or even half-a-crown; but I made my bow, and stood to see her safe out of sight for the sake of the family.

Then we were all bustle in the house, which made me keep out of the way, for I walk slow and hate a bustle; but the house was all hurry-skurry, preparing for my new master. Sir Murtagh, I forgot to notice, had no childer; so the Rackrent estate went to his younger brother, a young dashing officer, who came amongst us before I knew for the life of me whereabouts I was, in a gig or some of them things, with another spark along with him, and led horses, and servants, and dogs, and scarce a place to put any Christian of them into; for my late lady had sent all the feather-beds off before her, and blankets and household linen, down to the very knife-cloths, on the cars to Dublin, which were all her own, lawfully paid for out of her own money. So the house was quite bare, and my young master, the moment ever he set foot in it out of his gig, thought all those things must come of themselves, I believe, for he never looked after anything at all, but harum-scarum called for everything as if we were conjurors, or he in a public-house. For my part, I could not bestir myself anyhow; I had been so much used to my late master and mistress, all was upside down with me, and the new servants in the servants' hall were quite out of my way; I had nobody to talk to, and if it had not been for my pipe and tobacco, should, I verily believe, have broke my heart for poor Sir Murtagh.

But one morning my new master caught a glimpse of me as I was looking at his horse's heels, in hopes of a word from him. "And is that old Thady?" says he, as he got into his gig: I loved him from that day to this, his voice was so like the family; and he threw me a guinea out of his waistcoat-pocket, as he drew up the reins with the other hand, his horse rearing too: I thought I never set my eyes on a finer figure of a man, quite another sort from Sir Murtagh, though withal, *to me,* a family likeness. A fine life we should have led, had he stayed amongst us, God bless him! He valued a guinea as little as any man: money to him was no more than dirt, and his gentleman and groom, and all belonging to him, the same; but the sporting season over, he grew tired of the place, and having got down a great architect for the house, and an improver for the grounds, and seen their plans and elevations, he fixed a day for settling with the tenants, but went off in a whirlwind to town, just as some of them came into the yard in the morning. A circular letter came next post from the new agent, with news that the master was sailed for England, and he must remit £500 to Bath for his use before a fortnight was at an end; bad news still for the poor tenants, no change still for the better with them. Sir Kit Rackrent, my young master, left all to the agent; and though he had the spirit of a prince, and lived away to the honour of his country abroad, which I was proud to hear of, what were we the better for that at home? The agent was one of your middlemen, who grind the face of the poor, and can never bear a man with a hat upon his head: he ferreted the tenants out of their lives; not a week without a call for money, drafts upon drafts from Sir Kit; but I laid it all to the fault of the agent; for, says I, what can Sir Kit do with so much cash, and he a single man? But still it went. Rents must be all paid up to the day, and afore; no allowance for improving tenants, no consideration for those who had built upon their farms: no sooner was a lease out, but the land was advertised to the highest bidder; all the old tenants turned out, when they spent their substance in the hope and trust of a renewal from the landlord. All was now let at the highest penny to a parcel of poor wretches, who meant to run away, and did so, after taking two crops out of the ground. Then fining down the year's rent came into fashion – anything for the ready penny; and with all this and presents to the agent and the driver, there was no such thing as standing it. I said nothing, for I had a regard for the family; but I walked about thinking if his honour Sir Kit knew all this, it would go hard with him but he'd see us righted; not that I had anything for my own share to complain of, for the agent was always very civil to me when he came down into the country, and took a great deal of notice of my son Jason. Jason Quirk, though he be my son, I must say was a good scholar from his birth, and a very cute lad: I thought to make him a priest, but he did better for himself; seeing how he was as good a clerk as any in the county, the agent gave him his rent accounts to copy, which he did first of all for the pleasure of obliging the gentleman, and would take nothing at all for his trouble, but was always proud to serve the family. By and by a good farm bounding us to the east fell into his honour's hands, and my son put in a proposal for it: why shouldn't he, as well as another? The proposals all went over to the master at the Bath, who knowing no more of the land than the child unborn, only having once been out a-grousing on it before he went to England; and the value of lands, as the agent informed him, falling every year in Ireland, his honour wrote over in all haste a bit of a letter, saying he left it all to the agent, and that he must let it as well as he could – to the best bidder, to be sure – and send him over £200 by return of post: with this the agent gave me a hint, and I spoke a good word for my son, and gave out in the country that nobody need bid against us. So his proposal was just the thing, and he a good tenant; and he got a promise of an abatement in the rent after the first year, for advancing the half-year's rent at signing the lease, which was wanting to complete the agent's £200 by the return of the post, with all which my master wrote back he was well satisfied. About this time we learnt from the agent, as a great secret, how the money went so fast and the reason of the thick coming of the master's drafts: he was a little too fond of play; and Bath, they say, was no place for no young man of his fortune, where there were so many of his own countrymen, too, hunting him up and down, day and night, who had nothing to lose. At last, at Christmas, the agent wrote over to stop the drafts, for he could raise no more money on bond or mortgage, or from the tenants, or anyhow, nor had he any more to lend himself, and desired at the same time to decline the agency for the future, wishing Sir Kit his health and happiness, and the compliments of the season, for I saw the letter before ever it was sealed, when my son copied it. When the answer came there was a new turn in affairs, and the agent was turned out; and my son Jason, who had corresponded privately with his honour occasionally on business, was forthwith desired by his honour to take the accounts into his own hands, and look them over, till further orders. It was a very spirited letter to be sure: Sir Kit sent his service, and the compliments of the season, in return to the agent, and he would fight him with pleasure to-morrow, or any day, for sending him such a letter, if he was born a gentleman, which he was sorry (for both their sakes) to find (too late) he was not. Then, in a private postscript, he condescended to tell us that all would be speedily settled to his satisfaction, and we should turn over a new leaf, for he was going to be married in a fortnight to the grandest heiress in England, and had only immediate occasion at present for £200, as he would not choose to touch his lady's fortune for travelling expenses home to Castle Rackrent, where he intended to be, wind and weather permitting, early in the next month; and desired fires, and the house to be painted, and the new building to go on as fast as possible, for the reception of him and his lady before that time; with several words besides in the letter, which we could not make out because, God bless him! he wrote in such a flurry. My heart warmed to my new lady when I read this: I was almost afraid it was too good news to be true; but the girls fell to scouring, and it was well they did, for we soon saw his marriage in the paper, to a lady with I don't know how many tens of thousand pounds to her fortune: then I watched the post-office for his landing; and the news came to my son of his and the bride being in Dublin, and on the way home to Castle Rackrent. We had bonfires all over the country, expecting him down the next day, and we had his coming of age still to celebrate, which he had not time to do properly before he left the country; therefore, a great ball was expected, and great doings upon his coming, as it were, fresh to take possession of his ancestors' estate. I never shall forget the day he came home; we had waited and waited all day long till eleven o'clock at night, and I was thinking of sending the boy to lock the gates, and giving them up for that night, when there came the carriages thundering up to the great hall door. I got the first sight of the bride; for when the carriage door opened, just as she had her foot on the steps, I held the flam full in her face to light her, at which she shut her eyes, but I had a full view of the rest of her, and greatly shocked I was, for by that light she was little better than a blackamoor, and seemed crippled; but that was only sitting so long in the chariot.

"You're kindly welcome to Castle Rackrent, my lady," says I (recollecting who she was). "Did your honour hear of the bonfires?"

His honour spoke never a word, nor so much as handed her up the steps – he looked to me no more like himself than nothing at all; I know I took him for the skeleton of his honour. I was not sure what to say next to one or t'other, but seeing she was a stranger in a foreign country, I thought it but right to speak cheerful to her; so I went back again to the bonfires.

"My lady," says I, as she crossed the hall, "there would have been fifty times as many; but for fear of the horses, and frightening your ladyship, Jason and I forbid them, please your honour."

With that she looked at me a little bewildered.

"Will I have a fire lighted in the state-room to-night?" was the next question I put to her, but never a word she answered; so I concluded she could not speak a word of English, and was from foreign parts. The short and the long of it was, I couldn't tell what to make of her; so I left her to herself, and went straight down to the servants' hall to learn something for certain about her. Sir Kit's own man was tired, but the groom set him a-talking at last, and we had it all out before ever I closed my eyes that night. The bride might well be a great fortune – she was a *Jewish* all accounts, who are famous for their great riches. I had never seen any of that tribe or nation before, and could only gather that she spoke a strange kind of

English of her own, that she could not abide pork or sausages, and went neither to church or mass. Mercy upon his honour's poor soul, thought I; what will become of him and his, and all of us, with his heretic blackamoor at the head of the Castle Rackrent estate? I never slept a wink all night for thinking of it; but before the servants I put my pipe in my mouth, and kept my mind to myself, for I had a great regard for the family; and after this, when strange gentlemen's servants came to the house, and would begin to talk about the bride, I took care to put the best foot foremost, and passed her for a nabob in the kitchen, which accounted for her dark complexion and everything.

16

THE AMERICAN FRUGAL HOUSEWIFE, DEDICATED TO THOSE WHO ARE NOT ASHAMED OF ECONOMY

Lydia Marie Frances Child

Source: Lydia Marie Frances Child, Excerpts from *The American Frugal Housewife, Dedicated to Those Who Are Not Ashamed of Economy* (Boston, Marsh & Capen and Carter & Hendee, 1832), pp. 3–7

INTRODUCTORY CHAPTER

THE true economy of housekeeping is simply the art of gathering up all the fragments, so that nothing be lost. I mean fragments of *time*, as well as *materials*. Nothing should be thrown away so long as it is possible to make any use of it, however trifling that use may be; and whatever be the size of a family, every member should be employed either in earning or saving money.

'Time is money.' For this reason, cheap as stockings are, it is good economy to knit them. Cotton and woollen yarn are both cheap; hose that are knit wear twice as long as woven ones; and they can be done at odd minutes of time, which would not be otherwise employed. Where there are children, or aged people, it is sufficient to recommend knitting, that it is an *employment*.

In this point of view, patchwork is good economy. It is indeed a foolish waste of time to tear cloth into bits for the sake of arranging it anew in fantastic figures; but a large family may be kept out of idleness, and a few shillings saved, by thus using scraps of gowns, curtains, &c.

In the country, where grain is raised, it is a good plan to teach children to prepare and braid straw for their own bonnets, and their brothers' hats.

Where turkeys and geese are kept, handsome feather fans may as well be made by the younger members of a family, as to be bought. The sooner children are taught to turn their faculties to some account, the better for them and for their parents.

In this country, we are apt to let children romp away their existence, till they get to be thirteen or fourteen. This is not well. It is not well for the purses and patience of parents; and it has a still worse effect on the morals and habits of the children.

DOI: 10.4324/9780429321078-18

Begin early is the great maxim for everything in education. A child of six years old can be made useful; and should be taught to consider every day lost in which some little thing has not been done to assist others.

Children can very early be taught to take all the care of their own clothes.

They can knit garters, suspenders, and stockings; they can make patchwork and braid straw; they can make mats for the table, and mats for the floor; they can weed the garden, and pick cranberries from the meadow, to be carried to market.

Provided brothers and sisters go together, and are not allowed to go with bad children, it is a great deal better for the boys and girls on a farm to be picking blackberries at six cents a quart, than to be wearing out their clothes in useless play. They enjoy themselves just as well; and they are earning something to buy clothes, at the same time they are tearing them.

It is wise to keep an exact account of all you expend – even of a paper of pins. This answers two purposes; it makes you more careful in spending money, and it enables your husband to judge precisely whether his family live within his income. No false pride, or foolish ambition to appear as well as others, should ever induce a person to live one cent beyond the income of which he is certain. If you have two dollars a day, let nothing but sickness induce you to spend more than nine shillings; if you have one dollar a day, do not spend but seventy-five cents; if you have half a dollar a day, be satisfied to spend forty cents.

To associate with influential and genteel people with an appearance of equality, unquestionably has its advantages; particularly where there is a family of sons and daughters just coming upon the theatre of life; but, like all other external advantages, these have their proper price, and may be bought too dearly. They who never reserve a cent of their income, with which to meet any unforeseen calamity, 'pay too dear for the whistle,' whatever temporary benefits they may derive from society. Self-denial, in proportion to the narrowness of your income, will eventually be the happiest and most respectable course for you and yours. If you are prosperous, perseverance and industry will not fail to place you in such a situation as your ambition covets; and if you are not prosperous, it will be well for your children that they have not been educated to higher hopes than they will ever realize.

If you are about to furnish a house, do not spend all your money, be it much or little. Do not let the beauty of this thing, and the cheapness of that, tempt you to buy unnecessary articles. Doctor Franklin's maxim was a wise one, 'Nothing is cheap that we do not want.' Buy merely enough to get along with at first. It is only by experience that you can tell what will be the wants of your family. If you spend all your money, you will find you have purchased many things you do not want, and have no means left to get many things which you do want. If you have enough, and more than enough, to get everything suitable to your situation, do not think you must spend it all, merely because you happen to have it. Begin humbly. As riches increase, it is easy and pleasant to increase in hospitality and splendour; but it is always painful and inconvenient to decrease. After all, these things are viewed in their proper light by the truly judicious and respectable. Neatness, tastefulness, and good sense, may be shown in the management of a small household, and the arrangement of a little furniture, as well as upon a larger scale; and these qualities are always praised, and always treated with respect and attention. The consideration which many purchase by living beyond their income, and of course living upon others, is not worth the trouble it costs. The glare there is about this false and wicked parade is deceptive; it does not in fact procure a man valuable friends, or extensive influence. More than that, it is wrong – morally wrong, so far as the individual is concerned; and injurious beyond calculation to the interests of our country. To what are the increasing beggary and discouraged exertions of the present period owing? A multitude of causes have no doubt tended to increase the evil; but the root of the whole matter is the extravagance of all classes of people. We never shall be prosperous till we make pride and vanity yield to the dictates of honesty and prudence! We never shall be free from embarrassment until we cease to be ashamed of industry and economy. Let women do their share towards reformation – Let their fathers and husbands see them happy without finery; and if their husbands and fathers have (as is often the case) a foolish pride in seeing them decorated, let them gently and gradually check this feeling, by showing that they have better and surer means of commanding respect – Let them prove, by the exertion of ingenuity and economy, that neatness, good taste, and gentility, are attainable without great expense.

The writer has no apology to offer for this cheap little book of economical hints, except her deep conviction that such a book is needed. In this case, renown is out of the question, and ridicule is a matter of indifference.

The information conveyed is of a common kind; but it is such as the majority of young housekeepers do not possess, and such as they cannot obtain from cookery books. Books of this kind have usually been written for the wealthy: I have written for the poor. I have said nothing about *rich* cooking; those who can afford to be epicures will find the best of information in the 'Seventy-five Receipts.' I have attempted to teach how money can be *saved*, not how it can be *enjoyed*. If any persons think some of the maxims too rigidly economical, let them inquire how the largest fortunes among us have been made. They will find thousands and millions have been accumulated by a scrupulous attention to sums 'infinitely more minute than sixty cents.'

In early childhood, you lay the foundation of poverty or riches, in the habits you give your children. Teach them to save everything, – not for their *own* use, for that would make them selfish – but for *some* use. Teach them to *share* everything with their playmates; but never allow them to *destroy* anything.

I once visited a family where the most exact economy was observed; yet nothing was mean or uncomfortable. It is the character of true economy to be as comfortable and genteel with a little, as others can be with much. In this family, when the father brought home a package, the older children would, of their own accord, put away the paper and twine neatly, instead of throwing them in the fire, or tearing them to pieces. If the little ones wanted a piece of twine to play scratch-cradle, or spin a top, there it was, in readiness; and when they threw it upon the floor, the older children had no need to be told to put it again in its place.

The other day, I heard a mechanic say, 'I have a wife and two little children; we live in a very small house; but, to save my life, I cannot spend less than twelve hundred a year.' Another replied, 'You are not economical; I spend but eight hundred.' I thought to myself, – 'Neither of you pick up your twine and paper.' A third one, who was present, was silent; but after they were gone, he said, 'I keep house, and comfortably too, with a wife and children, for six hundred a year; but I suppose they would have thought me mean, if I had told them so.' I did not think him mean; it merely occurred to me that his wife and children were in the habit of picking up paper and twine.

Economy is generally despised as a low virtue, tending to make people ungenerous and selfish. This is true of avarice; but it is not so of economy. The man who is economical, is laying up for himself the permanent power of being useful and generous. He who thoughtlessly gives away ten dollars, when he owes a hundred more than he can pay, deserves no praise, – he obeys a sudden impulse, more like instinct than reason: it would be real charity to check this feeling; because the good he does may be doubtful, while the injury he does his family and creditors is certain. True economy is a careful treasurer in the service of benevolence; and where they are united respectability, prosperity and peace will follow.

17

MORTOMLEY'S ESTATE: A NOVEL

Charlotte Riddell

Source: Mrs. J. H. Riddell, Excerpts from *Mortomley's Estate: A Novel* (London, Hutchinson & Co, 1874), pp. 1–9

Chapter I

Introduces Mr. Asherill to the reader

DURING the course of the last ten or at most fifteen years, a new class of building has, mushroom like, sprung up in the Metropolis, which cannot perhaps better be described in a sentence than as

'The City of London Offices' (Limited).

True, none of the 'Houses,' 'Chambers,' 'Halls,' 'Buildings' that swell the ranks of this new army of offices, are so far as I know called by the above name, but they are all situated within the precincts of the City; they have been promoted by City men, they all belong to Limited Companies or to the liquidator of those Companies, and they all resemble each other more or less – more indeed rather than less.

They are to be met with in various lanes, alleys, streets, and courts. So far as a casual observer can see, they are principally remarkable for an utter absence of comfort. They possess longer corridors, smaller rooms, steeper and more unpromising stone staircases, than any other class of building, Newgate not excepted, east of Temple Bar.

So far as the mind can grasp, they are tenanted by a more wonderful race of men than Captain Cook discovered in the South Sea Islands, or Darwin conceived could ever have been eliminated from monkeys.

The windows are noticeable for having no front light, the edifices themselves are curious for the simple reason that they have been apparently built without the usual preliminaries of either architect or plan, while the men who during business hours inhabit the offices afford subject for the wildest speculation.

DOI: 10.4324/9780429321078-19

They have as a rule come from no one knows where; they live no one, save their victims, knows how; their business, though stated with sufficient distinction on the walls of the halls and corridors, and the glass and panels of the doors, is a sealed mystery to every one but themselves and the poor wretches who in those dreary offices are stripped of every valuable they possess, every rag of social consideration, every vestige of self-respect, and turned out naked as they came into the world to meet the world's opprobrium, and that which is tenfold harder to bear – the world's pity, and to try to make their way once again through a world it is unhappily necessary for them to pass through. And yet the men who are able to set up in business in the trade or profession (which?) that I have indicated, like the wicked, flourish as green bay trees; they gather riches, they purchase houses and inhabit them, they build barns and fill them, they lay by much treasure, they hug themselves on their balances, their position, the deference shown fearfully and servilely by those who are poorer than themselves, the familiarity of those who are richer, – never recking of that possible hour when poverty shall come upon them like an armed man, and when a hand more terrible than that of death itself shall be laid upon their shoulders and a voice whisper in their ear, 'Thou fool, this night thy substance is required of thee.'

As for their souls, they never think of them either. Money is palpable, spirit impalpable.

If in their blindness they ignore the probability of money making unto itself wings – even money coined as theirs has been out of the blood drawn from men's hearts, the anguished tears of women, the broken hopes of youth, and the disgrace heaped upon old age – it is not in the slightest degree likely they trouble themselves concerning the possible vagaries of their spirits.

Death, if the idea of dying present itself, is looked at either as an end of happiness or a cessation from anxiety.

It is bankruptcy in both cases. It ends a successful career; it smooths all difficulties in the path of those whose experiments have proved abortive, whose attempts have resulted in failure; and, as the earth-worm is no respecter of persons, it cuts short the career of worldly consideration, it renders men's good opinion valueless, it places the best-esteemed City magnate in a position where even a plum of money will not enable him to pass muster in a more creditable manner than the Bethnal Green pauper who has nothing to leave his family except his bones.

Death is bankruptcy. Can I say more in its disfavour when writing of a class who hold personal bankruptcy – their own, I mean – a calamity too great to contemplate; who estimate a man's standing, for here and hereafter, by the amount he has managed to rake and scrape together; and who live by swooping down upon his possessions, and selling the house which shelters him, the bed he lies on, the toys his children have played with, the dog he has fondled, the horses he has ridden, the harp his dead mother's fingers have touched?

Much more might be said of the race, but as one man of the genus waits, claiming particular attention, you and I, reader, will, leaving generalities, walk up to the first floor of Salisbury Buildings, Leadenhall Street, City, and enter the private office of Mr Asherill, senior partner in the firm of Asherill and Swanland, Public Accountants.

Well known was Mr Asherill in the City; his large frame, his high well-developed forehead, his massive head, his broad shoulders, his perfectly white hair, were as familiar to the *habitués* of Basinghall Street, and the thoroughfares conducting to that heaven for rogues and hell for honest people, as the faces of the ticket-porters in Lombard Street, or the livery of those stately gentlemen who lounge about the entrance to the Bank of England.

And indeed it must have been accounted a shame had it proved otherwise, for Mr Asherill was living, moving, and having his being in the City for five-and-twenty years at all events, before the new Bankruptcy Act developed that particular class of industry in which Mr Asherill is at this present moment employing the great and varied talents with which, to quote his own modest phrase, – 'The Lord has seen fit to bless him.'

How he employed the thirty-five years preceding the above-mentioned twenty-five of his sojourn in this wicked world, it would be tedious to specify.

His enemies – for even, such is the depravity of human nature, Mr Asherill had enemies – said a considerable portion of the period must have been spent in obtaining a practical knowledge of the roguery, vice, falsehood, and trickery, which he denounced so unctuously; and it is quite certain that in whatever school he may have graduated, his information on the subject of all the sins to which flesh is prone, his thorough acquaintance with all the forms of lying and cheating, to which what he habitually styled 'poor human nature' is addicted, were as complete as marvellous.

There must have been a black night at some period or other in his life; but no man in the City, at all events, could fix a date and locality when and where that event happened which caused Mr Asherill to conceive a dread of, and dislike for, gentlemen and ladies, which was the one weak spot in an otherwise almost perfect Christian character.

Mr Asherill's account of his own early life was that he worked in a cotton mill at Manchester; that through the kindness of a poor scholar who lodged in the house of his, Asherill's, sole surviving relative, his grandmother, he learned to read, write, and cipher; that, being steady and hardworking, he attracted the attention and secured the interest of a Christian blessed with worldly means and influence, who took him first into his own warehouse, and subsequently procured for him an appointment in India, where he remained for a long time, and might have remained till the end of his life, had not the delicate health of his wife compelled him, ten years after his marriage, to choose the alternative of parting from her or leaving India.

'Guided by Providence,' said Mr Asherill, 'I decided on returning to England.'

Which was all likely enough and plausible enough, only it happened to be untrue in one particular at least.

An unregenerate wag who met Mr Asherill at the Crystal Palace in the days when the mysteries of cotton spinning were expounded in the machinery department for the benefit of the masses, who were then supposed to be hungering and thirsting after solid information, persuaded that gentleman to inspect the process, and under pretence of ignorance beguiled the former factory lad into making various statements which proved conclusively he never could have been in a mill, save as a mere visitor, in his life.

One swallow, however, does not make a summer; and even though a man be convicted of having uttered one untruth, it does not follow that all his other statements are necessarily false.

That Mr Asherill had been in India there could be no question. He had been there long enough to place a very effectual gulf between his present and his past, and to render all attempts to fathom whatever mystery may have attached to his early life utterly futile.

It might be the case, as some people declared, that he had not risen from the ranks – that his real name was not Asherill – that he and his father, a respectable tradesman, having had some difference concerning the contents of the till, he was shipped out of the country and requested to stay out of it – all this might be so, but who was to prove it? and supposing it all capable of proof, who would be interested in the matter?

All the king's horses and all the king's men could not undo the fact, that for twenty-five years Mr Asherill had held up his head in the City – that he was a man of weight whom aldermen and common-councilmen delighted to honour – who had been connected with every form of speculation which the fashion of the day and the opportunities of each commercial year brought into repute. He had made money by railways and lost it, and come up again fresh and smiling as the director of various banks and insurance companies, the very names of which are now almost forgotten, so rapidly is the memory of one swindle wiped out by the collapse of another more recent. He had something to do, directly or indirectly, with nearly every 'big thing' which was floated in the City. To a nicety he knew the price of a lord, and was once clever enough to bait a hook which enabled him to land a bishop. He was acquainted with baronets and knights, whose names looked remarkably well on the list of directors' whilst he had an army of generals, colonels, and majors ready at any moment to take the financial field.

A ready man and an able – a man, a Yankee speculator, a canny Scot, a German adventurer, or a religious philanthropist, might have sat up all night to catch napping, and eventually found the intended victim wider awake than themselves.

If there were one thing more than another, always excepting sanctimoniousness, which distinguished Mr Asherill from other people, it was his intense respectability. From the crown of his head to the sole of his foot he looked the incarnation of that god which is the Englishman's Fetish.

The folds of his immaculate white cravat were in themselves letters of recommendation. Whenever any especially profitable and delicate piece of business had to be manipulated in the Bankruptcy Court, Mr Asherill always made it a point to be present in person; and, with the exception of one Commissioner, no

Judge had ever yet been known to urge an objection to any course Mr Asherill suggested, and throw cold water on any scheme that emanated from the brain which found no mean habitation in the massive head covered with thick but perfectly snowy hair.

And whatever Mr Asherill engaged in, he carried on and through respectably. Had his lot been cast in a different sphere, he would have made a splendid butler, a model parish clerk, or a magnificent hall porter.

As it was he associated himself with company after company, and then almost wept for those who lost their little savings, their policies of insurance, their deposits, and their incomes.

Whoever else might be to blame in the affair, he never was. He was always deceived; if there were one especial enterprise in which Mr Asherill had invested his largest stock of faith, it always proved to be that which came to the most utter grief, which collapsed with the mightiest shock.

Not only this, but the amount of money Mr Asherill, according to his own showing, lost on each of these occasions was positively appalling. He would shake his head and beg that the subject might not be mentioned to him, it was all so terrible; and then he would contrive to drop a hint as to how far he was 'in,' and the majority of people believed him, and the minority who did not believe was too small to count.

After that especial Friday, in eighteen hundred and sixty-six, when, had any former citizen liked to get out of his coffin in the vaults of St Edmund the King and Martyr, adjacent to the notorious Corner House, he might have fancied a second South Sea Bubble had just burst, after that Black Afternoon which brought ruin to thousands, Mr Asherill quietly packed up a few clothes and left town.

Perhaps he had been waiting for some such opportunity; perhaps some stray brick of that mighty pile touched him. Be this as it may, he went quietly down to Lewes, got himself decorously arrested and lodged in gaol, and then without the slightest fuss or useless publicity passed his examination, received his certificate, joined his wife at Brighton, and spent the summer at the sea-side. It was then he became a Christian and began to wear white neckcloths.

As he said it himself, there can be no harm in my remarking that up to the period of Overend and Gurney's collapse, he had not been a Christian. He was not one when he visited Lewes – he was not one when he reached Brighton, where, after more than a quarter of a century's bad health, his wife was at length dying with a commendable if late rapidity.

Whilst engaged in this occupation, she made the acquaintance of a widow lady, who was serious and possessed of an ample competency, and who being, moreover, amiably and charitably disposed, took the invalid drives, and furnished her with many luxuries luxuries and comforts to which she had always latterly been accustomed, but which, in the then state of the Asherill finances, she might otherwise have sighed for in vain.

"When Mr Asherill once more returned to business – the City, his old haunts, and companions – he was a changed man. If he had been respectable before, he was ten times more respectable now.

He was a widower, and he mourned for his deceased wife in a hat-band a foot deep, in black clothes of the best quality and of regular City make; in jet studs, a ring containing her hair, and a white cravat which would have made the fortune of an undertaker.

Nor was this all. Short as had been his absence, it proved long enough to enable him to acquire the language and manners of the people amongst whom he meant for the future to cast his lot; and he went about the City lanes and streets, informing all with whom he stopped to speak, of the irreparable loss he had sustained, of the great change which had been wrought in himself. If he heard naughty words uttered in railway carriages, he was wont to say, 'Hush,' and then read his dear young friends a homily on their thoughtlessness and profanity.

He did not hesitate to tell them he had once been sinful, even as they, and he always finished by expressing a hope they might be converted earlier in life than had been the case with him.

He was always sowing good seed; and though some of it was necessarily wasted, upon the whole, I am bound to say, Mr Asherill found the harvest pay him remarkably well.

His bankruptcy, his wife's death, the religious convictions which he was able to receive, proved the making of his fortune.

Never had Mr Asherill done better than when other men were doing as badly as they knew how. Everything he touched turned out well for him, at least; and nothing turned out a better speculation than the widow.

Naturally, after Mrs Asherill's death, she imparted to the widower a vast amount of religious consolation, and likewise naturally Mr Asherill found her conversation comfort and uphold him exceedingly.

Indeed, he found it so comforting that at the expiration of two years from the period of this failure, that is, in the summer of eighteen hundred and sixty-eight, he ventured to offer himself and his prospects to the widow.

He was a man and a convert, what could a lone woman desire or ask more? Nothing perhaps, and yet the widow had her doubts.

She had been so often angled for, that she looked rather closely at the bait before she rose to it, and hinted that whilst friendship urged her to say 'Yes,' prudence advised her to say 'No.'

She knew so little of Mr Asherill's antecedents, she was so ignorant even of the names of any of his friends, that –

'The name of Samuel Witney is familiar to you, doubtless,' interrupted Mr Asherill.

Yes, the widow knew it well. He was a shining light in his own particular denomination, and she had read his speeches, and listened to his lectures with delight and instruction.

'I suppose then,' suggested Mr Asherill, 'that if he writes to you saying he has known me for twenty years, believes me incapable of a mean action, and can vouch for my perfect respectability, I may hope –'

What he hoped was not exactly conveyed in words, but it resulted in the widow saying,

'Oh ! Mr Asherill,' and setting her cap, which had suddenly become disarranged, straight.

I do not wish to enlarge upon this theme, however; the loves of elderly couples cannot be made attractive by any sort of writing yet discovered, and the billing and cooing of a pair of old doves is music which no art can render sweet in the ear of the listener.

Immediately on Mr Asherill's return to town, he informed Mr Witney of his wishes, as well as of the great change he had experienced, thus killing, as was his wont, two birds with one stone.

He secured a second wife with a handsome income, every penny of which he insisted should be settled on herself; and he cemented the friendship, so called, which had after City fashion subsisted between himself and Mr Witney.

'It is so pleasant to think you are at last one of *us*,' said that gentleman, and undoubtedly Mr Asherill thought so too.

18

"THE TYRANNY OF THE KITCHEN," *THE NORTH AMERICAN REVIEW*

Catherine Selden

Source: Catherine Selden, 'The Tyranny of the Kitchen', *The North American Review*, Vol. 157, No. 443, Oct. 1893, pp. 431–40

There are found among those who enter domestic service certain defects of character which belong to the human race in general, supplemented by deficiencies peculiar to the class itself. These deficiencies are no longer matters of conjecture; they are of the nature of ascertained facts, and come home to each of us with the force of accumulated experience. It may safely be predicted that the servant girl of the future, as of the past, unless forced to do so, will make no adequate preparation for the duties she assumes; that the housekeeper must continue to teach her ignorant employee, and at the same time to pay her the price which is due to skilled labor. Judging from the present tendencies, there will be a steady demand for increase of wages (although few, if any, of the necessary articles purchased by the servant girl have risen in price within the past ten years), and a steady diminution in the amount of work that is done in return. The housekeeper must, however, recognize that ease and luxury play a large part in the ideals of life which take the strongest hold upon the masses; also that there is a very great inequality in the demands of different households. The chance which awaits every girl, of finding a situation in a luxurious home, where the work is light and wages high, is one never lost sight of. This, together with the innate love of change which secures relief from monotony, serves to bring about transitory engagements, and a chronic state of unrest.

Although the hours of labor cannot be definitely fixed, or the nature of the work so accurately defined as in a mill or other workshop, the employee in the private house has, as a rule, such wholesome accommodations, such excellent food, such good care in sickness, unattended by anxiety of mind concerning loss of wages, that these advantages and indulgences far outweigh any gain in other directions

 DOI: 10.4324/9780429321078-20

that the shop or factory may afford. She is, moreover, the recipient in the average household of a degree of care and consideration which she gets nowhere else, and which would be even greater than now, if the housekeeper found any substantial element of loyalty upon which she could repose. Fortunately the drudge or *slavey*, as she is known in Europe, does not exist in America in the houses of those who employ labor. She is only to be met when the chambermaid or cook marries and enters a house of her own.

In this question of domestic service, whatever apologies its defects may elicit, or whatever may be the inferences drawn from apparent or real causes, the effect remains the same. We find a condition of society wherein the advantages lie almost exclusively with the class which we are in the habit of regarding as one of the least intelligent in the community; a class, however, which has shown itself capable of being both aggressive and tyrannical; but we can hardly blame the servant girl, who, by means of a certain force of character, singleness of purpose and the aid of circumstances, has won a controlling position for herself, and has taken advantage of it. We rather look with astonishment upon that other class which has allowed itself to be thus dominated by persons of an inferior social grade. It seems surprising that employers should have so long postponed using their combined education and intelligence to mitigate some of the evils from which they suffer.

When an evil, such as we are considering, is so widespread, and is so little dependent, as we have noted, upon the character of particular housekeepers, there must be a deep-rooted cause which lies beyond the power of any one individual to create or to conquer. This cause is undoubtedly involved in the question of supply and demand, and such being the case there is no basis for the hope that the present state of things will pass away so long as there are more desirable situations ready to be filled than there are persons capable of filling them. One means of remedy lies in the more frequent employment of the Chinese and the Italians, since they combine many qualities essential to good servants. They are versatile, silent and economical. The great advantage of the Chinaman is that he is not a politician; that he minds his business, makes his money and goes home. We could not have a better tool to work with if it had been deliberately planned for our use. We have still another resource in a cooperative enterprise of some kind which by furnishing meals at a definite time or place, or by distributing them for home consumption, would lessen the demand for household service. Other palliatives will doubtless be thought of, and when this subject is once submitted to intelligent discussion we hope to receive many valuable suggestions, which, taken collectively, will furnish a basis for an enlightened policy.

The difficulties of the housekeeper are mainly due to the scarcity of a particular kind of labor. There is no scarcity of women laborers, taken as a whole. The labor market is indeed overstocked with them. It is, therefore, a question of distribution rather than supply. The heads of factories, stores and restaurants have no trouble, as a general thing, in getting all the labor they want. The problem is how to check the excessive competition in these quarters and divert a share of the labor seeking employment into channels where the services of women would yield a better return, both to the employer and employee. It is a well recognized fact that the women who seek situations in shops will not willingly enter domestic service. Their unwillingness to do so may be looked upon as an unreasonable prejudice. Nevertheless, it is a fact which cannot be overlooked in any effort which may be made to introduce this class of bread-winners into the household. It is a needless waste of energy to try and overcome this deep-rooted dislike to domestic service. The sensible thing to do, therefore, is to devise some plan of housekeeping which, so far from conflicting with this prejudice will, on the contrary, make it easy to secure the much-needed aid of those who entertain it. There are many self-respecting, capable girls who are willing to work faithfully and well under the roof of an institution who would not for a moment submit themselves to the control of a mistress in a private house.

Owing to the absence of external facilities, the American house is the scene of a heterogeneous and persistent industry, which has taxed to the utmost the powers of those whose task it is to direct it. We can safely assert that no other women of the same social grade and standard of living, as those in this country, have ever had so heavy a burden laid upon them as that which is due to the variety of their undertakings and the inadequate and incompetent force at their command to achieve them; but out of their necessities has arisen the need and the opportunity for the development of some new system of living more in keeping with the social conditions of modern times.

The work of cooking is the most troublesome and necessary part of domestic life. It requires more intelligence than all the other tasks of housekeeping, and is the one upon which the comfort of the family most largely depends. Experience has taught us there are some things which can be better and more economically done elsewhere than in the average house. We are already accustomed to buy our confectionery and many other articles from establishments organized especially for their production. There seems no reason why cooked meat and vegetables should not be brought from similar sources of supply.

It would not be difficult to found establishments of the nature of club-houses from which wholesome and well-cooked food could be distributed. The club has not hitherto been reckoned an advantage to the household. In many ways, indeed, it has been a detriment to it; but the form of organization of which it is an example might with profit be made use of for the benefit of the family. Indeed, it would be well if some of the clubs which already exist could be so enlarged as to include a department for the distribution of food. This could be effected without interfering to any great extent with their original purposes. A modification of this sort would, at the same time, give strength where at present there is an acknowledged weakness. The clientele of the family would furnish a much more certain basis for the purchase of supplies than the unforeseeable orders which now occasion one of the great difficulties in the management of clubs. Furthermore, the same capital, or perhaps it would be better to say the same plant, while subserving this double purpose might, in the nature of things, be expected to yield a larger return.

Ever since "the four thousand men, besides women and children ate and were filled" in Galilee, the simultaneous feeding of large numbers of people has been a matter of everyday occurrence. In the plan which we propose there is but one element of novelty and that is the sending out of food; but even this, so far as the least essential articles of the table are concerned, is already a matter of common experience. The task of distributing and keeping hot the more substantial and necessary varieties of cooked food ought not to present any great difficulties to a people so habile in solving mechanical problems as our own, nor ought the cost of so doing to be greater than the indirect tax that is now paid for the distribution of uncooked provisions from the different stores.

The men who belong to club-houses give as one of the excuses for their membership the diminished cost of living, the excellence of the food and the greater degree of comfort that is secured. It is frequently urged, however, that food cooked in large quantities is insipid and without its distinctive flavor; but such is not the case in first-class restaurants, and even if it were so, dishes prepared in the ordinary kitchens are not of such exquisite flavor or of such uniform excellence as to justify this criticism. But the membership of the family club should not be so large as to interfere with the gratification of individual taste. Indeed, one of the chief functions of its executive committee should be to see that no element which goes to give a home-like character to the institution is neglected. In other words, what we want to do is to combine the conveniences and organization of commercial life with the privacy of home and the independence of the individual.

In the ordinary club there is one great difficulty which is always met with, and that is the unwillingness of its best members to serve on its committees. To do so necessarily interferes, to a certain extent, with their regular occupations, and many would rather pay the indirect tax which comes from maladministration than give their time to preventing this evil. The same difficulty might be expected in any other association of a similar nature, but it doubtless will be far easier to get a body of good housekeepers to give their time and attention to the practical details of such establishments than it would be in the case of men.

The exact nature of the cooperation necessary for the experiment of keeping house on a large scale had best be determined upon by those who take an active part in such an enterprise. The idea of cooperative housekeeping was first set forth and advocated some years ago, but the experiment then made was incomplete and was never carried to the point of cooking and distributing food. An organization similar to that of the club-house especially commends itself, for the reason that this kind of cooperation is already familiar to the public and has proved itself a success, an advantage not to be underrated in endeavoring to overcome the inertia, if not positive resistance with which every novel enterprise is greeted. The initiatory management of the family club, whatever might be its final administration, ought to be undertaken by men. They are not only used to organizing large enterprises, but from habitude such burdens are lightly borne, and moreover such an undertaking in their hands would have the prestige which comes from experience and past success.

The one prime requisite for success and the principal element of cost presented by the scheme under discussion lies in the need of administrative ability of the order necessary to run a first-class restaurant. This difficulty, however, is not insurmountable, for talent of this order is not infrequently found among men, and there is no small amount of it lying dormant among women, which in their case needs to be called into activity, either by the benevolent motive or by pecuniary reward, or by both. But the direction of such an undertaking should be in the hands of the comparatively young and enthusiastic. The mature housekeeper who has been cooped up in this one occupation has had the vexation but not the enlargement which, under other circumstances, might be derived from the net work of industrial relations which encompass the household. Accustomed to the perpetual conflict and triumph in daily life of the commonplace over the ideal, she has a settled belief in the unconquerable and ever present power of evil as embodied in servants, pots and kettles, dust-pans and sewing machines. The skeptical state of mind induced by her experience is enough to check the enthusiasm of the most confirmed optimist.

There can be no doubt that the task of nursing, feeding and clothing humanity has had the effect of making women the most practical and disillusioned part of mankind. There is, nevertheless, a strong disposition on their part to seek consolation and refuge in the ideal when it is possible to do so. Such an organization as the above would serve as an outlet for aspirations founded upon practical ends, with a better chance of their realization than under ordinary conditions. It must be a very degenerate housekeeper who is not aroused to enthusiasm and emulation by the sight of a well-appointed, orderly, clean, and attractive kitchen and store-rooms, such as are to be found in good hotels and club-houses, and who does not find in these conditions the fulfilment of an ideal.

Without question the task of supplying a number of families with food is attended by its difficulties, but with our present system of labor it is hard to conceive anything more unsatisfactory, expensive and troublesome than the multiplied task of feeding small numbers. Indeed, the private kitchen is in many ways a monument of inefficiency. There is no doubt that the expense and labor in a restaurant is very much diminished in proportion to the numbers of its patrons. Thirty families might just as well have their dinners cooked in one kitchen by two or three cooks, as in thirty kitchens by thirty cooks. Instead of thirty ranges with their enormous consumption of fuel, one fire would be sufficient for the same purpose. There are also many labor-saving contrivances, economical devices and facilities now wanting in the home which could be made available, with the capital at its disposal, in the family club-house. The New England creamery serves in this connection to illustrate a very successful application of the cooperative theory. The unequal capacity and skill of the different farmers in a given district, and their unequal supply of water and other facilities for making good butter, have been avoided by the creamery. To these establishments, provided with such conveniences and resources as can only be secured by an expenditure of money out of proportion to the means of the average farmer, the dairyman brings his milk and has it converted into butter and cheese of far greater average excellence than could otherwise be secured.

Even in cases where there has been no previous training, and where it is a question of saving rather than of making money, several very successful efforts have been made to feed a comparatively large number of men at a very small cost. The Foxcroft Club in Cambridge, Mass., was organized by some gentlemen entirely without experience in the caterer's art, for the purpose of enabling students to obtain at moderate prices a sufficiency of plain and wholesome food. This they are enabled to do for about $2.50 a week. At Memorial Hall board is obtained at from $3.50 to $4 a week; but young men at the most vigorous and active period of their lives undoubtedly consume far more food than would be the case with the members of an average family. Memorial Hall and the Foxcroft Club are both managed by the students themselves; persons whose business experience must of necessity be small. If the above share of success is obtained under circumstances, which from a business point of view are somewhat unfavorable, far better results might be attained with experience and the application of the best business methods.

Mr. Atkinson's tables of the cost of food afford encouragement, and show how far our present methods lag behind economic and gustatory possibilities. Besides the unnecessary direct tax that has been placed upon mankind by ignorance and inattention to proper feeding, the indirect tax from this source is beyond computation. The question of food enters largely into the problem of intemperance, and many instances of reform have been due, not to any great moral uplifting, but to good food taken at proper intervals and in sufficient quantities to give strength and vigor to the bodily frame, thus diminishing the craving for stimulus and increasing the power of resistance to temptation.

So far as household service is concerned, the distribution of food would lessen the demand which now exists for domestic labor or rather distribute it more equably. By such an arrangement many persons who ordinarily employ two or three servants might dispense with one or more; those who have none might find it easier to get one, and those who so desired might altogether dispense with them. A liberal order for dinner might well include enough for luncheon, thus leaving but one meal to be prepared at home, and this the least troublesome of the three. The French have already taught us the sufficiency of coffee, eggs and bread for breakfast and the perfection to which these articles can be brought. It only remains for us to apply this lesson, together with other practical household experiments that have been made by these ingenious people.

The club as a centre of distribution should be conveniently placed with reference to its clientele, and being so placed might well have a restaurant attached for the benefit of such members as may prefer to take their meals abroad. There are conceivable instances where such a plan might afford greater comfort and diversion than the other, and in any enlarged scheme of life there should be room for all varieties of wholesome living. Multiplied opportunities and ways of healthful living give multipled chances for happiness. There are many households restricted within such narrow social limits, so impoverished in their occasions for diversion that any additional resource which gives a change of scene and relief from deadening monotony is to be welcomed. We cannot afford to despise any legitimate aid to enjoyment, and the embellishment, even of trifles, is, as Mr. Emerson suggests, not the least part of our duty in life.

It is needless to say the business of feeding humanity upon which every other enterprise is founded is of sufficient importance to awaken the interest of the imaginative, the practical and scientific minds. Indeed, it needs a cooperation of all these elements of thought; it offers a line of research which would seem to be especially fitted for women, and there can be no doubt that better education in the future will lead to the application of knowledge where hitherto ignorance only has prevailed. Such club-houses as those we propose afford ample opportunities for intelligent women of all grades to find useful employment; not only in the administrative offices but in all departments of practical work, and as we have before intimated, after the club-house had once been set on foot, its management might very properly devolve exclusively upon women. These establishments might be so conducted as to attract the better class of labor, and by means of promotion and reward retain it permanently in service. Booms simply appointed, to be used by the employees for recreation and reading might well enter into the plan of such a club. It might also in the course of time become a training school of the highest value; for the one thing of all others which commends institutions as such is the sense of continuity which they give. A great deal of teaching which elsewhere is dispensed in infinitesimal quantities and lost in dispersion is here crystallized into tradition, and an atmosphere is created in which it is easy to absorb knowledge without any tangible influence being exerted.

If, however, the choice were to lie between benefiting any any one class above another, we should say that,whatever pleasure and profit might accrue to others from such establishments, their primary object should be to give relief to the housekeeper, to diminish her daily task, and to free her mind from the hopeless attitude towards the problems of every-day life; but more especially to arouse her from her fatal predisposition to submission, when resistance, cooperation or organization of some kind would diminish her cares.

19

"THE WIFE'S CONTRIBUTION TO FAMILY INCOME," *THE ECONOMIC JOURNAL*[1]

Ada Heather-Bigg

Source: Ada Heather-Bigg, 'The Wife's Contribution to Family Income', *The Economic Journal*, Vol. 4, No. 13, March 1894, pp. 51–8

IT is matter of common knowledge that there are large numbers of women who work under terrible conditions, toiling long hours for starvation pay in the midst of filthy and unhealthy surroundings. A little time ago it was the fashion to ascribe this appalling state of affairs to the sweating system, and to define sweating as a method of employment involving subcontract.

The painstaking inquiries of Mr. Charles Booth, Mr. David Schloss, and Mrs. Sidney Webb, soon proved that the evils in question were constantly present in cases where there was no system of sub-contract, and were likewise absent in numberless cases where the method of employment *was* that of sub-contract. Sub-contract having thus been shown not to be in fault, the next cry raised was that home work was to be held responsible, and particularly the home work of women.

The outcry against sub-contract had been swelled by the antagonism of labour to capital, – the dislike felt by the man who works for wages to the man who works for profit. The outcry against home work is swelled by the hostility of the working man to the woman wage-earner. This feeling of resentment at women's presence in the wage market is based upon fundamental ignorance of social and industrial history. The popular impression seems to be that women to-day are taking a larger share of the world's work than they have ever done before – that this is a new departure, the outcome of the factory system.

As a matter of fact the share taken by women in the work of the world has not altered in amount, nor even in intensity, only in character. Even in character it has not changed as much as the working man imagines.

Leroy Beaulieu has good ground for hazarding his assertion that if only our classical education had familiarized us with something more than mere details of

DOI: 10.4324/9780429321078-21

the Camp and the Forum, we should see that the organization of labour amongst the ancients differed far less from our own before the introduction of machinery than is generally supposed, and that women took a vastly larger and less sedentary part in productive industry than our prejudices will allow us to admit.

Confining our attention to later times however, and dealing with the more precise data to which we here have access, we find that it was in France that woman's industrial position was earliest secured. Under the feudal system the serfs in that country had not only to yield to their lords part of the produce of the land, but to render to them linen yarn, pieces of stuff, tunics and other garments, the work of their female belongings.

'Long before the tenth century the old seigniorial manor included, besides farms and fields, work-rooms of men and women.'[2] Light work such as spinning, weaving, bleaching, dyeing, and the making of clothing, fell to the women, most of whom worked in their own homes, but many of them in the gynæceum. Sometimes the gynæceum was under the direction of the wife of the feudal lord, who allotted the tasks and herself shared in them; sometimes, as in the case of the monastic manor, it was controlled by the abbey intendant, who supplied all the material and saw that no time was wasted.

As early as the ninth century, too, associated work entered upon a new phase through the introduction of industries into monasteries and convents. The spinning and dyeing of wool engrossed a considerable portion of the nuns' existence. Not only in many cases did they make everything needful for their maintenance, from bread down to shoes, but they worked for the outside market as well.[3] This, as every one knows, they have still gone on doing all through the centuries. Not the least interesting detail in the life of the great Galileo, – contained in an incidental mention in his correspondence with his daughter, Sister Celeste – shows that he had all his needlework and washing done at the convent of St. Matthew, in Florence, and was a good customer to it for candied fruit and citron. Convents indeed were active centres of industrial life, and in their efforts to supplement their revenues competed largely with outside labour and promoted improvements. Thus the Flemish nuns, in their convents near Ghent, brought out that point lace which was so largely produced during the fourteenth and fifteenth centuries.

When we come to the latter half of the middle ages we get a still better notion of the extent and nature of the industries engaged in by women. In the production of luxuries for the nobles, in countries where the industrial arts had made any progress at all, women early bore their share, and that this share was no inconsiderable one is apparent to any one investigating the history of ecclesiastical embroidery, white embroidery, the manufacture of such light fabrics as battiste, muslin and silk textiles, and above all of lace.

The even larger share borne by women in that productive industry which supplied the coarse food and clothing of themselves and their families is less patent, because industry of this kind was domestic in a double sense – being carried on by the family *for* the family – each family supplying its own wants first and then disposing of the residue. Obviously, where all the members of the family work together it is difficult to estimate precisely the monetary value of the individual contribution to the total labour required.

The difficulty exists even when the work is being done for outside custom, as is very well illustrated in the present day by the East End tailoring trade. A daughter, receiving subsistence and a certain amount of pocket money, 'helps' her father; a wife, receiving subsistence and no pocket money, 'helps' her husband. It is not till the wife as a widow, and the daughter as an orphan, do precisely similar work at fixed rates for a tailor not related to them, that the world realizes that what is called '*helping*' father or husband is really '*maintaining* herself.'

In primitive industries the male head of the family disposes of the finished product, sweeps in the earnings and distributes them as his caprice or interest determines. What was the rule in pre-machinery days is even now the rule in some of the surviving domestic industries of England, for instance in the wrought nail trade of South Staffordshire, where the man's 'stint' of nails constantly embodies the labour of wife and daughter, though his name alone appears on the master's books. Something analogous to this is described by Mr. Scott in his interesting account of the Co-operative Society of Basket Makers at Villaines (ECONOMIC JOURNAL, Sept., 1893). 'The baskets,' he says, 'are entered in the workman's name by the secretary, whether he, or his family have actually made them, and he is credited with the amount.'

Where the financial arrangements are of this nature there is obviously no talk of women's work – the husband is the nominal worker. And I venture to think that a great deal of woman's work in the past has escaped the notice of economic inquirers through this practice of *throwing in* her work with her husband's.[4]

In sparsely settled districts and in industrially backward countries such as England was before the 15th century, women are not idle but are constantly associated with men in agricultural labour. In the *Crede of Piers Plowman* there is a graphic description of the peasant's wife leading the oxen while her husband guides the plough. 'Before the Plague,' says Thorold Rogers, 'women were employed in harvest work, in reaping the stubble after the corn was cut (for the thresher or for litter), in hoeing, in planting beans, in washing and shearing sheep, and sometimes in waiting on the thresher or tiler.'

In face of all this evidence of women's activity in the past, it is simply absurd to denounce their alleged increased employment in the present, or to seek to saddle nineteenth century civilization with the onus of having evolved the working woman and set up competition between the sexes.

This competition is no new thing. As early as the reign of Edward III. women's need to earn a living was recognized by a law prohibiting men from the use of the distaff and spindle, while, in 1789, just before the Revolution burst upon Europe, a petition of the women of the Third Estate to the king set forth that every occupation which involved spinning, knitting, or sewing, should be reserved exclusively for women.

Facts of this sort make the more cautious and thoughtful among the opponents of female labour content themselves with attacking not so much women's wage-earning altogether, as the practice of continuing wage-earning after marriage. This at least they declare is an innovation – and one which heralds the destruction of the home.

So obvious are the evils consequent upon the withdrawal of the wife and mother from the domestic hearth, that it would be impossible not to sympathise with the men's point of view, did they confine their opposition to the employment of married women in workshops and factories. But seeing that they oppose, quite as actively, work done for wages by married women in their own homes, it is clear that something else moves them than mere dread that maternal and household duties may be neglected.

Analysing carefully, we find that what they object to is the *wage-earning* not the *work* of wives. Home-work enables a married woman to become joint earner with her husband, and they profess to fear that facilities in this direction may lead to the gradual substitution of the wife for the husband as breadwinner. Such a fear is the veriest scooped-out, sheet-draped turnip that ever made a village dolt take to his heels and run. If being joint earners with their husbands could have led to the substitution of the wife for the husband as bread-winner, then this substitution would long since have been effected.

For, it is indisputable that women of the working classes always have been joint earners with their husbands. At no time in the world's history has the man's labour alone sufficed for the maintenance of his wife and children.[5]

So far from keeping his wife, the true account of the matter is that he and she have together kept themselves and the younger children, and this they continue doing to the present day.

It is not by economists that this truth has been overlooked. 'In order to bring up a family,' says Adam Smith, 'the labour of the husband and wife together, must, even in the lowest species of common labour, be able to earn something more than is precisely necessary for their own maintenance.'

Nassau Senior is equally explicit: 'We include as part of the wages of the married labourer those of his wife and unemancipated children . . . . The earnings of the wife and children of many a Manchester weaver or spinner exceed or equal those of himself.'

Again, Thorold Rogers states that in England before the Plague, the total earnings and perquisites of an agricultural labourer were £1 15*s*. 4*d*. a year, and that assuming that the wife worked only 100 days in the year, 8*s*. 4*d*., or a little less than one-fifth of the whole, was her contribution to the family resources.

According to Roscher, in France in 1832, a man working in the field earned on an average $1\frac{1}{4}$ francs a day, the wife $\frac{3}{4}$ of a franc (200 days to the year), and three children 38 centimes (250 days in the year), an aggregate of 650 francs per annum. The wife's contribution thus amounted to 23.0 per cent., or a little less than one-fourth of the whole.[6]

While economists have freely conceded that the wife's share in family maintenance, whether her labour be confined to her home or no, is an appreciable one, responsible statesmen have on occasions made and acted upon the same admission.

Thus in France, when a scheme of working class pensions was under consideration, some fifty years ago, the then Minister of Finance refused to entertain the project on the ground that it did not sufficiently recognize the claims of wives. It was out of the question, he said, that one alone of a married couple should reap the benefit of an annuity, the payments for which were made possible by the joint labours of both.

Amongst English statesmen Lord Brougham also seems certainly to have been alive to the large share taken by the wife in productive industry. Speaking at a meeting of the Society for the Encouragement of the Social Sciences in 1862, he stated that one-seventh of the married women of England were engaged in independent and isolated labour, while in addition there were large numbers of wives, daughters, and sisters who shared in the labour of their male relatives on farms, at the desk, behind the counter, and in domestic workshops.

Miss Edith Simcox, then, was within rather than beyond the truth when she affirmed before the Industrial Remuneration Conference, that in England 'not more than half the whole number of working class families are maintained by the labour of the father assisted only by the elder children.'

Even in America, where one would suppose men's wages would be on a sufficiently liberal scale to enable them unassisted to provide for wife and children, the wife's labour is an important and necessary factor in family maintenance. The United States Department of Labour recently conducted an inquiry into the industrial conditions of Europe and America, subjecting the industries of coal, iron, steel, and glass, and cotton, woollen, silk and linen textiles, to complete investigation, and collecting Budgets of Cost of Living from 770 workmen employed in Europe and 2,490 employed in America. As a result of these investigations, it was ascertained, that not only are the total earnings of the family highest in America, but the contribution of the husband thereto is both relatively and absolutely higher than elsewhere. Yet even here 'only in two cases – viz. the bar-iron and steel manufacture – was it possible for the husband unaided to support his family.' In Belgium, where the return to labour generally is small, it is calculated that only three-fifths of the family income come from the husband's wages.

But it may be urged, grant that wives have at all times earned their bread, is it not perfectly possible that they are beginning in these modern days to do more than earn their bread? Are we not witnessing a real displacement of male labour? To this the answer is a decided negative. There may be a change in the distribution of male labour, but that is quite another matter from its displacement. The woman's share in household maintenance is no more than it ever was. The facts have not altered, but the conditions of modern industry enable us to see what the facts are. In short, we are witnessing not a process of *substitution* but of *revelation.*

People who assert glibly that wives in the past had enough to do looking after their homes, seldom realize what looking after the home meant 150 years ago. It meant chopping wood, fetching water, baking bread, spinning flax, weaving, knitting, pickling, curing, churning, preserving, washing.[7] But now, water is laid on into the houses, bread is bought at the baker's, it is cheaper to buy garments than to make them, wood and coal are brought round to the door in carts, and jam and pickles, butter and bacon, are all to be had from the general shop. So that now, – for dwellers in big cities at any rate, – 'looking after the home,' means only cleaning, cooking, washing, mending, care of children being the same in both cases. Even washing is ceasing to be the essentially domestic occupation it used to be, many women finding it more profitable to work at some trade in their homes and to give their washing out to a poorer neighbour to be done in the municipal wash-houses, or in the places set apart for washing in model buildings.[8]

Though women did not earn wages for all the multifarious occupations which 'looking after the home' formerly involved, it is clear they did as much of the necessary work of the world as they do now. If, then, the fallacy that there is a limited amount of work to be obtained, and that the more the women take the less the men get, be supposed true, it is certain that female labour competed as much with male labour heretofore as now. The only difference was that each woman took an infinitesimal share of a great many different kinds of work, whereas now she takes, as a tailoress, clerk, jam-factory girl, or what not, an appreciable share of one particular kind of work.

Without drawing subtle distinctions however I may conclude by saying, what I think few will dispute. So long as the wife must contribute her quota to family maintenance, it is distinctly advisable that she should be allowed to do this in the way she herself finds least irksome. The ideal to be aimed at, I submit, is not that the man should be the sole bread-winner, but that bread-winning should go on under circumstances which secure the most comfortable life for the men, women, and children composing the family, which permit the fullest development of all powers, and which, openly substitute economic co-operation on the part of the wife for economic dependence. Tested by reference to this ideal, home work will always, in the very teeth of admitted drawbacks, find itself justified, for it indisputably allows the married woman to contribute her share to family maintenance in a way congenial to herself, and on lines which are consonant with the beauty and stability of family life.

NOTES

1 Read before Section F of the British Association, September 18, 1893.

2 *Le Travail des Femmes au XIX. Siécle*. – Leroy Beaulieu.

3 Levasseur, *Histoire des Classes ouvrières* II., ch. iv., p. 139.

4 Cf. *A History of Agricultural Prices in England*, by Thorold Rogers, p. 75. 'The Manor of Thorncroft, that is Leatherhead in Surrey, contained one tenant in villenage.' From him numerous labour rents were exacted, amongst others – 'To find one woman to wash and shear sheep and lambs, and to do this for nothing.' This woman would naturally have been either his wife or his daughter. Cf. also Craigie's 'Size and Distribution of Agricultural Holdings in England and Abroad,' *Journal of Statistical Society*, Vol. 1. 'A

special form of *petite culture* prevails in Sweden, whereby small plots called "torps" – about 180,000 in all – are let to labourers who pay rent not in produce or money, but in labour – one to three working days a week, and certain extra work by women at harvest, being the usual terms.'

5 'Cette société idéale,' says Leroy Beaulieu, 'où l'homme pourrait suffire aux besoins de la famille, et où la femme n'aurait qu'à vaquer aux soins de la maison et *à* l'éducation des enfants n'a nulle part existé dans le passé.'

6 Monsieur Baudrillart states that at the present day in the Arles district the annual income of a family of petty peasant proprietors and petty wage-earners is about 850 francs, of which the wife contributes 150.

7 An incident in the life of a notable American woman, detailed by Helen Campbell in an article on 'Women Wage Earners' in the *Arena*, shows what looking after the home has sometimes meant. 'In mid-winter, with neither money nor wool in the house, one of the boys required a new suit. The mother sheared a half-grown fleece from a sheep and in a week had spun, wove, and made it into clothing, the sheep being protected from cold by a wrappage made of braided straw.'

8 Le Play, with whose works Mr. Henry Higgs has done so much to familiarize English readers, predicted long ago that amongst Western nations washing would ultimately cease to be carried on as a domestic industry. Now that steam laundries are springing up on all sides and vast amounts of linen are washed by men and machinery, this prediction seems in a fair way of being realized.

20

THE MODERN MARRIAGE MARKET

Marie Corelli, Flora Annie Steel, Lady Jeune and Susan, Countess of Malmesbury

Source: Marie Corelli, Flora Annie Steel, Lady Jeune and Susan, Countess of Malmesbury. *The Modern Marriage Market* (London, Hutchinson, 1898)

Among the many ages or periods in this world's existence, ages and periods which have been separated and classified, according to the fancy of historians, as the "Dark," the "Mythical," the "Classical," or the "Mediæval," it is doubtful whether there has ever been one which has so richly merited the pre-eminent and prominent label of "Sham" writ across it as this, our own blessed and enlightened time. If any pride can be taken in the fact, let those who will be proud. For never in all the passing pageant and phantasmagoria of history did a greater generation of civilised hypocrites cumber the face of the globe than cumber it to-day, never was the earth so oppressed with the weight of polite lying, never were there such crowds of civil masqueraders, cultured tricksters, and social humbugs, who, though admirable as tricksters and humbugs, are wholly contemptible as men and women. Truth is at a discount, and if one should utter it, the reproachful faces of one's so-called "friends" show how shocked they are at meeting with anything honest. We are drifting our days away in a condition of false luxury, of over-ripe civilisation, which has bred in us that apathetic inertia which is always a premonitory symptom of fatal disease. If one should talk to us of heroic actions—even the simplest—our befuddled minds connect them vaguely with a necessity for the police or the law courts, if we should hear of a bold man's attempt to scale the heights of a seeming too lofty ambition, we express our sickly belief that he will fail, and if he succeeds, we are, in the same sickly spirit, more disappointed than gratified. We cannot abide boldness. We are too weak in our nerves to stand the warm and splendid fervours of enthusiasm. We shudder—we cry—we whine at things that threaten to disturb our slothful self-indulgence, our eating—our drinking—our sleeping in soft beds, guarded from draught and noise our dear, pet vices—our morbid egotism—our blind, idiot vanity: we cannot endure troublous emotions—the great stress and storm of heart which moulds

 DOI: 10.4324/9780429321078-22

noble character. Away with such! We cannot be expected to exert ourselves more than is absolutely necessary for the feeding of our bodies and the carrying of them about, carefully, to such places as may seem adequate for their entertainment and further nourishment. I am not speaking of the "millions underground," the vast, toiling, silent millions of unregarded and unrewarded workers, who labour out of sight as it were and with such ominous speechlessness, the speechlessness being only for a time. I am addressing you, women, most of you, who read the pages of this popular magazine because you expect you will find something therein to minister to pleasure or vanity, something in the way of advice of dress or the toilette, or the thousand-and-one little fascinations wherewith you hope to entrap the often silly souls of men, not because you want to be told where you fail in the very mission and intention of Womanhood. Some of you are sincere enough, no doubt, in the wish to do the best with the responsibilities invested in you: but "wishing to do" is one thing, and "doing" is another. Most women of Society find it more than difficult to carry out the good intentions with which they have perhaps begun their careers; and the more exalted their position, the less, as a rule, are they able to withstand the temptations, follies, and hypocrisies which surround them. Follies, temptations, and hypocrisies surround in a greater or less degree all women, whether in Society or out of it, and we are none of us angels, though to their credit be it said, that some men still think us so. Some men still make "angels" out of us in spite of our cycling mania, our foolish "clubs," where we do nothing at all, our rough games at football and cricket, our general throwing to the winds of all dainty feminine reserve, delicacy, and modesty, and we alone are to blame if we shatter their ideals and sit down by choice in the mud when they would have placed us on thrones. It is our fault, not theirs. We have willed it so. Many of us are more "mannish" than womanly; we are more inclined to laugh at and make mock of a man's courtesy and reverence than we are to be flattered by it. The result is that nowadays we are married, both men and women alike, for what we *have*, and not for what we *are*.

It is one of our many hypocrisies to pretend we do not see things that are plainly put before us every day, and also to assume a fastidious disgust and horror when told of certain "barbarisms" still practised in Europe, barbarisms which we consider we have, in our state of ultra-civilisation, fortunately escaped. One of these "barbaric" institutions which moves us to shudder gracefully and turn up the whites of our eyes, is slavery. "Britons never, never shall," we say. British women shall never, for example, stand stripped in the market-place to be appraised and labelled at a price, and purchased by a sensualist and ruffian for so much money down. No British man shall ever stand with bound hands and manacled feet, shamed and contemptible in his own eyes, waiting till some luxurious wanton of the world, with more cash than modesty, buys him with her millions to be her fetch-and-carry slave till death releases him from the unnatural bondage. These things are done in Stamboul. True. Stamboul is barbaric. What of London? What of the "season," when women are as coolly "brought out" to be sold as any unhappy Armenian girl that ever shuddered at the lewd gaze of a Turkish tyrant? What of the mothers and fathers who force their children thus into the open market? Come—face the thing out—don't put it away or behind you as a matter too awkward and difficult of discussion. It is an absolute grim fact that in England, women those of the upper classes, at any rate are not to-day married, but bought for a price. The high and noble intention of marriage is entirely lost sight of in the scheming, the bargaining, and the pricing.

What **is** marriage? Many of you have, I think, forgotten. It is not the church, the ritual, the blessing of the clergyman, or the ratifying and approving presence of one's friends and relations at the ceremony, still less is it a matter of "settlements" and expensive millinery. It is the taking of a solemn vow before the Throne of the Eternal, a vow which declares that the man and woman concerned have discovered in each other his and her true mate, that they feel life is alone valuable and worth living in each other's company, that they are prepared to endure trouble, poverty, pain, sickness, death itself, provided they may only be together, and that all the world is a mere grain of dust in worth as compared to the exalted passion which fills their souls and moves them to become one in flesh as well as one in spirit. Nothing can make marriage an absolutely sacred thing except the great love, combined with the pure and faithful intention, of the human pair involved. They have to realise first of all that a God exists; and that before that God, Whom they solemnly acknowledge and believe in, they are One.

What has the cash-box to do with this? The reply will be that in order to live, one must have the wherewithal for living. Quite so. But then, if it be once fully realised that there is a Supreme Creator of things, to Whom we are answerable for the breaking of any of His laws, we shall understand that no two human beings have a right to share each other's lives at all, if the result of such sharing should be to *drag each other down*. Marriage is intended to uplift—to consecrate—to inspire, and while these noble duties cannot altogether be properly fulfilled if extreme poverty bars the way, and starvation looks in at the door, it is not at all necessary that the married pair should be so grossly and vulgarly wealthy as to be free of every shadow of difficulty. Shadows of difficulty show best where love's sunshine falls. We are never as strong, as sweet, or as true as we might be if we lack the divine difficulties which nerve us to fresh endeavour. It is as easy—perhaps easier—to be happy on five hundred a year, as on five thousand, and a study of the faces of those who possess a hundred thousand a year will move us more to compassion than envy.

I know an artist who lives on the Island of Capri, a perfectly happy man. He earns about one hundred pounds per annum by painting charming little studies of the beauties of the island, and disposing of them whenever he can to chance visitors. He is a gentleman by birth, breeding, and education, he is essentially one in manners, and excels in the almost lost art of conversation. He is passionately in love with his wife, a pretty, coaxing little creature of the fair Sicilian type, and he adores his son, a sturdy small person of three years, whose exquisite baby beauty is the delight of every inhabitant of the place. Nature surrounds the little trio with her loveliest scenery—the melting charm of sea and sky and island picturesqueness is theirs to enjoy from every window of their flower-wreathed habitation, and they crave for nothing more than they possess. "We love each other," is the simple secret of the idyllic life they lead; and when you have been at one of the merry little Bohemian suppers which the artist often gives to friends coming over from Naples to Sorrento, when in the warmth of the Italian night the windows are set wide open to let the white moon light up with her full Southern brilliance the unpretentious "feast" of luscious fruit and genuine wine, and your fair hostess leans against the rose-twined porch, softly playing her mandolin in subdued accompaniment to the gay songs of her guests, you begin to think you have found something like the lost paradise, which, after all, was only a paradise just so long as the human beings in it were content to obey their Maker's commandment. Beyond that commandment lay the forbidden tree, the sting of the serpent-devil, and afterwards distrust—mutual reproach and misery.

It is the same now as it was then the old Biblical legend can be fitted to ourselves every day and every hour of the day. God's laws exist, and chiefest of them all is the Law of Love. Twist that great mandate into a decree of Mammon, and you have blotched with crime the bright face of the universe. The artist of Capri is happier than many a millionaire, and a hundred times better-looking than most. Nature has done her best for him in all respects, has given him a fine face and figure, a fearless look, superb health, and complete enjoyment of life, what more does any one want out of the vast storehouse of creation?

It is what we are all fighting and struggling for—life and the enjoyment of life: this man has it on a simple hundred pounds a year. And if another man as good, as handsome, as simple-hearted, and as worthy of respect, were to ask one of our modern young Englishwomen to-day to try and love him *on that income*, she would find her heart singularly impervious to his wooing, depend upon it! If he suggested living in some lovely nook of the world, where life is cheaply and easily maintained, such as Capri, she would begin to mope at the mere idea of the "dulness" involved and why? Because Love is not sufficient for her. Because in the rush of our time we are trampling sweet emotions and true passions under foot, and marriages are seldom the result of affection nowadays, they are merely the carrying out of a settled scheme of business. Mothers teach their daughters to marry for a "suitable establishment": fathers, rendered desperate as to what they are to do with their sons in the increasing struggle for life and the incessant demand for luxuries which are not by any means actually necessary to that life, say, "Look out for a woman with money." Heirs to a great name and title sell their birthrights for a mess of American dollar-pottage, and it is a very common every-day sight to see some Christian virgin sacrificed on the altar of matrimony to a money-lending, money-grubbing son of Israel.

Bargain and sale, sale and bargain, it is the whole *raison d'être* of the "season," the balls, the dinners, the suppers, the parties to Hurlingham and Ascot. Even on the dear old Thames with its delicious nooks, fitted for pure romance and heart betrothal, the clatter of Gunter's luncheon-dishes and the popping of Benoist's champagne-corks remind the hungry gypsies who linger near such scenes of river revelry that there is not much sentiment about only plenty of money being wasted. Here, for instance, is a little river-study taken from life:

> Time: late evening. Scene: Cookham. Sky-effect: moonrise. *Dramatis personæ:* He and She, lolling each in a deck-chair on a luxuriously fitted house-boat.

HE:
I heard a lot this season about the way you were going on with that poor devil of a So-and-So, people said you were fond of him, dontcherknow.

SHE (*casually*):
Did they? So I was. Awfully fond. But he hadn't got any oof-bird.

HE:
Oh! Then I suppose he's "off"?

SHE:
Off? I should think so! Why (*this with deep contempt*) he's become a *digger*.

HE (*laughing*):
Costume will suit him down to the ground. Rather good-looking fellow—fine figure and all that—jolly sort of chap. I say, then, if he's "off" I'm on—eh?

SHE:
If you like. I told you it would be all right when your governor died. Couldn't settle up till then. He might have lived ever so long.

HE:
So he might. But he hasn't. He's gone, sure enough. Then it's a tie?

SHE:
It's a tie. No don't kiss me I don't feel like it.

HE (*chuckling*):
Don't you? Well, I suppose you have got to be taken in the humour. I don't feel like it either, now I come to think of it.

SHE:
I am quite sure you don't. It's so idiotic, you know,

HE:
I bet you kissed the digger fellow. Come, didn't you?

SHE:
I may have done. I don't remember. Anyhow, it isn't your business. I want some ices.

HE:
Waiter! Ices! And a brandy-and-soda!

(*Slow music. Song by minstrels "Won't yer ketch 'im when yer sees 'im."*)

[*CURTAIN*.]

This kind of wooing is the way Mammon teaches his sons and daughters to jest with the most divine emotions of life, and the spirit of *fin de siècle* cynicism and mockery pervades all the preliminaries of marriage and marriage itself, to work dire results of discontent and wretchedness hereafter. For Nature will not be baulked of her rights. She gave us brains wherewith to think—hearts wherewith to feel—emotions to respond to every touch of human tenderness and sympathy—minds to educate in such wise that they should be able to grasp and realise all the dear and holy responsibilities of life; and when we will neither think nor feel, nor respond, nor be educated, nor realise what we were made for, she takes her vengeance upon us and an appalling one it sometimes is. There can be nothing more hideous, more like a foretaste of hell itself, than the life-to-life position of a man and woman who have been hustled into matrimony, or rather, as I prefer to put it, sold to each other for so many thousands per annum, and who, when the wedding-fuss is over, and the feminine "pictorials" have done gushing about the millinery of the occasion, find themselves alone together, without a single sympathy in common, with nothing but the chink of gold and the rustle of bank-notes for their heart-music, and with a barrier of steadily-increasing repulsion and disgust rising between them every day.

And this is what happens in nine cases out of ten in fashionable modern matrimony. "A marriage has been arranged" is a common phrase of newspaper parlance, and it has one advantage over most newspaper forms of speech namely, that of being strictly and literally true. A marriage is "arranged" as a matter of convenience or social interest; lawyers draft settlements and conclude the sale, and a priest of the Most High God is called in to bless the bargain. But it is nevertheless a bargain, a trafficking in human bodies and souls, as open and as shameless as any similar scene in Stamboul.

And yet there **is** liberty in our land if we will only avail ourselves of the glorious privilege. Women are free to assert their modesty, their sense of right, their desire for truth and purity, if they only will. Is it too much to ask of them that they should refuse to be stripped to the bosom and exposed for sale in the modern drawing-rooms of the "season"? Is it too much to ask that, in their natural and fitting desire to be suitably wedded, they should look for men rather than money, love rather than an "establishment," mutual sympathy and understanding rather than so much heritable property in houses and lands? And may not it even be suggested that men should be manly enough to refuse to set themselves forth in the market as "Heir to the estate of So-and-So, worth so much in hard cash" or "Only lineal descendant of the Earl of So-and-So, anxious to sell title, with body and soul attached to it, to any woman who can give the adequate millions necessary for immediate purchase"? A man who marries a woman for her money only is really one of the most despicable objects in existence. He who by natural law was intended to be the supporter, becomes the supported, he who by every proud prerogative of manhood is formed to be the conqueror and protector, is tamed and tied like a feeble nursling to a woman's apron-string, he loses the right to exert his independence, and must submit to be henpecked, "nagged at," or else treated with a callous indifference, and sometimes an infinite contempt.

The woman who marries for money is quite as blameworthy, and is likely to find her position equally as aggravating, only in another way. The man who has the "chinks" will never throw her poverty at her as a fault in the blunt and coarse terms which many a wealthy woman uses to a dependent husband, but he will involuntarily show her, by a thousand little unmistakable signs, that he knows he has bought her, and even in the very lavishness of his gifts to her she will gradually come to realise the "position" she holds with regard to him namely, one of social dummy, household figure-ornament, while he, free as air, amuses himself with other women, and soothes any pricking of his conscience by the reflection that after all, as his wife, she has everything she wants in the way of dress and jewels, food and firing, and that, in all the necessary items of sustenance and comfort, he has done his duty by her.

The real fact of the matter is that marriage is nothing more nor less than a crime if it is entered upon without that mutual supreme attraction and deep love which makes the union sacred. It is a selling of body into slavery, it is a dragging down of souls into impurity. The passion of love is a natural law, a necessity of being, and if a woman gives herself to a man in marriage without that love truly and vitally inspiring her, she will in time find that the "natural law" will have its way, and attract her to some other than her lawful husband, and drag her steadily down through the ways of sin to perdition.

I am addressing myself especially to women. In a woman's life **one** love should suffice. She cannot, constituted as she is, honestly give herself to more than one man. And she should be certain absolutely, sacredly, solemnly certain that out of all the world that one man is indeed her pre-elected lover, her chosen mate, that never could she care for any other hand than his to caress her beauty, never for any other kiss than his to rest upon her lips, and that without him life is but a half-circle, waiting completion.

How much of this kind of "certainty" enters into the "arrangements" of a fashionable marriage? How many women, as they pass up to the altar in all the glory of their bridal finery, are actually proud and happy to take the vows of love and fidelity? Very few. Yet it *should* be a proud moment for any woman; it should be the height of her life's triumph to submit to the mastery of love. Only, unfortunately, it is seldom this divine mastery of love which dominates her; it is a weak compound of toleration and resignation, mixed up with pounds, shillings, and pence, a farce of society fuss and feigning, in which poor Love gets crowded out altogether, and hastily spreads his wings for flight. He is the last of all the mythical gods to be tempted or cajoled by lawyers and settlements, wedding-cake and perishable millinery. His domain is Nature, and the heart of humanity, and the gifts he can bestow on those who meet him in the true spirit are marvellous and priceless indeed. The exquisite joys he can teach, the fine sympathies, the delicate emotions, the singular method in which he will play upon two lives like separate harps, and bring them into resounding tune and harmony, so that all the world shall seem full of luscious song, this is one way of love's system of education. But this is not all: he can so mould the character, temper the will, and strengthen the heart, as to make his elected disciples endure the bitterest sorrows bravely, perform acts of heroic self-sacrifice, and attain the most glorious heights of ambition; for, as the venerable Thomas à Kempis tells us, "Love is a great thing, yea, a great and thorough good; by itself it makes everything that is heavy light, and it bears evenly all that is uneven. For it carries a burden which is no burden, and makes everything that is bitter sweet and tasteful. Though weary it is not tired, though pressed it is not straitened, though alarmed it is not confounded, but as a lively flame and burning torch it forces its way upward and securely passes through all."

Is not such divine happiness well worth attaining? Is the cash-box better? And will the possession of jewels, gold, and estates, be of any avail as consolation in the hours of pain and loss? Think well about it, fair women, before deciding your destinies; and if you are inclined to shudder at the way in which your human sisters are sold in Stamboul, put a stop to the preparations you are making for selling yourselves. The London market will be open to you in May, and the bidders will assemble as usual. They will consider your value in face, figure, skin, eyes, hair, and general complexion. They will note in slang parlance as to whether you are "well-groomed" (i.e., well-dressed), just as they note the condition of their thoroughbred mares. They will look at you with the egotistical tolerance of men who have money and know that they are worth marrying. Your pretty ways, your little smiles, your blushes, your graceful attitudes, will be discussed at the clubs and restaurants in various forms, as, "She knows how to do it," or, "She is laying a neat trap for me," or, "I expect I shall have to give in to her in the long run," and certain other chuckling assertions of a like kind; and if you come up to the expectations of the Jews or the Gentiles, who are thus estimating your qualities, you will be sold.

That is, if you choose to be marketable commodities. It rests with you. You are not bound to listen to one of your own sex who asks you, as I do, in plain words **not** to sell yourselves. But if you do listen, albeit only for a moment, I shall not have written quite in vain. I want you to refuse to make your bodies and souls the traffickable material of vulgar huckstering. I want you to **give** yourselves ungrudgingly, fearlessly, without a price or any condition whatsoever, to the men you truly love, and abide by the results. If love is love indeed, no regret can be possible. But be sure it **is** love, the real passion, that elevates you above all sordid and mean considerations of self that exalts you to noble thoughts and nobler deeds, that keeps you faithful to the one vow, and moves you to take a glorious pride in preserving that vow's immaculate purity; be sure it is all this, for if it is not all this, you are making a mistake, and you are ignorant of the very beginnings of love. Try to fathom your own hearts on this vital question; try to feel, to comprehend, to learn the responsibilities invested in womanhood, and never stand before God's altar to accept a blessing on your marriage if you know in your own inmost soul that it is no marriage at all in the true sense of the word, but merely a question of convenience and sale. To do such a deed is the vilest blasphemy a blasphemy in which you involve the very priest who pronounces the futile benediction. The saying "God will not be mocked" is a true one; and least of all will He consent to listen to, or ratify such a mockery as a marriage-vow sworn before Him in utter falsification and misprisal of His chiefest commandment—Love. It is a wicked and wilful breaking of the law and is never by any chance allowed to remain unpunished.

BY LADY JEUNE

II

THE inevitable controversy as to the improvement or deterioration of one age over another still continues, and no comparison is ever satisfying. It is so easy to generalise and so difficult, when we particularise, to arrive at any accurate deduction. Each age has its vices and weaknesses, which alter according to the condition and influences which are then existing; and to say that one time is worse or better because the particular characteristics we contemplate have altered or disappeared, is entirely misleading. An idyllic life of peace and contentment, away from the storm and stress of life, is theoretically perfect, but it is perfectly possible for such a life to develop the worst qualities of mankind. Egotism, self-indulgence, indolence, and a thousand other weaknesses might ride rampant under such conditions; while in an existence where luxury, wealth, and pleasure appeared to be the sole ambition, some of the noblest virtues of humanity might exist. Therefore, in generalising and condemning the weaknesses of the age in which we live, we are apt to form too hasty conclusions of the life which we see around us, and in condemning its weaknesses to lose sight altogether of the higher and better part which lies close beside.

Human nature is stronger than all the forces and influences opposed to it, and it does not alter materially, though conditions of life, and changes, modify it. We are always inclined to be pessimistic in comparing the time in which we live with the past. We are always being told that we were once more virtuous and brave, more simple and self-reliant; that our women were more beautiful, our men more Spartan and courageous; that modern civilisation, and the gigantic changes which the nineteenth century has witnessed, have demoralised and degraded us; and that the great qualities which inspired the makers of our Empire have died away in an effete and worn-out civilisation.

If we were to admit the accuracy of all the conclusions at which the pessimists arrive, it would still be possible to prove that a "remnant" remains, sufficiently pure and wholesome to mitigate greatly the evils that undoubtedly exist; but we maintain and it is easy to prove our contention that the pessimists are wrong, and that not only are we not worse in the main than our forefathers, but that our times have called into existence qualities of the highest nature, which could be only produced by the particular conditions of to-day.

It is impossible, in the complex life of our time, that there should not be a large and powerful element in society whose influence is not altogether for good. The great wealth and luxury of to-day must produce effects which are demoralising and weakening to the characters of those who live under their influence; but every age has had the same evil, though perhaps to a less intensified degree. Where there is great wealth there must be great extravagance and display; but if only controlled and properly directed, its effect may benefit the community.

A demand for luxuries means employment to many poor people. Large entertainments, with all their accessories—smart clothes, carriages, and all the adjuncts of wealth which modern moralists condemn—have, after all, some advantages; and those who live in London and work amongst the poor can truthfully testify to the vast difference in their comfort and prosperity when a season is a good one, and to the severe pinch of poverty when the spending power of the wealthy classes is curtailed. Therefore, while deploring and admitting evils which are the inevitable result of an age of luxury and expenditure, one cannot help feeling that the outburst against them is sometimes exaggerated, because people are too apt to jump to hasty conclusions from not carefully analysing the criticisms they make.

A very powerful indictment against the evils of modern Society appears in these pages from the pen of one of the most popular writers of to-day—one who has studied human nature, and knows much of the life of to-day; and while admitting that some of her criticisms are accurate, we think she is a little carried away by a righteous feeling of indignation at some things which belong to every age and society, and are not in themselves a definite sign of the decadence of this. It is very easy to write the word "Sham" across this age, and by a free and hasty generalisation to condemn it to make it seem as if courage, heroism, and all other manly qualities have disappeared in a "slothful self-indulgence," and, that the aim of our life is to shut our eyes and ears to everything save the gratification of the lowest desires of human nature. We fail to see any signs of such a decadence when we know that for every post of danger and responsibility there are thousands of men ready to volunteer, and glad to serve their country, giving their life for the pay that a well-paid artisan would not look at. In the daily record of the papers we read of acts of heroism and self-sacrifice which show no indication of a decay of the heroism and bravery which have been the glorious characteristics of our race. In great shipwrecks, in the terrible naval disasters of the last few years, the same cool, heroic courage has been displayed, not only by the officers, but the men as, for instance, when the Victoria was sinking. The taking of Chitral, the march on Dongola, are incidents in our history just as glorious, though of less importance than some in more well-known military expeditions. They all prove that when the necessity arises England can send her sons to fight her enemies with the same confidence as of old, knowing that they will prove themselves as worthy as the veterans of Trafalgar and Waterloo.

Our vast colonial empire, which is the growth of this "effete" century, is surely an unanswerable argument to the cry that we have become unable to hold our own in the council of the nations. Wherever new fields of enterprise and colonisation are opened, there English men and women are found ready to people them; and it is because they possess the qualities which we are now told are in a state of decay that they succeed where every other people fail. It seems to us, in this age of independence, that there never was a time when self-reliance and individuality were so pre-eminently the characteristics of a people; and that, so far from having sunk into a condition of decay, we are as ready as ever to emulate the deeds of our sires.

In the history of any Western country the influence which women exercise must largely affect its destinies: where the women are strong and virtuous a country must prosper in just the same proportion as it will decay if they are the reverse. The change that has come over the lives of women in England during the last thirty years is so remarkable that it cannot but have produced enormous differences in English life and society; and opinions will always differ as to whether it is beneficial or the reverse. For our part we have no hesitation in saying it is all for good. There may be excrescences and anomalies which the large measure of independence women now enjoy have created, and which time will modify, and has, indeed, already modified. But when we contrast the position of women now with that of thirty years ago, the change is surely for good. If the sexes were equally distributed, and every woman could become a wife and follow the natural career which nature intended for her, the changes which so many deplore would perhaps never have come or certainly much more tardily. But in a community where the female element is largely in excess of the male, and where modern thought and education have raised them intellectually on a more equal basis, it was not possible for women to remain the colourless, dependent creatures of the past. And as they have become emancipated they have more or less chosen their own careers, and thousands of women are now living proofs of the advantages of a change that has given them an aim in life which they can pursue successfully.

In our very complex state of society there must necessarily be great varieties and differences in the lives of the different sets into which so large a society must be divided, and we cannot deny that there are aspects of modern life which we deplore. Whether such conditions are worse than formerly must ever be an undecided question; but that we have done with the coarseness and brutality of the last century no one will deny. Where there are great riches, a high standard of comfort and luxury, and a moneyed class, there must be extravagance and less moral restraint than in a more primitive state, where the conditions of existence are harder and the life is more simple. An existence such as Marie Corelli tells us of is poetical and idyllic to the highest degree; but in our country, and under the conditions of modern life, it is an impossible one. It does not, however, necessarily follow that a life equally pure and happy is impossible in our modern Babylon. "Love in a cottage" is a delicious thing, but the wherewithal to provide the cottage and its accessories is an absolute necessity. The higher standard of comfort which modern society requires, without any superfluities, makes marriage more difficult than formerly, not because there is not the same capacity for affection and self-denial among us, but because the whole conditions of our life have changed and are still changing; and it must be evident to the most Spartan of us that, however simple and rugged may be our theories, it is an impossibility to carry them out in their entirety. The modern mother is not the heartless, selfish creature described to us because she shrinks from letting her daughter link her life with some one (however deep her attachment to him may be) who cannot at least provide her with the necessaries of life. We think that Marie Corelli is mistaken in drawing the picture she has done of the "modern marriage market." The same reproaches have always been heaped on Society which she makes; women have always been accused of sacrificing their daughters for money, for the sake of the jewels and settlements of a rich husband; and the cry of the "slave market" is as old as the world itself. But is it true? Or rather, is not the accusation so grossly exaggerated as to be as false as if there were no foundation for its existence? There are, and always have been, women who are sufficiently worldly to allow and even to persuade their daughters to marry for the material advantages which a rich husband can provide; but that such women represent the average mother is an accusation we distinctly deny. There may be circumstances surrounding some marriages which lend colour to the suggestion that girls have sold themselves for money; but such cases are exceptions, and because some exist it is false to affirm that all are the same.

In the same way we object and protest most strongly against Marie Corelli's statement that girls are "brought out" in the "season" to be sold as "any unhappy Armenian girl" a statement as false as it is ridiculous. Does she really believe that the bright, happy, pretty girls we see in London ball-rooms all go there for the purpose of exhibiting their charms to the richest and most desirable suitor? Does she think that every girl starts in life with the avowed and open intention of making the best of her looks for such a purpose? We say that such an idea is monstrous; absolutely false of the girls, and equally untrue and unjust as regards their mothers. In the heart of every girl lies the hope that some day she may marry the man she loves, and, in joining her life with his, taste the sweet joys of life together; but the thought is one quite apart and outside any of the motives which make her wish to go into the world, or add to the enjoyment of her season.

Girls enjoy society because of the fun, the gaiety, the change, and the wholesome excitement which a season gives them, and not because in the distance they see the millions and the millionaire they are supposed to be hunting. Take any young, wholesome-minded girl with a happy home, and suggest such a thing, and see her indignant denial of an accusation the thought of which had never darkened the pleasure of her life. If we watch girls in ball-rooms or in following any of their amusements, listen to their hearty laugh, and see the bright, happy expression of their faces, and the zest with which they throw themselves into all they do, can we honestly say that we see a trace of the demoralising influences which Marie Corelli tells us are sapping all that is pure and sweet in their nature? If such an accusation as Marie Corelli's were true, it certainly needs more confirmation than the facts she brings forward to prove it, and our experience leads us to regard it from an entirely opposite point of view.

We agree with her that women, to use her own expression, are much more "mannish" than formerly; and that has grown out of the greater freedom and independence they now enjoy. It may have taken away some of the dependence and softness of women, but it has given them a strong individuality, strong opinions, and an independence which makes anything like maternal coercion an impossibility. Girls think and act for themselves, and have their own most distinct ideas on all subjects; and any mother would find it very difficult nay, almost impossible to force her daughter to marry a man solely because he was hugely rich. With a gentle, docile nature, without much strength of character or will, persuasion, or even stronger measures, might influence them; but the majority of girls could not be forced to such a step. Nay, we go still further, and say that there are, we believe, very few women who would urge their daughters to marry a man they did not love.

Girls may marry hastily, perhaps marry too young, without knowing their own minds; but in these days no girl is forced into a marriage that is repugnant to her because her mother wishes it, and there are few women wicked and cruel enough to blast the life of their child by acting as Marie Corelli would have us believe. Every year the increased independence which girls enjoy, and the feeling of the time in which they live, make them less anxious to marry, or to marry so early; and their position with regard to men and the feeling of *camaraderie* which exists between the young of both sexes do not tend to increase a girl's desire to take a husband. Marie Corelli says truly, "Nature will not be baulked of her rights; she gives us brains to think, hearts wherewith to feel, emotions to respond to every touch of human tenderness and sympathy, minds to educate in such wise they should be able to grasp and realise all the dear and holy responsibilities of life." Because this is so, it is also true that modern thought and education make mothers realise those responsibilities with regard to their children, and so refrain from using any influence except what tends to their happiness; and the same influences also make girls understand the profanation and wickedness of a loveless marriage.

We can hardly believe that the little sketch of a waterside proposal which Marie Corelli gives us is descriptive of any class of society. We cannot, of course, presume to guess how the question is asked or answered, the question that is old as time and yet sweet and fresh as the spring flowers; but we are certain Marie Corelli does not know either, and we cannot suppose she expects us to take the two actors in her little comedy as typical of English life and manners; for however barren a marriage may be of any sentiment or passion, we hardly think it possible a proposal of marriage could be conveyed in such language or accepted in a like fashion. We cannot help feeling that Marie Corelli generalises too much, and takes a class, and a very small class, as typical of the whole of English Society.

If what she says is the case, the society in which we live is indeed corrupt and rotten to the core, and the end to which it is tending must be utterly disastrous. But we are sure she is wrong—wrong in her facts and her conclusions. The mass of English men and women are as strong and morally pure as their predecessors. There never was an age when the standard of life was higher, or the obligations and responsibilities of wealth and position were more recognised, than the present.

In selecting a very small clique as typical of the whole of English Society, Marie Corelli has overstated her case; and if we look around us, among the people to whom we belong and to the wider circle of English homes, we see that she is mistaken in every respect. There may be people whose life and example are bad; that we do not deny: but we say that the whole of English Society is essentially pure, and the standard of life and morality a high one. There may be cases where a *mariage de raison* is the only alternative left to a woman, and there may be women who, from circumstances of poverty or necessity, are driven to marry men with whom they are not in love; but all these are exceptions, and the ordinary English marriage is one of affection and sympathy. If any other reason but this was the rule, where would be all the happy homes we see around us? How, otherwise, can we account for the peaceful and happy family life which is so distinctively English and of which we are so justly proud?

There are spots on the sun, and there is no such a thing as an ideal society. Perfection in this world is what we are all striving after, and which, like the magician's stone, is not to be found. Our ideals are high, even if we do not attain to them, and no Englishwoman would, we imagine, admit that the picture which Marie Corelli draws of the English is correct. We do not deny that there may have been, and are, cases such as she describes in a society which represents only a very small feature of English life, and is, in no sense of the word, representative.

In spite of all the allurements of riches, the ostentation and extravagance of to-day, and the temptations which money offers to women, we maintain that the hearts of girls in England are pure and single-minded, that the men they choose to be their helpmates and companions in life are the men they love, and however well gilded or attractive may be the advantages which money without love holds out, they have no chance in competition with the affection which develops into the glamour and ecstasy of a pure, genuine passion. It would be useless to ask Marie Corelli to pause in her denunciations of the mother who, however much she may see her child suffer momentarily, prevents a marriage where poverty would be the inevitable companion of a lifetime. But she would surely not deny that the mother is justified in stopping a marriage (however great might be the affection) where the whole of two lives would be spent in an unequal struggle with privation and need. It is so easy to blame such a woman and inveigh against her worldly-mindedness. But a mother can never forget that there are wider considerations than the present happiness for two people who enter into a marriage where there is barely enough for them to make two ends meet. The destinies of unborn children have to be considered, and she may well be justified in putting her veto on a contract which may bring beings into existence for whom no adequate provision is possible.

Marie Corelli may say what we urge is a justification of her contention, and she may so construe it if she likes. All we maintain is, that the evils of which she complains are only exceptional, and if they exist, they exist only in a society which is not to be taken as representative in any sense of the word, nor are they the outcome of any age or system, but have always existed. There have been mercenary, selfish women since the creation of the world, and to some natures the temptations which wealth offers will always be irresistible. But because this may be true of a few, it is unjust to brand and condemn all Englishwomen, as Marie Corelli is prepared to do. We may be more selfish, more luxurious than formerly, and the weaknesses engendered by such influences may be more apparent; still, we maintain unhesitatingly that the Englishwomen of to-day are no less governed by the sentiments of affection and passion than their ancestors, and are just as ready to join their lives with those of the men they love. Every day we see men and women in every class marrying, who have neither great wealth nor even the prospect of it, but who are content to lead lives of self-denial, consecrated by that love, the very best and purest of which human nature is capable, which will never be tarnished or destroyed by any of the changes which affect the more mutable affairs of life.

BY FLORA ANNIE STEEL

III

THIS title, "The Modern Marriage Market," conveys to my ear a distinct flavour of blame when taken as a whole; but when I come to dissect its alliterations, I find myself in doubt where to lay the accent of accusation. Should it be on the "modern," the "marriage," or the "market"?

So far as the adjective is concerned: I think the plaint may be dismissed summarily. Personally I confess myself unable to see the slightest difference in the principles on which marriages are made nowadays and those on which they were made a hundred two hundred five hundred years ago; briefly, since chivalry beguiled the world from the straight path of duty. The theory of marriage, as set forth by Western civilisation, has practically remained the same for centuries; such theory being simply that the feeling, passion, emotion call it what you will which we designate as Love with a big L is the only reason which an honourable man or modest woman can possibly admit, even to themselves, as a reason for marriage. In other words, herein lies the only justification, sanctification, and purification of what would otherwise be unjustifiable.

I think that even the most cynical and *blasé* frequenter of houseboats at Cookham would, if confronted with his own soul, admit that it had a sneaking belief in this theory; while even the most cursory glance at our literature proves that it has as many signatories as the Thirty-nine Articles. Briefly, it is and has been the foundation-stone of our marriage system.

It is scarcely fair, therefore, to blame it as modern. Nor, when we come to analyse the next word, have we any right to condemn marriage as it is. Viewed in the purely personal aspect which is all that a marriage conducted on such purely personal lines as the mutual gratification of feeling can claim, marriage seems to touch a very high average of content. It can boast quite as much success as is consistent with the natural evanescence of all feeling.

Are we, then, to let our tongues slide over "modern" and "marriage" to dwell reproachfully upon "market"? Are we to lay the burden of blame upon the very idea of commerce in the Temple of Hymen?

One of my predecessors has used the whip of words both to buyers and sellers in this connection, and the other, while deprecating the justice of the reproof in regard to actual facts, has not denied the iniquity of barter.

Nor do I; but I would like to remind my readers that it was not only the tables of the money-changers which the scourge of the Master drove forth from the Temple, but also the seats of them which sold doves! I would ask them what ethical difference there is in selling yourself for love or for money, if mere personal pleasure lies at the bottom of the bargain?

I make bold to say that there is none. The girl who gives herself for exchange in pure passion is quite as mercenary as the one who sells herself for gold. Both claim their own desire, irrespective of everything but themselves. It is merely a question as to the relative dignity of their ideals in regard to such personal pleasure. A market is therefore inevitable under our present system, since, whether Mammon or Eros ratifies the bond, English girls are taught to take their equivalent in something which is valuable to themselves, and themselves only.

So it seems to me that the phrase "modern marriage market" should have no accent at all. It must be taken as a whole, or rejected as a whole. We must either say that marriage is honourable in all if we get an equivalent which satisfies our personal ideals, or we must say that neither for love nor for money have men and women the right to enter into a contract which only concerns themselves for a few short years, but which may influence the world for generations.

Which shall we do?

To most, no doubt, the very idea of condemning the fundamental principle of our marriage system wholesale may seem more absurd even than sacrilegious. The world, they will say, has got on very well with the help of the little blind god. Lads and lasses have sold their birthright for love since the beginning of Time, and will continue so to do until Time is no more. It is natural, it is proper, it is above all easy for them to do so. The majority of such marriages are happy, decorous, respectable; and though our social morality is not quite what it should be, that has nothing to do with the question. Our qualms as to what may be going on round the corner in Piccadilly have no right to make our own voices quaver in singing about the one "which breathed o'er Eden" during a marriage service in St. George's, Hanover Square.

Perhaps not; and yet the uncomfortable remembrance that the first wedding in this world was rather the reverse of a panacea for all evil makes some of us doubt if this theory of ours, of which we have spoken, is not responsible for a large portion of the confusion which undoubtedly exists in the minds of many men and women regarding what is called the relation of the sexes.

To say so may seem almost an insult to the hundreds, the thousands of honest men and women who, as their children grow up to take their place in the world, hold each other bravely by the hand till death do them part, and smile at each other even then, knowing that they have done their duty that they have given their mortality to the immortality of the world; but the heroism, the virtue of these thousands must not blind us to the fact that the very things we admire in them the faithful comradeship, the dutiful devotion, the self-denial are the very things which would have been scouted as a justification of marriage long years before: must not blind us also to the fact that the passionate, absorbing Love—again with a big L—which, according to Marie Corelli, is the only safeguard against making souls and bodies "the traffickable material of vile huckstering," has in nine cases out of ten disappeared.

I shall be told that I am wrong in saying this—that it has not disappeared. It has strengthened, changed, sobered, risen into a far more excellent thing than it was at first. Then why, in Heaven's name, condemn those who prefer the gingerbread without the gilt upon it to begin with? Why should we extol the man or woman who says openly, "I expect 'Love to teach me exquisite joys,' to 'bring our lives into resounding tune and harmony, so that all the world shall seem full of luscious song.' I wish to appropriate to my sole use and benefit that which personally makes 'my life worth living.' I feel that I must have that 'kiss and no other on my lips,' that hand 'and no other to caress me'"?

Does not that—put, not as I put it, but as the advocates of Love as a purifying element between man and woman put it—sound quite as much like an apotheosis of personal delights as "I expect money to give me exquisite joy, to bring resounding tune and luscious song, etc., etc."?

Compare it, for instance, with the position which our present system condemns, which nine out of every ten women would be ashamed to confess. "I do not expect intense personal gratification, but I wish to marry, to have a home and children, to take my share in the glory and toil, and here is my chance." If you come to analyse this, you will find, not only that it brings with it a far higher ideal of life, but that it emphasizes something that sorely needs emphasizing: the distance—if I may be allowed so to put it—between Piccadilly and St. George's, Hanover Square. It leaves us with something more as a foundation for marriage than a mutual physical and mental attraction which overpowers other considerations: an attraction which the individual experience of nearly every man and woman in the world teaches them is evanescent. That it lasts sometimes need not be denied. But its persistency certainly seems to vary in inverse ratio to its intensity: those who feel it most keenly being, as a rule, those who are liable to feel it most frequently. This, indeed, is almost inevitable, since both the strength and the frequency argue the same cause, an emotional nature.

I shall be told, of course, that I have utterly failed to grasp the very idea of Love; that I am confusing it with passion.

I do not think I am, if the latter word is meant to carry even a suspicion of blame with it. Briefly, it is one thing to fall in love to be, let us say, very much in love; another to think that it is not only a pleasant but a virtuous act. As a matter of fact, it is a very commonplace, a very natural one. In many cases such Love may prove quite a safe guide; but it is not a virtue to yield obedience to the instinct, as if it were the voice of God.

Yet that it is so, is the teaching which nine-tenths of us almost give to our girls. Nay, more! It is the universal teaching to both sexes on this point. Take up the most sentimental fiction of the English school, or the most realistic of the French, and you will find them alike in this underlying assumption that the attraction of sex for sex is something praiseworthy. In the former the mutual self-sufficiency of hero and heroine, when it dawns upon them that they are really in love with each other, would be unbearable if it were not comic. And if Providence is kind enough to endow their superiors in age with a few sensible doubts, the young people almost burst with importance over the discovery that the course of true love never did run smooth.

The same thing is observable in the realistic novel. The blind little god's arrow is sufficient excuse for murdering one's grandmother, to say nothing of one's lawful wife. No doubt the treatment of this theory differs, but a careful reader can scarcely avoid coming to the conclusion that the emotion which leads, in the sentimental novel after an intolerable amount of strong love-making to wedding bells, is virtually the same as that which culminates in the necessity for propriety to use the "candle, the bell, and the book."

The drama in both, begins on the old classical lines; youth, propinquity, an all-absorbing selfishness, a mental and bodily exaltation which is intoxicating as wine. Now, if this be so, the wrong if wrong there be must be in the end which differentiates the two similar beginnings.

But if the end in both be a purely personal gratification, it is hard to see why one should be blessed and the other cursed utterly. Still harder it is for any one to lay down the law and say, as the advocates of "all for love and the world well lost" theory do say, that you may seek the happiness of personal self-gratification through the mind but not through the body; through the sensual pleasures which can be bought by love, and not through those which are to be bought by money. The distinction is a purely arbitrary one. Self lies at the bottom of both decisions. The money-changers and the sellers of doves alike turn the Temple into a market-place.

Of course, the retort will once more be that I fail to understand what Love with a big L means, and that, even admitting the earthly element, which must count for something, there still remains the mental sympathy—the friendship, the honest, unselfish desire to stand by each other to do the best for each other, in every way, which is the essence of real love.

Undoubtedly it is. So much so, that I retort, in my turn, by asking why this should need the sanction of an ephemeral passion? Why, briefly, should it be right for a woman to crave a "luscious song," and wrong for her to be content with the still small voice of an approving conscience? Why should she be allowed to forget duty in pleasure, and forbidden to forget pleasure in duty?

Women have not so learnt their rights, their privileges, their duties in those Eastern lands with which I am best acquainted. There, hidden under a thousand blemishes, a million abuses, still lingers the great truth so unpalatable to our Western individualism—that man and woman stand related, not to each other, but to the immortality of their race—that immortality which comes to the world through the generations on generations of men and women who are born into it. There, even nowadays, when error has obscured so much, marriage is not a purely personal matter, as it is with us; it is a duty to the race.

I am not, however, going to advocate the Indian system here (with child-marriage, female infanticide, and sati thrown in as make-weights)—though my personal experience is that, even with polygamy superadded, the percentage of rational happiness derived from wifehood and motherhood is as high in India as it is in England. I only wish with all diffidence to ask each thinking woman if our present ideal of what justifies marriage does not put St. George's, Hanover Square, into dangerous proximity with Piccadilly. To use one and the same bell for weddings and exorcisms is confusing to the multitude, which has but the one sense of hearing; yet, if we admit the sanctifying power of mere emotion, it seems to me impossible to avoid so using it. For experience—every-day experience of the world—teaches us that it is impossible even for the principals themselves to tell beforehand whether the Love which prompts their marriage will stand the strain. They may hope it so, wish it so, pray that it may be so; but very few men or women either, for that matter could truthfully say, as they stand at the altar, that they never felt a similar emotion before, or predict that they would never feel it again. Perhaps it may be said that I exaggerate this teaching. Let us go back to what has been written in these pages about it.

"What is marriage?" asks Marie Corelli; then answers the question by saying that it is the taking of a vow before the Throne which declares that the "man and woman concerned have each discovered in each other his or her true mate that all the world is a mere grain of dust in worth as compared with the exalted passion which fills their souls, and moves them to become one in flesh as well as one in spirit."

Lady Jeune, again, gives it as her opinion that with a pure and single-minded English girl, nothing has any chance in competition with "the glamour and ecstasy of a pure, genuine passion."

These are no uncertain utterances. They point unerringly to the thesis that this personal emotion—call it what you will—is in itself sufficient to warrant entering into a lifelong contract into which, to say the least of it, many other considerations should enter: a thesis which is largely responsible for making the standard of social morality in the West so low.

For it is low. Whatever the theory of twin souls may have done towards personal happiness, it has certainly not enabled us to rise one whit higher in regard to social and conjugal morality than those who hold marriage to be a thing apart from Love.

In truth, the quarrel goes deeper than a mere dispute as to the relative greed for pleasure of the Englishwomen of to-day and their sisters of yesterday. What has to be settled is the question whether, as Marie Corelli puts it, "marriage is nothing more nor less than a crime if it is entered upon without the mutual supreme attraction and deep love which makes the union sacred"; whether a marriage without ecstasy is a "*selling of the body into slavery*" (the italics are mine). Is this so? Or do we touch here on the mother error which has done more to lengthen the record of our divorce courts than any other cause, and which, even when it stops short of that, sells the soul of many a good woman into something worse than slavery, into the loss of her own self-esteem, into a sense of perpetual degradation: the assertion, briefly, that the duties of wifehood and motherhood are in themselves debasing?

"Try," goes on Marie Corelli in her eloquent appeal, "to feel, to comprehend, to learn the responsibilities invested in Womanhood."

Never was more admirable advice given; but why stultify it by setting as the highest responsibility the duty of "being kissed" as she likes to be kissed, caressed as she likes to be caressed, of giving herself "without any consideration whatever to her pre-elected lover"?

Would it not be better advice to bid our daughters claim that right of reasonable judgment which Lady Jeune excuses in the much-abused mother—the right of remembering "that there are wider considerations in marriage than the present happiness of two people, since the destinies of unborn children have to be considered"?

It seems almost incredible that at this time of day it should be necessary to insist on such a palpable truism. That it should be so speaks volumes of blame, not so much for the Modern Marriage Market as for the theory of marriage which has inevitably led to it.

It is time this was altered. The changing conditions of woman's life in this nineteenth century of ours make it imperative that some more certain guide should be chosen than that which leads alike to Piccadilly and St. George's. In the old days, when women had little else to do, and still less to choose, this dream of personal happiness was not so dangerous as it is now, when we have begun to ask questions and insist upon answers. Take a middle-class family of girls, for instance; nice girls, good girls, pretty girls. Half of them cannot hope to marry. But which half? There is the crucial point. If, when they were born, Providence wrote on their foreheads, "This one is to be married, this one not," it would be well and good. But it can never be safe to din the claims of personal pleasure and pure passion as they are dinned by most purveyors of fiction "*pour les jeunes filles*" into ears which may never have the chance of listening to the passion itself, or, what is worse, may have to listen to it without the mysterious sanction of marriage.

It is always unsafe to live in the mental condition of that large section of unreasoning humanity which loves to sit in a basket and then lift itself up by the handles. Pure passion is the sanction of marriage—marriage is the sanction of pure passion. Here is the position with a vengeance!

In truth we need a surer guide, a more bracing and wholesome gospel.

We must go back to what our Eastern sisters have never left; to the sanction of home and motherhood—a sanction which there is grave danger, in this age of individualism, will soon be lost sight of altogether.

Men have already almost lost their fatherhood, from the very extent of their personal freedom in regard to it; and though this is not the place in which to discuss that aspect of the question, the fact that this is so must fill the minds of the thoughtful among us with dread, lest the emancipation of women should lead to a like loss of the highest function of humanity.

For it is the highest. The Angel of the Annunciation carries to woman the most honourable of all messages, gives her the most noble mission she can have. For the world still waits for the child that shall be born for its greatest poet, its greatest statesman, its greatest philanthropist: briefly, for the man who shall right the wrong in all times, all places.

And it is to the thought of that child which is to come—that child with its message of peace through self-sacrifice, lying in its mother's arms, perhaps in our own—that we women must look for the solution of many a problem which now angers the world and us. As of old, the purification of the Temple will come through that message of Annunciation; but the hand of the Messiah must overthrow the seats of them that sell doves, as well as the tables of the money-changers.

BY SUSAN, COUNTESS OF MALMESBURY

IV

"Lord Thomas was a bold forester,
And a chacer of the Kings deere.
Faire Ellinor was a fine woman,
And Lord Thomas he loved her deere."

THE condition of mind so artlessly described in the old ballad quoted above, belongs to the aboriginal class of emotions which is neither ancient nor modern, but co-existent with human nature, and against which education, civilisation, and luxury fight in vain. As every creature born into the world presents a fresh and sensitive surface to the impressions of experience, and only learns too late, as a rule, to profit by that of others, so the successors of Lord Thomas and Faire Ellinor, as they walk together in the vernal pageant of their youth, contemplate themselves and their heart-adventure with astonishment, awe, and an honest, hearty, wholesome belief that no one ever loved before as they do, nor ever can again so much as guess at the unearthly beauty of a light which seems to shine for them alone. Upon this simple but solid foundation the edifice of marriage mainly rests, and I fully believe that in the majority of the unions of to-day feeling plays an important part.

If any one should doubt this statement, let him spend a week in a country-house alone with any young engaged couple, chosen at random among his acquaintance. It will probably be a painful experiment, since his unhappy personality, unillumined by the Shekinah of their mutual interest in one another, will remain plunged in a gloom which will seem all the darker for the brilliant radiance near at hand.

But the foundations of a building, though first in importance, are only the beginning of a complicated structure, and it is my desire to follow as closely as I can the details of an institution which has existed so many thousands of years, and has, from age to age, learnt, partly to adapt itself to the needs of a nervous and impulsive race of beings, and partly to act as a restraint on qualities, not in themselves actually bad, but hurtful when exercised without control. I wish to guess at what should and perchance might be, and at what seems practically attainable in the present state of society. But first I must glance at the three views of marriage now laid before me: the Romantic, as presented Marie Corelli; the Social, as understood by Lady Jeune, and the Practical, of which Mrs. Steel is the prophet.

The first of these writes with a skilful pen, a warm heart, but an undisciplined mind. It is, no doubt, a happy state to be in, that in which we are unable to see more than one side of every question, and one which, in addition, seems calculated to endow the world with saints and martyrs whom it piously reveres, but whom it shows no signs, at this stage of its existence, of emulating. The fly, with the thousand facets of its eye, must be fairly puzzled at times, one would suppose, to choose its path in life, unless its brain corrects the myriad images the retina receives. It is for us, in the same manner, to order and arrange the many different facts and sides of life which pass before our gaze. A good delusion and a strong prejudice serve as a goal in the steeple-chase of our career, and as blinkers to keep us in a narrow and perhaps a useful path; but in studying a question in order to arrive at the truth, whether palatable or not, and above all in claiming to advise our own sex for its highest good, so far as is possible, every point of view should be considered, every element in the case weighed in the balance. To look at marriage from its purely romantic side, or, on the other hand, to bring its utilitarian aspects into too great relief, is unskilfully to mix the ingredients which go to form that compound of experience and intuition which we call a ripened judgment. Marie Corelli draws a pretty picture of simple, loving hearts in Sicily, but is she very sure that those whom she so touchingly describes as passing rich on over twice as much again as forty pounds a year exhibit more than the negative virtue of content? Would they refuse comfort and affluence if offered them? Comfort, which might mean life or death to either in ill-health; affluence, which would certainly afford advantages to their children such as they could not hope to obtain under present circumstances, and such as they would scarcely have the right to decline?

The sum, in truth, we have to spend is nothing: the all-important question is, What must that sum be made to buy? What are necessaries? What are luxuries? For I need hardly point out to any one who has felt the grip of an English winter, that what constitutes riches in Capri would mean poverty and privation in a climate like ours. So much depends on the class we happen to associate with, and the sky under which we live. The deprivation of accustomed luxuries, or such easements as we have enjoyed in life, is so serious a matter that it is a well-known factor in punishment as administered to criminals.

Are we, then, purely mercenary if we urge these considerations on those who have yet to grapple with reality, and have never known the crushing hug of want? To turn to another point: is there a mother in this world who, if she could prevent it, would allow her daughter to give herself "without conditions of any sort" to the first man for whom the woman-nature in her breast had faintly stirred in that slumber where it lies bound by the opiate of custom, education, and hereditary proclivities? To such dreams of Heaven, natural though they be, there is a cold awakening in the chilly dawn of human experience. Few men, worthy of the name, would accept such a sacrifice or undertake such a charge. Those who have done so, for selfish reasons, have forged fetters on their limbs of which they sometimes hear the clanking all their days. Not the most advanced woman among the vanguard which leads that section of our sisters can live happy and content under the disapproval and avoidance of those she has been accustomed to associate with. The enthusiasm which armed martyrs for the rack or death is sadly cooled by the daily pin-pricks which accompany any irrevocable step taken in defiance of custom and society, just as a heavy shower of rain will do more to disperse a mob than more heroic measures. No woman, whose heart is single, would recommend another to follow in such a thorny path.

Lady Jeune, who follows Marie Corelli in the discussion, writes from the practical standpoint of a woman who has a wide and intimate knowledge of the special class which she describes; but she confines herself to that alone. And Mrs. Steel, who succeeds her, is, by her own confession, more conversant with the matrimonial affairs of our Eastern than of our Western sisters. Moreover, she evidently considers the former to be the highest and happiest development of home-life, and that the duties of wives and husbands towards each other should be entirely or chiefly merged in their mutual care for their offspring, which, I may suggest, but for that gilt on the gingerbread which Mrs. Steel condemns, would probably never come to be a factor in the case. She is evidently of opinion, with Mrs. Malaprop, that it is better to begin with a little aversion; but even that stern lady does not condemn us to indifference all our lives. Why, because a feeling is both beautiful and evanescent, are we not to enjoy and prize it while it lasts? Beauty and evanescence are two of the chief characteristics of existence—beauty which the human eye may never see, and evanescence which oft-times enhances that very beauty we desire or regret. And will the memory of love not serve to prevent our judging coldly and harshly the faults of those to whom our faith is pledged? And if that only, and no more, does it not fulfil a high purpose between a man and woman whom only death or shame can part, whose interests and whose duties are the same? Love is the fulfilment of the law, the willing, cheerful sacrifice of self for the happiness and good of others, either of a single individual or of the race. It is this that Mrs. Steel constantly confuses with passion.

Another point. Her special reference to the greater regard of Indian women for their children than is displayed by our sex in this country seems to me to be an unfortunate one. Take, for instance, the motive for bringing children into the world which is well known to exist in many cases: the belief that, if they die without descendants to perform their obsequies, their souls go into the body of an unclean beast. This is certainly purely selfish, and has its root in what Mrs. Steel ought to feel compelled to call a personal gratification, though one which we should consider imaginary. All true love, whether between parents and children or husband and wife, is, in its essence, free from self; but in both cases it is founded on the strongest and most abiding instincts of the human race. Neither can be said to be higher than the other, as they are not intrinsically good, if I may say so, nor are they bad. They are simply natural; their absence is unnatural, and tends to the deterioration, as their presence does to the preservation, of our kind, having still, as Mrs. Steel would say, a selfish origin, though on the widest basis.

All things, as St. Paul himself admits, are lawful, but all are not expedient. Self-preservation is a notable example of an impulse admirable in itself and necessary to human life, which must be controlled, or sacrificed even, where wider interests are at stake. Instincts, to be useful, must be recognised as such, not placed on a pedestal and elevated into transcendent virtues, but put into harness, so to speak, and made to draw the cart of life.

Another factor in marriage has eluded Mrs. Steel's quick eye—one that is of the highest consequence to the race. It was touched upon by *Punch* many years ago in his picture of the Noble Owner and his Prize Short-horn:

> **NOBLE OWNER** (*very attenuated*):
> You certainly are a magnificent fellow.
> **PRIZE SHORT-HORN:**
> Well, my lord, if as much trouble had been taken to select your father and mother as you took with mine, you would be a magnificent fellow too!

History does not relate what the Noble Owner replied, but he might have pointed out that difficulties of selection increase as higher tests of fitness are required. With us not only physical, but moral and intellectual gifts are looked for, and it is a recognised, if melancholy, fact that the first and last, at any rate, rarely exist together in any high degree. Different qualities also are needed in the various ranks of life—a fact which our modern system of education does not always condescend to notice; while it is evident that certain natures require certain others as the complement to their own. "The heart of a little man," said a friend of mine the other day, "goes out like a rocket to a big woman," and we see the converse happen every day; while what he said of physical is equally true of mental gifts.

The exhilarating and stimulating effect of certain minds upon our own is within the experience of most of us, while another perhaps superior intellect may leave us cold and dull.

Not even the Purdah or the Yashmak can entirely disguise or obliterate a determined character or powerful will, and this we know was as true in the days of Lady Mary Wortley Montagu as it is in certain notable instances at the present time.

The little tenement in which, for a few brief years, our soul crouches in unrest, and of which it is in some degree both the cause and the effect, so effectually separates us from other beings of our kind that each must live apart and die in solitude. This loneliness grips every heart that beats and every mind that stretches forth a feeler in the dark. To find a sister-being one with our own, complete community of thought and aspiration, is the deep longing which consumes both men and women; and to the thoughtful mind, denied fulfilment of its holiest and dearest wish, the most convincing proof of life beyond the grave. This desolation of the soul, "divine despair," which feeds upon our inmost heart, and which spurs a noble nature to exertion, is the same force, but transformed, which drives the weaker creature to perdition. We cannot live alone, and, meeting with another isolated entity, we think to find in it the silver key to loosen our disquietude, and to unlock, each for another, the guarded secrets slumbering, scarcely dreamt of, below the surface we present to the open, if inscrutable, book of persons and events, whose pages slowly turn before our eyes. We search, as did Faust of old, for the Helen of our lives, and when, at last, like him, we say to the flying moment, "Stay! thou art so fair!" it melts beneath our touch. No reality if, indeed, there be such a thing can reach the beauty of our pictured thoughts, and we are doomed from childhood to smart beneath privation and regret.

This bitter discipline, rightly endured, moulds the character and develops the muscles for the Olympic Game of life. Nerve feeds on danger, and courage on necessity; while sorrow, nobly borne, weaves a steel strand into the cable of experience, which strengthens it for those who follow in our traces.

This hope of fellowship and effort to attain perfect union, the practical outcome of our solitude of heart, is the motive power which drives some of us to marriage and some of us to sin.

After an early stage of existence, men are much less likely to "fall in love," as it is called, than women, and especially girls who are less in contact with the real world, and unacquainted with its sterner side. It is therefore far more important that they should be protected against themselves, and it is certainly the plain duty of every mother to lay before her child the inevitable consequences of an imprudent marriage. Most girls in the upper classes know nothing of the value of money; they are brought up in comfortable, or even luxurious, homes, by parents generally indulgent, and are as incapable of judging of the merits of a possible husband as they would be of the points of a horse. Such a girl might, as likely as not, choose a high-stepping, flashy screw, and pay for it the ruinous price of a spoilt life. It is the act of a friend, though a painful task, to tear aside the veil which ignorance or native innocence and a pure heart hang before her eyes, if by so doing she can be saved from an irretrievable blunder, the punishment for which is as heavy, alas! as for a crime.

Girls are now highly educated so far as book-learning can make them so; they are allowed freedom undreamt of twenty years ago, and the superficial knowledge of life they thus acquire is one of the most dangerous elements in their present condition. An attitude of independence, an indisposition to listen to advice, combined with total ignorance of the real situation they are bent on creating for themselves, is a spectacle which would be ludicrous if it were not melancholy to those who know by experience the difficulties which beset a woman's life, even under the most favoured conditions. Authority being admittedly obsolete, all a mother can do is to create and maintain, with infinite patience and affection, such an influence over her child's mind as will allow of the latter being guided aright when she comes to the place where two roads branch. To know how to look for the qualities which stand the wear and tear of life in common, and to learn that all that glitters is not gold, is one of the first steps in our education. Neither brilliant personal qualities alone, nor wealth and position by themselves, can satisfy the heart which is formed to look, often against its conscious will, for something higher, for that invisible but possible perfection to which the caged bird sings its sweetest songs. It is this search for the ideal, and the fond belief that it has at last been found, which wrecks so many lives and makes the searchers do wrong in secret, or bear open shame for the sake of the treasure which they think at length is in their grasp, but which often turns to ashes in their hand.

It is therefore inevitable that marriage should produce a large amount of disappointment, which may best be overcome by reflecting on our own shortcomings rather than on those of our companion. Partners in a happy marriage must bring a certain capital of youth and health, and in addition qualities, moral and mental, such as are necessary to advance them in their condition of life.

"Choose not alone a proper mate, but a proper time to marry."

You do not require your carriage-horses to wait at table, neither does your pet dog pay the household bills; but in human beings we are apt to look for qualities quite as incompatible as these, and to marry in the fond hope that the particular thistle we have selected, unlike all others, will bear a fine crop of figs.

Marriages between different classes in Society rarely turn out well. Early influences are seldom, if ever, eradicated, and where two people look at life from opposite points of view there must be constant straining of the tie which binds them to each other.

Those who marry into a class above their own are almost invariably huffy, and constantly on the outlook for slights. Where this is not the case they may easily become overbearing or purse-proud. When, on the other hand, they marry beneath them, they find their new surroundings impossible to conciliate, and themselves accused of pride or "airs." Most frequently is this the case where a lady marries a working man. The tie shortly becomes as irksome to him as to her, and he finds her delicate and useless, unable to do the hard work expected of the women to whom he is accustomed; while the very sense of inferiority, which constantly haunts him, renders him uneasy in her presence, and sometimes even drives him to ill-treat or desert her altogether.

I came across an instance of this kind, not long ago, in a pretty creature, still young, but roughened by toil, who had formed a union with a working man. Shunned by her own people, and finally abandoned by her husband, she had been found and rescued from the lowest depths of degradation by a kind and charitable lady.

Difference of race is generally a great handicap to contentment in conjugal life. Even between European nations difficulties are apt to arise: how much more, then, where colour prejudices step in. This sad lesson many of our girls have learnt in India, where they find their position almost untenable, while the men they marry, returning to their own people and former habits, undergo a strange and terrible transformation in the eyes, at least, of their English brides, who are awakened too late to the truth and to the inherent differences of race and inherited characteristics which even a European education is powerless to remove.

Imprudent marriages, where means of support are inadequate, are more frequent with us than on the Continent, where, particularly in France, the whole affair is treated more as a family arrangement. The position of the woman in her own house seems to gain, rather than not, by this way of looking at the matter, and on the whole the average results appear to be satisfactory.

Restrictions on marriage are common in Continental armies, where, in certain cases, officers are obliged to ask the consent of their colonel, who is instructed to institute a full inquiry into the lady's character and financial position.

With us these regulations are confined to the men, four or five per cent. of whom only can marry "with leave." This does not, of course, compel the remainder to remain single, like Zulu warriors, but excludes their wives from certain privileges which those who are "on the strength" enjoy; free quarters, for instance, and such employment as can be reserved for them.

Mercenary motives are far from being confined to the upper ranks of life, and from inquiries I have made I learn that a woman of the working classes, with "a little bit of money," is just as much run after as great heiresses in Society by fortune-hunters, and just as likely to be cast aside when that little bit of money is spent.

I have said that equality in social position is an important factor, and that serious racial divergences should act as a bar to marriage. Furthermore, for the sake of any children which may be born, persons suffering with hereditary diseases ought to remain single, and the very immature unions which take place so frequently for instance, in the East End of London should be discouraged and prevented as much as possible.

Beyond these initial points, I hold that we ought to look for physical beauty, which in itself includes so many other qualities; for evenness of temper, and the greater moral and intellectual gifts which go to widen and heighten the horizon of our life, and which bring unfailing consolation in time of privation or sorrow. The power to occupy the mind, to divert it from cares when by no taking thought can trouble be averted or suffering relieved, is one of the most precious gifts that a man or a woman can receive or acquire, and one which must tend to sweeten the life they have solemnly undertaken to spend together.

These, I shall be told, are all counsels of perfection; but in reply I may remind my readers that he who "aimeth at the sky, shoots higher far than he who means a tree." We can at least look up, and some day hope to scale the snow-clad heights which look so inaccessible from below.

And in the meantime let us say with the Preacher:

> "Two are better than one; because they have a good reward for their labour. For if they fall, the one will lift up his fellow: but woe to him that is alone when he falleth; for he hath not another to help him up."

21

"THE COLLEGE WOMAN AND THE FAMILY CLAIM," *COMMONS*

Jane Addams

Source: Jane Addams, 'The College Woman and the Family Claim', *Commons*. Vol. 3, 1898, pp. 3–7

The daughter as a family possession

It has always been difficult for the family to regard the daughter otherwise than as a family possession. From her babyhood she has been the charm and grace of the household, and it is hard to think of her as an integral part of the social order itself; to believe that she has duties outside of the family to the State and to society in the larger sense. This assumption in regard to the daughter that she was solely an inspiration and refinement to the family itself and its own immediate circle; that her delicacy and polish were but outward symbols of her father's protection and prosperity, worked very smoothly for the most part, so long as her education was in line with it. When there was absolutely no recognition of the entity of woman's life beyond the family, when the outside claims upon her were still wholly unrecognized, the situation was simple, and the finishing-school harmoniously and elegantly answered all requirements. She was fitted to grace the fireside and to add lustre to that social circle which her parents selected for her.

The new individuality versus the old ideal

This family assumption was notably broken into, however, when the daughter was sent to college. Her individuality was then recognized quite apart from family or society claims, and she received the sort of training which for many years has been deemed successful for highly developing a man's individuality and freeing his powers for independent action.

Perplexities often occur when the daughter returns home from college, owing to the fact that this recognition has been but partially accomplished. When she attempts to act upon the assumption of its accomplishment, she finds herself

 DOI: 10.4324/9780429321078-23

jarring upon ideals which are so entwined with filial piety, so rooted in the tenderest affections of which the human heart is capable, that both daughter and parents are shocked and startled when they discover what is happening, and they scarcely venture to formulate it because it implies the outrage of something sacred.

Wounded affection is sure to be the result when parental control and the family claim assert their authority in fields of effort which belong to adult judgment, and which pertain to activity outside of the family life. Probably the distinctively family tragedy, of which we all catch glimpses now and then, is the assertion of this authority through all the entanglements of wounded affection and misunderstanding. We see both sides acting from conscientious motives and with the tenderest affection, hiding their misery from each other – a misery which is quite needless did they but recognize the existence of more than one claim.

The ideal for the education of woman has doubtless changed under the pressure of a new claim. The family has responded to this claim to the extent of granting an education in line with it, but they are still jealous of it, and assert the family claim as over against it.

Unnecessary conflict between the social and the family claim

The modern woman finds herself educated to recognize a stress of social obligation which her family did not in the least anticipate when they sent her to college. In their view she has been educated that she might well fulfill the duties of a daughter in a good family and those belonging to a member of polite society. She responds to these expectations, but she finds herself, in addition, under an impulse to act her part as a citizen of the world. She accepts her family inheritance with loyalty and affection, but she has entered into a wider inheritance as well. She has strongly felt what the writer has ventured to call, for lack of a better phrase, the human claim or the social claim. The college woman submits her mind to the latter for four years, only to find, after her return from college, that the family claim is exclusively and strenuously asserted, and that her attempts to fulfill the other are resented. The situation has all the discomfort of transition and compromise. The daughter finds a constant and totally unnecessary conflict between the social claim and the family claim. In most cases the social is repressed and gives way to the family claim, because the latter is concrete and definitely asserted, while the former is vague and unformulated. In such instances the girl quietly submits, but she feels in some way wronged whenever she allows her mind to dwell upon the situation. She either hides her hurt, and splendid reserves of enthusiasm and capacity go to waste, or her zeal and emotions are turned inward, and the result is an unhappy woman, whose vitality is consumed by vain regrets and desires.

A share in the race life completes the family life

If the college woman who is freed from the necessity of self-support is not quietly reabsorbed into her family, she is even reproached for her discontent. She is told to be devoted to her family, inspiring and responsive to her social circle, and to give the rest of her time to further self-improvement and enjoyment. She expects to do this, and responds to these claims to the best of her ability – even heroically sometimes. But where is the larger life of which she has dreamed so long? that life of the race which surrounds and completes the individual and family life? She has been taught that it is her duty to share this life, and her highest privilege to extend it. This divergence between her self-centered existence and her best convictions becomes constantly more apparent. The situation is not even so simple as a conflict between her affections and her intellectual convictions, although even that is tumultuous enough; the emotional nature is divided against itself. The social claim is a demand upon the emotions as well as the intellect, and in ignoring that she not only represses her mental convictions, but lowers her springs of vitality. Her life is full of contradictions.

Does marriage satisfy the universal claim?

There is no doubt that the period when this tumult is greatest is the period between the daughter's graduation and her marriage, altho marriage by no means satisfies the universal claim. The young wife can offer us an excuse for a non-fulfillment of it that she gives much time to her household and to the care of her little children; but this excuse, like Ralph Touchet's weak lungs, alleviates her pangs of conscience, but does not satisfy her sense of unfulfilled obligation. The family claim in its highest form is being fulfilled, yet her full human claim is not thereby discharged. Many a young mother says to herself, "When my children are grown, then I shall give my time and ability to these outside things, which I really ought to do." There is no doubt that he who finds the family life in its sweetness and strength is he alone who fulfills the larger claim, just as truly as he who finds his individual life is he who first loses it.

Need of initiative to action

The girl, however, cannot formulate this for herself. She looks out into the world longing that some demand be made upon her powers, for they are too untrained to furnish an initiative. When her health gives way under this strain, as it often does, her physician invariably advises a rest. But to be put to bed and fed on milk is not what she requires. What she needs is simple health-giving activity, which shall mean a response to all of the claims which she so keenly feels, and which shall involve the use of all her faculties.

It is quite true that the family often resents her first attempts to be part of a life quite outside their own, because the college woman frequently makes these first attempts most awkwardly; "visiting shiftless families; attending foolish meetings for the promotion of everything under the sun, and so on." Her faculties have not been trained in the line of action. She lacks the ability to apply her knowledge and theories, to Life itself and to its complicated situations. This is largely the fault of her training and of the one sidedness of educational methods. The colleges have long been full of the best ethical teaching insisting that the good of the whole must ultimately be the measure of effort, and that the individual can only secure his own rights as he labors to secure those of others. But while the college teaching has included an ever broadening range of obligation, and while it has insisted upon the recognition of the claims of human brotherhood, the college training has been singularly individualistic, it has fostered ambitions for personal distinction and has trained the faculties almost exclusively in the direction of intellectual accumulation.

Practical defect in woman's education

Doubtless woman's education is at fault in that it has failed to recognize certain needs and has failed to cultivate and guide the great desires of which all generous young hearts are full. During the most formative years of life it gives the young girl no contact with the feebleness of childhood, the pathos of suffering or the needs of old age. It gathers together crude youth in contact only with each other and with mature men and women who are there for the purpose of their mental direction. The tenderest promptings are bidden to bide their time. This could only be justifiable if a definite outlet were provided when they leave college. Doubtless the need does not differ widely in men and in women. But in the case of women, for whom we may perhaps claim a more tender conscience, those who are not absorbed in professional or business life in the years immediately following college, are brought baldly face to face with the fact that their faculties have been stimulated in one direction and trained in another . . . .

While the student is still in college the incongruity between the ethical teaching and her training is largely reconciled by dreams of future activity and it does not bear upon her with unmitigated harshness. Because of the ethics she has been taught but is not able to formulate into action, – the same ethics which her family much admire when actualized by a missionary or a philanthropist but which when undeveloped they insist are clashing with and disclaiming the family ties – we have all the elements of a tragedy . . . .

The attitude of modern parents

. . . Parents insist that the girl is carried away by a foolish enthusiasm, that she is in search of a career, that she is restless and does not know what she wants. They will give any reason, almost, rather than the recognition of a genuine and dignified claim. Possibly all this is due to the fact that for so many hundreds of years women have had no larger interests, no participation in the affairs lying quite outside of personal and family claims. Any attempt that the individual woman formerly made to subordinate or renounce the family claim was inevitably construed to mean, and often quite justly, that she was setting up her own will against that of her family for selfish ends. It was concluded that she could have no larger motive, and her attempt to break away was therefore selfish. That the family should consent to give her up at her marriage when she was enlarging the family tie by founding another family, was of course logical, or that they should permit and promote her going to college, traveling in Europe, or any other means of self-improvement, might merely mean the development and education of one of their own members; but an honest attempt to fulfill the universal claim was breaking away with every tradition. That the outward manifestation of the selfish attempt and of the larger attempt are so similar, is of course an excuse for the family's attitude . . . .

Readjustment between the claims

. . . As we have learned to adjust [the] two claims of the personal and family, and to find an orderly development impossible without a recognition of both, so perhaps we are called upon now to make a second adjustment, between the family and the universal, in which neither shall lose and both be ennobled.

The family as well as the State we are all called upon to maintain as the highest institutions which the race has evolved for its safeguard and protection. But merely to preserve these institutions is not enough. There come periods of reconstruction, a task is laid upon a passing generation, to enlarge the function and carry forward the ideal of a long-established institution, that all coming generations may live in a larger conception of it. There is no doubt that many women consciously and unconsciously are struggling with this task. The family, like every other element of human life, is susceptible of progress, and from epoch to epoch its tendencies and aspirations are enlarged, although its duties can never be abrogated and its obligations can never be canceled. It is impossible to bring about the higher development by any self-assertion or breaking away of the individual will. The new growth in the plant, swelling against the sheath which at the same time imprisons and protects it, must still be the truest type of progress. The family in its entirety must be carried out into the larger life, it must lose none of its affection but it must enlarge its affections and goodwill until it embraces more than those held together by ties of consanguinity. To bring the notion of human brotherhood to bear upon active human life is not an easy undertaking. The harmonious, intelligent and consistent development of such a movement is as yet impossible; but let us at least cherish the manifestations of it even where they may seem ill judged. Let us avoid the error of considering those attempts unrighteous and something to be deplored, simply because our code of ethics has not yet been revised to fit this enlarged relationship.

22

"ECONOMIC INDEPENDENCE OF MARRIED WOMEN"

A Paper Read at the Fourth Session of the National Council of Women (New Zealand), 1899

Kate Sheppard

Source: Kate Sheppard, 'Economic Independence of Married Women', A Paper Read at the Fourth Session of the National Council of Women (New Zealand) (1899)

The idea of the partnership of husband and wife is not new, and, I am happy to say, the financial equality of the partnership is freely conceded by many husbands. Especially is this latter the case among our working classes, in which, more frequently than not, the wife is the purse-keeper.

But while the majority of men at their marriage solemnly declare that they endow their wives with all their worldly goods there is no legal recognition of the equal partnership of husband and wife in income or property. Both income and property are by law considered to be possessed by the husband alone. In the Municipal Reform Bill, passed last session, provision was made whereby husband and wife may vote by virtue of property held by either. This is a slight recognition of the principle of the economic equality of husband and wife, for which we are thankful. Our representatives have declared that men and women are partners in municipal matters, and having taken the first step, which is usually the hardest, we may hope that they will go on to a fuller declaration of the economic equality of married women. It may be added that in connection with the Government relief works it has been the rule that, when a man is working away from home, the half of his wages is paid to his wife, which is a distinct acknowledgement of the principle we are urging.

Colonel Higginson, in his book entitled "Common Sense About Women/' under the heading of "A Co-partnership," says: "Marriage, considered merely in its financial and business relations, may be regarded as a permanent co-partnership. Now, in an ordinary co-partnership, there is very often a complete division of labour among the partners. If they manufacture locomotive engines, for instance, one partner perhaps superintends the works, another receives and pays out the money. The latter is not necessarily the head of the firm. Perhaps his place could be more easily filled

DOI: 10.4324/9780429321078-24

than some of the other posts. Nevertheless, more money passes through his hands than through those of all the others put together. Now, should he at the year's end call together the inventor and the superintendent, and the traveller and the correspondent, and say to them, 'I have earned all this money this year, but I will generously give you some of it,' he would be considered simply impertinent, and would hardly have a chance to repeat the offence the year after. Yet precisely what would be called folly in this business partnership is constantly done by men in the co-partnership of marriage. For instance, a farmer works himself half to death in the hay-field, and his wife meanwhile is working herself wholly to death in the dairy. The neighbours come in to sympathise after her demise; and during the few months' interval before his second marriage they say approvingly, 'He was always a generous man to his folks! He was a good provider!' But where was the room for generosity any more than the member of any other firm is to be called generous when he keeps the books, receipts the bills, and divides the money? In the case of the farming business the share of the wife is so direct and unmistakable that it can hardly be evaded. If anything is earned by the farm she does her distinct and important share of the earning. But it is not necessary that she should do that to make her, by all the rules of justice, an equal partner, entitled to her full share of the financial proceeds. Let us suppose an ordinary case. Two young people are married, and begin life together. Let us suppose them equally poor, equally capable, equally conscientious, equally healthy. They have children. Those children must be supported by the earning of money abroad, by attendance and care at home. If it requires patience and labour to do the outside work, no less is required inside. The duties of the household are as hard as the duties of the shop or office. If the wife took her husband's work for a day, she would probably be glad to return to her own. So would the husband be if he undertook hers. Their duties are ordinarily as distinct and as equal as those of two partners in any other co-partnership. It so happens that the out-door partner has the handling of the money; but does that give him a right to claim it as his exclusive earnings? No more than in any other business operation. He earned the money for the children and the household. She disburses it for the children and the household. The very laws of nature, by giving her the children to bear and rear, absolve her from the duty of their support, as long as he is alive who was left free by nature for the purpose."

In spite of writers like Colonel Higginson, however, we are still asked by those who are too indifferent to read books on the subject, and who have given the matter little or no thought, "Seeing that the husband earns the money, why should the wife desire economic independence?"

The answer is: 1st. *BECAUSE IT IS JUST*. When a woman consents to undertake the duties of wifehood and motherhood, she gives up her opportunities of earning money for her present need, and future comfort. She undertakes to share all the privations that may be brought about by her husband's blunders, weakness, and misfortune. By her maternal functions she imperils her life, and, in the majority of cases, finds it necessary to spend the greater part of her years in a ceaseless round of duties that involve far more toil and care than would be the case if she were earning her own living as a single woman. It is, therefore, only just that she should have at her disposal for her own needs, and for her share of the joint expenses of the household, a moiety of the family income.

2nd. *BECAUSE IT IS NECESSARY FOR HER OWN PROTECTION.* In entering into marital partnership a woman undertakes the most dangerous, arduous, and wearisome part of the partnership. If there should be financial disaster, it will fall more heavily on her than on her husband. By being fully aware of the source and amount of the income, and by having an equal voice in the joint expenditure she will, at least, have an opportunity of averting financial difficulties by prudent counsel. Further, she needs legal protection from the indignity suffered by many wives of having to sue for money for personal needs. Perhaps I may be pardoned if I again quote Higginson on this latter point. In his Chapter on "Asking for Money," page 114, he says: "One of the very best wives and mothers I have ever known once said to me, that whenever her daughters should be married, she should stipulate in their behalf with their husbands for a regular sum of money to be paid them at certain intervals for their personal expenditures. Whether this sum was to be large or small was a matter of secondary importance – that must depend on the income and the style of living, but the essential thing was, that it should come to the wife regularly, so that she should no more have to make a special request for it, than her husband would have to ask her for a dinner. This lady's own husband was, as I happened to know, of a most generous disposition, was devotedly attached to her, and denied her nothing. She herself was a most accurate and careful manager. There was everything in the household to make her financial arrangements flow smoothly. Yet she said to me, 'I suppose no man can possibly understand how a sensitive woman shrinks from asking for money. If I can prevent it my daughters shall never have to ask for it. If they do their duty as wives and mothers they have a right to their share of the joint income within reasonable limits; for certainly no money could buy the services they render. Moreover they have a right to share in determining what those reasonable limits are.'

"It is unreasonable to say of such women, 'Too sensitive! Too fastidious!' For it is just this quality of finer sensitiveness which men affect to prize in a woman and wish to protect at all hazards. The very fact that a husband is generous; the very fact that his income is limited, these may bring in conscience and gratitude to increase the restraining influences of pride, and make the wife less willing to ask money of such a husband than if he were a rich man or a mean one. The only dignified position in which a man can place his wife is to treat her at least as well as he would treat a housekeeper, and give her the comfort of a perfectly clear and definite arrangement as to money matters. She will not then be under the necessity of nerving herself to solicit from him as a favour what she really needs, and has a right to spend. Nor will she be torturing herself, on the other side, with the secret fear lest she has asked too much, and more than they can really spare. She will, in short, be in the position of a woman and a wife, not of a child or a toy.

"I have carefully avoided using the word 'allowance' in what has been said, because the word seems to imply the untrue and mean assumption that the money is all the husband's, to give or withhold as he will. Yet I have heard this sort of phrase from men who were living on a wife's property or a wife's earnings; from men who nominally kept boarding-houses, working a little, while their wives worked hard; or from farmers, who worked hard and made their wives work harder. Even in cases where the wife has no direct part in the money making, the indirect part she performs if she takes faithful charge of her household, is so essential, so beyond all compensation in money, that it is an utter shame and impertinence in the husband when he speaks of 'giving' money to his wife as if it were an act of favour.

"It is no more an act of favour than when the business manager of a firm pays out money to the unseen partner who directs the indoor business or runs the machinery. Be the joint income more or less, the wife has a claim to her honourable share, and that as a matter of right, without the daily ignominy of sending in a petition for it."

I have quoted thus lengthily from Higginson's book because he puts the case in a plain and common-sense manner, and also because it is written from a man's point of view.

While we know there are many husbands whose conduct towards their wives in money matters is all that could be desired, there are also many who practise so petty a tyranny as to make sensitive women stint themselves of necessaries rather than suffer the humiliation of asking for money for personal requirements.

Again, a woman needs protection from the unjust whims and peculiarities that a husband may have regarding the disposal of the property after death. To illustrate this point let me give you a case that came under my own notice. The woman was strong, healthy, and in the prime of life. She was a thoroughly-trained and very clever cook, able to earn her £60 a year, as well as her board and lodging. In a weak moment she accepted the proposal of a struggling farmer. For many years she did, single-handed, the heavy work of a farm house and dairy, being the first up and the last to lie down.

The farmer became wealthy, but, being of a penurious bent, they lived in apparent poverty, and the wife not only found no relief, but found it difficult to preserve even an appearance of decency. For nearly forty years she, who before marriage had enough and to spare, did not know what "pin-money" meant, and her scanty clothes were bought by her husband with great reluctance and grumblings. At length the farmer died, and his wife found that he had bequeathed his many thousands to his own relatives, and that she, at 70 years of age, had been left the use of a leaky cottage and £20 a year. Had she not married she would have lived an easier life, and would have been able to make a suitable provision for her declining years. Had economic equality of married women been the law of the land, the whims of the husband could only have affected his moiety of their joint earnings and possessions.

3rd. *IT IS NECESSARY FOR THE PROTECTION OF THE CHILDREN.* Just as a man can, under the present law, bequeath his property away from his wife, so may he act in precisely the same manner towards his children.

In the last session of the New Zealand Parliament a Bill was introduced by Mr McNab, M.H.R., entitled the "Testator's Family Provision Out of Estate" Bill.

This Bill provides that any person leaving a will, and failing to make due provision for wife (or husband) and children, the Supreme Court may, on application made to it by or on behalf of the said wife, husband, or children, order that due provision be made for the maintenance and support of the said applicants.

The very fact of such a Bill being considered necessary shows that the public mind is being exercised in this matter. I quote it to show how cruel the present law allows a man to be, and to reiterate that the economic equality of husband and wife would prevent a man from bequeathing the whole of his estate away from his family. Again, if a man is sordid, he can prevent his wife from expending on the children what may in her view be necessary for their physical and mental education. This may be a real deprivation to the children, and one which may affect their whole life. There is also the fact to be deplored that children, often unconsciously, learn to respect their mother less through observing that she is obliged to accept a subject position when money, and indeed almost every other matter, is concerned. The purse necessarily dominates the positions, and the purse-holder thus acquires an artificial superiority in the eyes of the children, which is undoubtedly detrimental to them in many ways.

Instances of men who waste the greater part of their earnings or income in the indulgence of drunken or dissolute habits, while their families suffer want and privation, are known to all of you. In a recent number of the *Mercantile and Bankruptcy Gazette of New Zealand*, in connection with the Destitute Persons Act, the question was raised as to the advisability of preventing a man from squandering his estate by drinking, or by any other form of dissipation. The article in question states that such cases are none too isolated, and waxes indignant at the idea of the wife and children being imposed as a *burden on the community*. The sufferings of the unfortunate wife and children are not discussed, nor does the idea of giving the wife power to protect herself and her children seem to have entered into the mind of the writer of the article; and yet this latter method would, I am sure, go a long way towards solving the difficulty.

Cases are also well known where the death of the husband has deprived the family of the only individual in it possessed of any business knowledge, and poverty and distress have come through simple ignorance. He may have been most kind and affectionate, but in keeping his wife ignorant of money matters and business usages he has been in reality most cruel, and the children have to suffer the penalty of their father's reticence and their mother's ignorance.

4th. *IT IS NECESSARY TO PROTECT A MAN FROM HIMSELF.* When considering the necessity of economic equality for the protection of the children, I referred to the case of a man who wasted his substance on drunkenness and other vices. Surely anything that would prevent a man from following such a ruinous course would be a boon to himself as well as to his family.

There are also instances where men are imbued with the gambling spirit, and are prone to rush recklessly into mining or land speculations far beyond their legitimate means. If economic independence were legalised a woman could at least protect her own share of the joint income or property, so that a portion of the disaster to the family could be averted, and she and her children would not be left helpless to face the world. But I believe that the financial discussions which would become imperative between husband and wife under such conditions would often lead to the abandonment of reckless plunging and the adoption of a more prudent course.

5th. *IT WOULD IMPROVE THE POSITION OF MARRIED WOMEN*. Mona Caird, in her essay on "Motherhood under Conditions of Dependence", makes what at first sight seems to be a strong and sweeping statement. She says: – "It is not a little remarkable that the present position of the married woman corresponds, in outward features, with that of a slave in early ages . . . In return for maintenance and the sum paid for his possession, the bondsman surrenders himself with all his service for life, and gives up his liberty. He may be well-treated, well-lodged and fed, but his toil brings with it no right to self-direction or hope of respite, should the condition of his lot prove painful. This constitutes the real difference between freedom and slavery. To be maintained, however luxuriously, without earning anything over which there is undisputed control is to be, in so far, in the position of a slave.

"Other conditions may, indeed, be very unlike those of servitude, but such a situation presents its essential features. It will be seen that the married woman is exactly in this position, inasmuch as her work in the home does not procure her independence. She is the working partner in a firm in whose profits she has no share. Her share is only in the labour. Yet her husband imagines he is supporting her!"

"Whence has arisen among good men the state of conscience which approves this injustice? Many changes must take place before it can be entirely removed; but it is important to recognise the wrong and to work to eradicate the false ideals on which it rests."

This author goes on to say that "wives who have begun their married life without private means and acquired them afterwards, notice that a marked difference is discernible in the husband's attitude towards them. It is the unconscious "recognition of the new status" – that is to say, that the wife has, in the eyes of her husband, acquired a new dignity.

It is this recognition of the true dignity of women that we seek to bring about by law, for, as the Apostle truly says, "The law is our schoolmaster." While law is the visible expression of the highest thought of the majority, it is also a standard to which even the lowest may in time be levelled up. As soon as a certain number of citizens are strong enough and persistent enough to get their views focused into an Act, the other members of the community, whether hostile or indifferent previously, accept what has been decided by Parliament as a matter of course. Thus the legal recognition of Economic Independence would give women a status not previously possessed, and which it is right and just they should possess.

6th. *IT IS A RACE QUESTION*. "Dependence, in short," says Mona Caird, "is the curse of our marriages, of our homes, and of our children who are born of women who are not free."

Those who are acquainted with the law as it now stands, know that all a married woman can claim is the barest shelter, food, and clothing. Everything that affects her mode of life, her home, and her children is decided according to her husband's code of justice and morality. If he is generous she fares well, if the opposite she has no redress. What a mortifying position in which to place a human being! Sensitive women must necessarily feel the depression of the situation, and this very depression must affect her children both before and after birth. Surely the mothers of the race should be free from all unnecessary care, from petty tyranny, from unjust conditions.

Economic Independence would raise women from their present position to one of dignity and freedom, while helping men to act justly. To sue as a favour for what belongs to one as a right is to create a subject on the one hand and a tyrant on the other. The subject condition is a degrading one, and must tend to enfeeble our women and retard their highest development.

Mary Woollstonecraft [sic], in her famous book, "Vindication of the Rights of Women," written over a hundred years ago, says: "The laws respecting women make an absurd unit of a man and his wife; and then by the easy transition of only considering him as responsible, she is reduced to a mere cypher. The being who discharges the duties of its station is independent; and, speaking of woman at large, their first duty is to themselves as rational creatures, and the next in point of importance as citizens is that which includes so many, of a mother. To render woman really virtuous and useful, she must not, if she discharge her civil duties, want, individually, the protection of civil laws, she must not be dependent on her husband's bounty for her subsistence after his death, for how can a being be generous who has nothing of its own? Or virtuous who is not free? . . . . It follows, then, I think, that from their infancy, women should either be shut up Eastern fashion, or educated in such a manner as to be able to think and act for themselves."

"We are mothers. Through us in our bondage,
Through us, with a brand in the face,
Be we fettered with gold or with iron,
Through us comes the race!

We were ignorant long, and our children
Were besotted, and brutish, and blind;
King-driven, priest-ridden! – Who were they?
Our children? – Mankind.

We were kept for our beauty, our softness,
Our sex; – What reward do ye find?
We transmit, must transmit, being mothers,
What we are to mankind!

At the meeting of our Council last year, when the motion, "That the legal recognition of the Economic independence of married women is desirable for the attainment of justice and for the furtherance of truer marriage relationship" was put, one of our members moved as an amendment, "That the Council endeavour to educate public opinion to the recognition of the money value of a woman's worth as wife and mother." I ask, Can such work be measured in money, or can it be replaced by money if lost? Higginson says, "If a business man loses his partner he can obtain another, and a man no doubt may take a second wife; but he cannot procure for his children a second mother. Indeed, it is a palpable insult to the whole relation of husband and wife when one compares it even in a financial light, to that of a business partner. It is only because a constant effort is made to degrade the practical position of woman below this standard of comparison that it becomes her to claim for herself at least as much as this."

And here I would state that in asking for Economic Independence we are not seeking privileges. The day of privilege is fast passing away, and the day of right and justice is dawning. We hold that if a woman shares in her husband's income, she shall also share in his financial and legal responsibility. And let it be clearly understood that in asking for Economic Equality we are doing so from the standpoint of Freedom and of the highest morality.

I should like, in conclusion, to answer some of the most frequent abjections which have been urged against this reform. It is said that

IT WILL CAUSE HUSBAND AND WIFE TO QUARREL. This objection is an old friend. We met with it frequently during our Franchise campaign. Husbands and wives disagree now on money matters. They would be less likely to quarrel when the position of each is clearly defined by law.

Again, it is said that "A man may marry a woman who has no idea of the value of money, and will squander her share, and leave him to maintain the family out of the income." That is true. But in that case legal relief may be obtained by a decision of the Magistrate, as provided in the draft Bill brought before the Council at its last annual meeting (see clause vi.). Moreover, mothers would be anxious to educate their daughters to financial responsibility. Even as the law now is, a man has to suffer if he marries a wasteful wife, just as a woman has to suffer if she marries a spendthrift man. With the economic partnership legally defined, both men and women will be much more protected than they are now.

To this reply the retort has been made, "You will have men and women constantly flying to the courts to settle money matters." I do not think that this would be so. As a rule, people object very much to airing their grievances in public. But such an Act would be a deterrent to those husbands or wives who were wasteful and careless; and the fact that it was in existence would prevent them from transgressing its behests, and incurring its penalties. Another objection that we hear is, that "*It is impossible in many instances for a man to say what his income is.*" The answer to that is, he can find out his income for his wife's information in the same way that he does it for the Income Tax Commissioner.

It has been urged that "*It is a woman's own fault if she doesn't get all the money she wants*" – a woman should be able to manage her husband.

If "managing" means using artifice and cunning to gain her ends, then no surer proof of the harm to character that results from present conditions can be urged.

To obtain by artifice what one should be able to claim as a right, is a demoralising and humiliating method.

It is also urged against any change in this matter, that *some women are quite content with things as they are*. So were many slaves in the United States before their emancipation. Many thousands of people are content to live in slums, in a dirty, ragged condition today, without wishing for anything better. Some of the prisoners released from the Bastille, after many years of incarceration, begged to be allowed to return to their prison cells. Their eyes could not bear the light of the sun, and their freedom seemed a burden to them, as it brought with it responsibility of action.

Yet the fact that there were contented slaves and dwellers in slums and prisons was not accepted as a good reason for withholding freedom and healthy conditions from those who suffered from the want of these things. And so with regard to the proposed law for the economic equality of husbands and wives. It will not apply to the large number of men who already treat their wives with justice. It need not apply to those women who are content with things as they are. But if there should be, as there are now, women who are so unfortunate as to feel that for the best interests of their children and for the preservation of their own self-respect an appeal to the law is necessary, it will be there for their protection.

"*If you give economic independence*," says another, "*you will do away with the beautiful old ideal of marriage – the man to protect, the woman to lean and cling, ivy-like*." I deny the beauty of this conception. A woman may cling like a loadstone round a man's neck until she drags him down to earth and crushes him, just as the tree is eventually killed by its parasite, the ivy.

"He for God," sang Milton, "She for God *in him*." It was Milton's ideal, doubtless, but we, knowing what harmful results have grown out of such artificial ideals, think that we have a higher and truer standard.

One of our modern poets has written –

"And so these twain upon the skirts of time
Sit side by side, full-summed in all their powers,
Dispensing harvest, sowing the To-be,
Self-reverent each, and reverencing each,
Distinct in individualities.
But like each other, e'en as those who love.
Then comes the statelier Eden back to men,
Then reign the world's great bridals, chaste and calm,
Then springs the crowning race of human kind.
May these things be."

I shall be sorry if anything I have said should give rise to the idea that we consider the interests of husbands and wives antagonistic. I firmly believe that they are one and the same. All good and thoughtful men and women recognise the importance of working together in the interests of the home. The home is the unit of the State, and whatever is for the elevation of the home must lead to a higher life for the community. To give due respect and dignity to the mistress of the home is for the true welfare of the State, for

> "If *she* be small, slight-natured, miserable,
>   How shall *men* grow?"
> . . . "let her make herself her own
> To give or keep, to live and learn and be
> All that not harms distinctive womanhood."

23

"THE ECONOMIC IMPORTANCE OF THE FAMILY," IN *THE STRENGTH OF THE PEOPLE: A STUDY IN SOCIAL ECONOMICS*

Helen Bosanquet

Source: Helen Bosanquet, 'The Economic Importance of the Family', in *The Strength of the People: A Study in Social Economics* (London: Macmillan, 1903), pp. 180–92

CHAPTER VI

The economic importance of the family

Economic motives arise mainly from disinterested affections – The burden of the next generation; why do we accept it? – Having accepted, what is the best method of fulfilling our duty towards it? – Is the institution of the family an efficient instrument? – Necessity for some definite policy; either family or some more efficient instrument – Claims of the expert, not sufficient to meet the needs of childhood – State can never be, or provide, a substitute for parents – Highest qualities and economic motives developed in the family – Further, family only safeguard against "surplus population" – Comparison between French and English ideals – Relation between overcrowding and family life; tendency to disintegration of family – When and why does the family fail?

At first sight it seems entirely alien to our ordinary way of thinking to regard the family from an economic point of view. We like to think of it as the centre of hopes and affections and motives which have nothing to do with the more mercenary motives of business life. It is the consecrated corner of the world into which business man and wage-earner may retire from the friction of bargain and exchange, of work and wages, into the sunshine of disinterested services, of mutual affection, of intercourse which brings pleasure and not merely profit.

DOI: 10.4324/9780429321078-25

And yet, when we begin to seek about for the motives which give rise to economic activities, we find them largely, if not mainly, in the disinterested affections of family life. There is no such striking instance of the way in which non-economic causes may give rise to the most important economic results. The parent's care for his children may be entirely without an eye to any future recompense, and yet lead him to the most strenuous exertions on their behalf. In economic language we say that the motive which induces a man to work is the wage he hopes to earn; but without the prior and deeper motive of love for wife and child the wage he earns would often fail to seem worth while. And even if we allow that to some extent his action may take the form of conscious investment of capital, and that he looks for a return from his children in his old age, yet the fact remains that it is the bond of family life upon which is based the more purely economic motive.

If we were able to estimate to what extent our activities are directed towards our own maintenance, and to what extent towards that of the next generation, we should probably come to the conclusion that, directly or indirectly, we were very largely engaged in the latter task. We could keep ourselves alive and amused at a very much less expenditure of exertion than we actually undergo; and though, no doubt, a certain amount of our work is due to sheer lack of the imagination necessary to play, yet it is the nourishing and education of the next generation which is responsible for the greater part of it.

This has been so, of course, from the beginning, and will continue to be so to the end; for failure here would be the beginning of the end. From the point of view of Nature, each generation must replace itself with a well-equipped and capable successor, or utterly fail of its purpose in the world.

The particular methods by which we achieve this end may, indeed, be sometimes called in question; but no one, I believe, has ever ventured to suggest that the duty does not exist, and that any generation should live for itself alone, regardless of posterity. Questions of practical importance may arise from time to time for the statesman, as to how far we have a right to burden posterity with debts incurred for our own needs, or with evils incurred by our own recklessness; opinion may differ as to what kind of legacy will best enable our descendants to take up their burden when the time comes; but that in some way or another we are bound to leave them at least as well equipped as we have been ourselves, seems to be one of the principles so bound up in our very nature as human beings, that no one has as yet thought it worth while to deny it.

If we look for the reason, not so much of the principle as of the absoluteness with which we feel and accept it, it may probably be found to lie chiefly in that homogeneity of the different generations which is rooted in family life. Not only our children, but our children's children, are a living interest to us – a present existence, and not merely a contingent future. Through the welding power of the family life the three generations form one homogeneous whole with identical interests; nowhere is there any sharp break dividing us from the past and future. Our welfare was one with that of parents and grandparents, and is one with that of children and grandchildren; the "family fortunes" knit all generations together, and make it impossible for us to disregard, whether in private or public action, the welfare of those who come after us.

There are, of course, individuals who by their lives deny the claim, who live for their own satisfaction or advancement alone; but they are rare, except amongst those who have fallen lowest in the scale of human life, who have dropped out of all organic connection with their fellows, and are no longer capable of entering into so delicate an organism as that of a family. But the fact that these degenerate specimens exist, does not affect the general principle that the duty in question is one accepted by the human race as such.

But though the duty itself is not denied, it has from time to time been questioned whether the method adopted by the community for meeting this duty is the best which could be devised. That method is, of course, primarily the institution of the family. The family is, we have seen reason to think, a powerful means of making the duty recognised and accepted, by welding together the generations through their inseparable interests; but is it also the best means of carrying it out, of securing the efficiency of the young? is it the best nursery for developing and training the rising generation?

There are not wanting those who will tell us that the family has had its day, that it is breaking up and disappearing in civilised countries, and that the responsibility for the next generation really rests with, and can be much better managed by, the State. They protest, on the one hand, against the weight of the burden imposed upon parents; on the other hand, against the dangers of entrusting the helplessness of childhood to the possible irresponsibility, ignorance, or poverty of the parents. And even those who would shrink from any open attack upon the family as irreligious – the mass of the benevolent public – are continually bearing witness to their belief in its inadequacy by their attempts to transfer its functions to public bodies, or to committees and societies created *ad hoc*.

Now, it is quite clear that on this question of the care of the rising generation there must be some definite policy; it must be entrusted to some one in particular if it is to be properly carried out. Everybody's business is nobody's business, and the children would fare badly indeed if they were left to the chance benevolence of the ratepayers in general. The question is, To whom in particular shall it be entrusted? From a purely economic point of view we might put it in this way. Here are so many children, the property of the community into which they are born, estimated roughly at a present value of £5 per unit. How shall the community develop this property to the best advantage? It is true that the generation which accepts the burden may reap but a small share of the profit, especially if it takes the line of weakening the main link which exists between the generations; but laying aside this divergence of interests, and allowing, for the sake of argument, that the State has an absolute right to choose its policy in this matter, what is the most efficacious method of developing the property? Opponents of the family will say, with some degree of plausibility, by entrusting it to the care of experts instead of to the bungling stupidity of any ignorant woman who may happen to have a baby. The nurture and training of children, they may urge, are matters of such importance as to call for all the knowledge and skill available; but we leave it to people of whom the vast majority hardly know that such skill and knowledge exist. And, indeed, it does seem to all of us, in some moods, as if less care and attention were bestowed upon the development of the human race than upon the cultivation of our gardens or the breeding of horses.

But in this matter at least there is a great intuitive wisdom underlying our apparent carelessness. It is lamentable, indeed, that there should be so much ignorance among parents, and for that the community may well be to blame. It is lamentable that many children should be stunted physically and mentally for lack of proper nurture; and yet it does not follow that the institution of the family is not – with all its shortcomings – the best conceivable one for the end in view.

It is worth while in this connection to consider in general what are the most important needs of childhood. There is always a danger lest the clumsy adult, forgetful of his own childish days, strengthened and perhaps a little coarsened by contact with the world, should lose sight of the characteristic features of childhood, and represent its needs as a mere repetition of his own on a smaller scale. Instruction, not so "advanced" as his, but not necessarily less difficult; food, less in quantity, and probably of a less expensive quality than he himself requires; clothing, again, his in miniature; and recreation of a very elementary character – these are the needs which he attributes to the child. And the result is not unlike that attained by the "old masters" in their portraiture of children, who are little old men and women, with nothing but their diminutive size to indicate the wonderful fact of childhood, in its innocence and tenderness and appealing helplessness.

Now, with such a little-old-man image in his mind, it is not wonderful that the reformer is apt to rely too strongly on the power of the State. There is nothing in all this range of wants which it is inherently impossible for the State to provide; and since of these it *can* ensure the punctual and regular, if somewhat mechanical, provision, it is arguable that it should undertake to make them a certainty.

But this is to leave out the most important fact of all – much as if God should have made a world without sunshine in it. For what is it that the child, especially in infancy, needs beyond everything; without which no abundance of food and clothing can make it other than a forlorn little creature, and with which it will thrive and be joyous in the poorest and coarsest surroundings? It is, of course, the tenderness and caressing love which it can be sure of receiving from its mother alone; a tenderness and love which is something different from the most conscientious discharge of duty, which may exist, indeed, quite apart from any sense of duty at all, but which overflows spontaneously – the outsider might even say to a superfluity – into the life of the child. Children may be made to live and grow without it, as plants may be made to live and grow without sunshine; but neither child nor plant will ever develop to its full perfection.

And it is the mother's instinct alone which can secure to the child its birthright of tenderness; the State is powerless to provide it at any cost. There are those, indeed, who have the mother's instinct towards everything which is feeble, who can no more resist the appeal of helplessness than the mother can resist the cry of her child; but it is a quality which cannot be supplied to order like instruction, food, and clothing. And of all human qualities, this instinctive love of the mother is the last to fail: women who have sinned against every other law of man and of nature will still cling to the infant whose helplessness they can defend; and so long as this is so, to intervene between them is sacrilege.

And the mother's instinct is essential all the more because in infancy the child is little likely to possess any attractive qualities; nothing but the mother's love is strong enough to be blind to all its shortcomings and triumph over all its defects. And as the child grows older, this sun of love, which shines alike upon the just and the unjust, is no less necessary to enable it to develop its highest qualities, to open out into blossom and fruit. It alone can create the atmosphere in which the diffident child can learn self-confidence, the weakly courage, the dull insight. The blind belief of the mother in her children is more than prophetic, for it creates the very qualities which it insists upon seeing. And since this love, with all the patience and faith and tenderness involved in it, is far more likely to exist in the parents than in any one else, to whom is it possible that the child should be normally entrusted but to its parents? They, indeed, may fail to give it many valuable things which the trained expert might give; but the trained expert is almost certain to fail to give it the one invaluable thing which they can give.

To many, no doubt, it will seem almost like sacrilege even to discuss the rights of parents to bring up their children, and the advantages of family life; but since there are many also who hold that the sacredness is merely sentimental and the advantages very questionable, it becomes necessary to endeavour to give expression to facts which are so close to us that we are apt to lose sight of them.

What we urge, then, is, that children can develop their highest qualities only in the sunshine of personal tenderness and affection, and that this sunshine can be maintained only in the family. It is to the family, therefore, with all its possibilities of failure, that we must continue to entrust the care of the rising generation. Its work may be supplemented in school; but no matter how wise and patient the teachers, nor how sufficient the apparatus and curriculum, it can never be superseded. The school may give knowledge, discipline, the habit of good comradeship and intercourse with the outside world. It can never give that refuge from one's own defects, that unity of interests and affections, that deep, underlying sympathy rooted in a common nature with its common difficulties and aspirations, which form the very atmosphere of home life at its best.

And it is in this atmosphere also that the more purely economic virtues flourish best.

If we endeavour to induce the average young man to take an interest in any stray baby, no matter how nicely washed and dressed, he will in nine cases out of ten turn from it with disgust. He will certainly have no impulse to sacrifice any of his leisure and amusements on its behalf. But let that baby be his own – his own by right of creation, and his own to make a man of, – and it becomes the most absorbing and fascinating interest in the world, worthy of any and every sacrifice. The more complete its dependence upon him, the more strenuously he will strive on its behalf, and the more complete his motive will be to efficiency and steadiness. The man who has a family dependent upon him is likely to be a far more productive member of society than the man who has only his own needs to consider. The children supply a motive-power to the parent, which few other interests are strong enough to afford to the mass of mankind; while the parents supply the material, both physical and moral, for the life of the children.

Now, it is clear that a great part of this gain would be lost if, by way of compromise, the child should be left with the parents but the cost of its maintenance be provided by the State. This compromise was tried with disastrous results under the old Poor Law. The parent who no longer feels himself responsible for the maintenance of his child, has lost the chief source of his interest in it; and has lost therewith all the stimulus to exertion, the motive for efficiency, which it would naturally provide. Moreover, as the child grows old enough to appreciate the situation, it is inevitable that his knowledge should react upon his feelings towards his parents: he will no longer owe everything to them, probably he will owe very little; for where less effort has been made for him, there will not only *seem* to be less affection – there will actually *be* less.

The family, again, when even moderately efficient, is the best school for the child, not only in affection and mutual services, but in the more economic arts of life. He learns there, not by hearsay and as a set lesson, but by practical experience every hour of every day, what can be done with the income earned by the sort of man he will be when he grows up. He becomes familiar in every detail with the organisation of life on a given plane. No one would wish that a child should suffer privation, and yet it is well that he should learn how to economise in bad times and how to expand in good; to share the fortunes of a family is a far more vitalising experience than the well-fed monotony of institution life. Experiences of this kind cannot be introduced into institution life, for they would have no meaning there, no relation to the facts of real life; it is only within the circle of the family that the child can safely be made familiar with the working of economic cause and effect. There he will learn with all the vividness of actual experience the importance of the little store laid by for the rainy day, of the club-money in times of sickness, of the credit which follows upon good repute, of the holiday taken in good times and forgone in bad. He will be trained also in the qualities of mutual forbearance and mutual service which are of the essence of family life; and as he begins to earn he will learn the pleasure and responsibility of contributing to the family welfare. The girl, meanwhile, will be learning with more or less completeness the function of the woman in the home: she will learn by actual experience the art of laying out the family income to the best advantage, and she will begin that long apprenticeship to baby which will form so large a part of her future life and be of such infinite importance to the next generation. If she has been "well grounded" in a good family, no amount of after schooling or industrial training will spoil her for home life; they will only put the finishing touches to her efficiency in the home.

One writes naturally of the life of the wage-earners, because they form so much the larger part of the community; but the same facts hold good in all ranks of life.

It is in the family that the child learns most naturally and completely to organise his life on a sound economic basis, so that credit and debit may properly balance, and that he may neither incur responsibilities which he cannot meet, nor fail to meet those which are attached to his position.

The family being, then, the best available institution for securing the efficiency of the next generation, another important economic fact reveals itself. The family, developed to even a mediocre degree of efficiency, is the one sufficient safeguard against a surplus population.

24

MOTHERS WHO MUST EARN

Katharine Susan Anthony

Source: Katharine Susan Anthony, Excerpts from *Mothers Who Must Earn* (New York: Survey Associates, 1914), pp. 18–24, 85–9, 199–200

THE condition of the family depends primarily on the condition of the principal breadwinner. Whether the father is dead or absent, or whether he is living at home and is unemployed or at work, will roughly determine the economic circumstances of the family. For the sake of greater accuracy, the 370 women studied are here divided into six groups, – those whose husbands were withdrawn from the family through death, desertion, or separation forming three of them, and those whose husbands were living at home in a state of incapacitation, idleness, or employment forming the remaining three. Table 1 shows the number and percentage of mothers in each group.

It must be noted that the distribution of women according to family status, shown by the table, is not representative of family conditions in the district. Naturally, the proportion of widows, deserted wives, and separated wives would be much higher among wage-earning women than in the general population of the locality. It must be noted also that "incapacitated" in the following table means invalidity through specific disease and not old age alone. Mere age as a test of incapacitation is difficult to apply. Whatever the man's years, he was not put into this class unless his infirmities placed him there. Husbands were counted "idle" only when they had been out of work for at least a year. Among those "at work," many intermittent or irregular workers were therefore included. Men who worked only three or four days of the week, those who were out of work on account of illness or a strike, those who worked regularly at a low-paid occupation, and those who earned more but drank and did not "give their money in" – all these fell into the group "at work." In a district like the West Side, which offers so many opportunities for casual employment, it would be unfair and inaccurate to class as "idle" the men who were simply fitting into their industrial environment as they found it. Hence several men whose work histories for the year showed long and repeated gaps were nevertheless assigned to the class of working husbands.

 DOI: 10.4324/9780429321078-26

Table 1. Conjugal condition of 370 wage-earning mothers

Group	*Conjugal condition*	*Mothers*	
		Number	*Per cent*
I	Widows	125	33.8
II	Deserted wives[a]	40	10.8
III	Separated wives	9	2.4
IV	Wives with incapacitated husbands	21	5.7
V	Wives with idle husbands	12	3.2
VI	Wives with husbands at work[a]	163	44.1
	Total	370	100.0

[a] Among the women visited were two who had formed irregular unions and were the mothers of illegitimate children. As one of them had been deserted and the other was still living with the father of the child, they were assigned respectively to the groups of deserted wives and wives with husbands at work.

One-third of the women visited were widows. There were 125 of these fatherless families where the mother was compelled to perform the duties of two parents and to support wholly or partially a family of several persons on an income scantily adapted to the needs of one. To all these homes disease or accident had dealt a blow which had permanently altered the family structure. The deserting husband may return and take up his responsibilities once more; the loafer may reform and go to work; the man who has lost his job may find another next week or tomorrow – vague hopes like these play their part in the lives of the women whose husbands are still whole and sound.

But where disease and accident have done their work the situation of the family is comparatively static. It is true that the widow's children are growing on toward the day when they also will become wage-earners. The precariousness of the family's position is proportioned exactly according to whether that day is in the near or distant future. It is also true that the widow herself may remarry. This is by no means unlikely on the West Side where remarriages are frequent.[1]

The subject of marriage was frequently discussed, for the shrewd wisdom of the women on this head was not to be lost. It is not the fashion among them to speak in praise of "marriage life," as the Irish women say. "If I had it to do over, I'd never marry," was almost the universal remark. At first I set this down as the conventional language of disillusionment, the kind of remark which the women thought proper for middle age to make. As I came to know them better, I realized that there was a much deeper reason. The strain of bringing up a family on the average working-man's wages, reduced as this is likely to be by unemployment, sickness, or drink, constitutes, indeed, the dark age of the tenement mother's life. It is not strange that the goodwill existing between husband and wife often gives

Fifty-five Years of Age and Forty-five Years of Toil

way beneath it. "I tell my husband," said Mrs. Gurney, "it's not right for us to be quarreling all the time before the children. But it seems like we can't help it. He's so worried all the time and I'm so tired. If we were easy in our minds we wouldn't do it."

Occasionally there was a sad story of cruelty at the hands of a man degraded by drink or brutalized by every influence from his youth up. There were sordid stories such as are rehearsed daily in the domestic relations court. There were tales of men who, deprived by circumstances of everything but their power over wife and child, found their greatest pleasure in the exercise of this power; wretched types "who know no influence but that of force, no reason, and no gentleness, since these have never come their way; who know only that they must keep that little which they have, since that which they have not is so great and so desirable."[2]

Some of these sad histories ended in desertion or separation; 40 deserted wives and nine who had separated from their husbands were among the group studied. Divorce is unknown on the West Side. Legal counsel is too expensive and the societies which furnish legal advice free to the poor are not willing to undertake this kind of case. Other histories equally grim or sad were only terminated by death. More than one woman candidly confessed that her husband's death had been a relief. Mrs. Brunig, a sincerely religious woman, said to me, "You may think we are having a hard time. But I don't mind it. It's nothing compared to what it was when Brunig was alive. I never had a happy day then."

In contrast to these dismal homes there were others where mutual affection and sympathy had survived every strain, and where one found instances of absolutely heroic loyalty on the part of a wife toward an unlucky husband. Some of the men were sick and a hospitable institution was waiting to receive them and relieve the over-burdened wife of this care and expense. Yet a woman would say, "He was good to his family as long as he had work. It's not as if he were a drinking man and wasted his money. I won't send him away now." And then there was Mrs. Cary whose husband's earnings fell so low – he was a longshoreman handicapped by hernia – that she started out to find work. The neighbors all said, "You'll spoil him." To which Mrs. Cary replied firmly and proudly, "Everybody knows their own best," and went her way.

But whether the situation has been relieved by goodwill or aggravated by ill feeling, the strain of making a home for a family under the usual West Side conditions is a stern experience. The woman who has gone through it looks on a second marriage from a practical point of view based on something more than the normal amount of disillusionment which goes with the middle years even under happier conditions.

Few women are likely to be as extremely practical as Mrs. Cooley was in her second marriage. If her attitude seems somewhat materialistic, it must be remembered that Mrs. Cooley's life had been spent in the pursuit of food, clothes, and shelter, and not of ideals. Here is the story as she told it:

"My first husband was a hoisting engineer. It was easy work, but only a sober man could do it. Barney was sober enough – and jolly, too, when he wanted to be. He could make others laugh, but he only made me cry. He never drank, but he beat me. Even before I married him, up to the day of the wedding, I was always dreading it. The night before, I looked him in the eye and said, 'Barney McBride, will ye be good to me?' I would have left him after Henry was born, but he was sickly and I knew he wouldn't live long. I took care of him till he died, but it's God's truth, I was glad when I saw him in his coffin.

"I was working over at the carpet factory at Greenpoint then, going all that way back and forth every day because I didn't want to break up my home. After awhile Samuel Cooley began to come around. He was a boiler maker. He'd be waiting at the gate of the factory when we come out at night and walk along with Maggie and me a ways. But I had had enough of marriage life. So I left the Greenpoint factory and come back to New York so's to get rid of him. Then I went to scrub in a hotel. But one day I come home and there was Samuel standing before the door. He told me he was married thirty-two years to his first wife and she never did a day's work outside her house all that time. I left him waiting three months and then I married him in the fall. That was October. I didn't mind working in the summer, but when winter came I wished I had a husband so's I wouldn't have to go out."

As I have said, Mrs. Cooley's frankly materialistic attitude was unusual. The women were not as a rule inclined, as girl wage-earners generally are, to look forward to marriage as a means of escaping work. Experience had taught them better. They were more likely to marry for companionship.

Mrs. Grant, a middle-aged silk weaver and a shrewd observer of life, analyzed thus the motives of her own two marriages. "I was married the first time when I was only eighteen. Because my sister, a year younger than me, was getting married, I thought I couldn't let her beat me and took the first chance. It was just as well, too, for it kept me out of harm's way. After my husband's death I went back to the silk mill. The second time I married was thirteen years after the first time. I expected to go on working, but I wanted a good companion."

Perhaps in a worse plight than the widows was a small group of women, 21 in number, whose husbands were either sick or maimed, as in the case of Mrs. Cary. Each of these unfortunate men was an added responsibility for his wife. Besides requiring care and, in some cases, constant nursing, he made another member of a family which had to be supported on an income scarcely sufficient to supply the needs of one person.

. . .

A more helpless figure than the middle-aged mother of a family starting out to look for work would be hard to imagine. Sometimes she buys a newspaper and reads the advertisements. This is called "following the papers." Hotel positions are often secured in this way. Through the women's exchanges, neighborhood churches, settlements, day nurseries, and charitable agencies, she can find opportunities to go out and work by the day. Having one satisfied patron, she is usually able to secure another through the recommendation of the first. There is perhaps more organized effort to place the work of women who go out by the day than any other class of labor done by middle-aged women of the West Side.

But the women who do day's work derive at best a varying and uncertain income. They complain that "you never know what you'll have on a Saturday night." Those who must have "something regular" look for a factory job or an office cleaner's place. Like their sixteen-year-old daughters, their usual plan is simply to "apply on the premises." They walk about for hours, following up poor chances and, worst of all, wearing out their shoes.

With the women, as with the men, it is often the "pushing sort" that gets the job rather than the industrious steady worker. Mrs. Rudden, who hadn't a "lazy bone in her body," as all her acquaintances could testify, had nevertheless a shy, apologetic air which was a distinct disadvantage in looking for work. Applying at one laundry after the other, she was always among those who were turned away. On the other hand, young Mrs. Snyder with her hustling manner and her engaging smile used to declare that "she could always get taken on, even if there was 20 turned away." She explained her success by declaring that she was "ambitious." Her invalid husband, who had himself been "ambitious" before tuberculosis laid him low, would say to her, "Pop's kid, the reason you always get work is because you're *lookin'* for work. The others *ain't.*"

Mrs. Snyder's husband was not altogether right about the 20 women who were turned away. Certainly Mrs. Rudden was looking for work. She had six children to be supported on her husband's wage of $12, with insurance to pay every week, with three or four pairs of shoes to be bought every month. She was giving her children coffee for breakfast against her own better judgment, because she could not buy milk for so many. On top of all this had come a slight misfortune and a debt of $30. No one was ever looking for work more sincerely than Mrs. Rudden.

With Mrs. Williamson the search became a desperate one as the months went by. At her husband's death she had been left with two children, a boy of three years and a girl of eleven months. Williamson had left no insurance, but there were considerable savings in the bank. He had been a "tight" man with his money on board the ship of which he was second officer. His bill at the bar for a three months' voyage would not be over 45 cents. Consequently his wife had funds on hand to tide the family over a year and a half during which, of course, the children were growing older and less helpless. But the end of the savings inevitably came.

Mrs. Williamson began to look for work at the beginning of summer. A few odd days' cleaning and a little sewing was all that she managed to pick up. When November came she was still looking for work. Her story of how she finally got a job shows what a desperate frame of mind she was in by this time.

"There was a woman in the next house that worked at the hospital. One night she came by and said they wanted another regular cleaning woman. The next morning, as I walked up to the hospital, I kept saying to myself, if I didn't get that job I would go home and do away with my children. I don't know what might have happened if they hadn't put me to work that morning. But they gave me the job. I'm working there four months now."

The job which probably saved the lives of the Williamson children was scrubbing stairs and floors nine hours a day, six days in the week, and it pays the grateful woman who does it $6.50 a week.

Very often the news of a vacant place comes through a friend or neighbor, just as Mrs. Williamson's opportunity finally came. Those who have work act as scouts for those who have none. Thus it sometimes happens that several neighbors from the same or adjoining tenements work at the same office building, theater, or factory. A woman who has much opportunity to act as agent for her employer develops a good deal of judgment in selecting the right kind of person.

There was a Mrs. Tomlin who had worked for two years at the same theater with only one week's absence during that time. When the "boss" needed a new woman or extra help, he simply commissioned Mrs. Tomlin to bring a recruit up from the West Side. One day when the investigator happened to be calling on Mrs. Tomlin, a neighbor woman dropped in to advertise her need of a job. "I wouldn't recommend her," said Mrs. Tomlin after the woman had gone. "She wouldn't be steady. Didn't you hear her say there was a place she would have gone to see about this morning, but she had company and couldn't go? I'd like to see company that would keep *me* from going to see about a job."

The women feel a strong mutual responsibility to help one another to find employment. It does not occur to them to seek any immediate reward for their services from either side. It is enough for them if they can thus "square themselves with the boss" and secure a friendly fellow worker.

One woman, an office cleaner, was exceptional in that she had been inducted into the art of exploitation by her employers. She worked for a commercial agency which contracted to clean offices and public buildings by the day. Mrs. Nieman was paid $1.50 a day on the condition that she would find other women to work for $1.25 a day. Her method was simply to pretend that she herself was getting only $1.25 a day. Apparently she had no scruples about deceiving other women as poor as herself and thus helping to lower the standard of wages. Nor did Mrs. Nieman's husband, once a building trade worker and now a casual teamster, see anything morally awry in his wife's proceedings as middle woman. Had he not often enough had to "pay for his job"? It seemed to him only natural that the scrub-women should pay for theirs.

There is no free municipal or state employment agency at which these women may apply, as they might if they were, for instance, in the state of Massachusetts or Wisconsin. The National Employment Exchange of New York, maintained by public spirited citizens, is an agency which aims to bring together the job and the man, with the least possible waste and expense to both sides. But the field of the exchange is limited to manual labor for men, and office work for men and women. It does not handle the manual work of women. In the meantime, the women of the tenements roughly cooperate to help each other in work. Massed together as they are, the news of a vacant job is quickly passed around. The employer needs only to send word to the tenement quarters and he promptly has applicants at his door. Over half of the West Side women, when asked how they had secured their position, replied that they had got it "through a friend."

It is true that the local churches, settlements, and charity organization offices handle manual labor, especially domestic labor, almost exclusively, and give their services free. But it is apparent that all these methods are haphazard for the worker and unselective for the employer. In the meantime, many women who have only unskilled work to offer must earn in order to keep a home for their children. Their necessity renders them liable to exploitation by irresponsible contractors.

. . .

CONCLUDING NOTE

. . . Our study of this group of 370 West Side women completed, we cannot do better than recur to the questions which were uppermost in the minds of the workers when the investigation was begun. Why were these women wage-earners? How many of them worked because they must and how many for other reasons? There was one inevitable conclusion which resulted from the analysis of economic conditions in their homes. It was that not one of the mothers could afford not to earn. They had become wage-earners in obedience to the most primitive of maternal instincts. Their children would have suffered seriously had they failed or refused to earn. Small as were the wages of their unskilled occupations, the amount, as we have seen, played an important part in a family budget correspondingly small. Moreover, they were found to be doing all their own housework before and after their wage-earning hours, instead of paying others to do it for them. By overworking themselves they made their earnings clear gain for their families.

Finally, it may be asked to what extent is the West Side mother of more than local significance. Is she, or is she not, a part of a much larger trend? When we consider the tremendous increase in recent years of the number of girls and unmarried women at work, we can scarcely doubt that the wife and mother has also felt the influence of the current. The swift translation of women from the home to the field of commercial employment is being felt in varying degrees by women everywhere. The compulsion to earn which the West Side mother has felt and obeyed is a far-reaching and significant one. It presents a problem of vital importance which demands the best efforts of social welfare workers for its solution.

NOTES

1 Of the 370 women visited, 10 per cent had already contracted second marriages. We may suppose that a certain proportion of the 125 widows will take second husbands. Indeed, there were several who were on the eve of doing so.

2 Galsworthy, John: A Commentary: Demos, p. 39. New York, G. P. Putnam's Sons, 1911.

25

"WOMEN WHO WORK AND BABES WHO WEEP – WHAT 'HOME INDUSTRIES' MEAN," IN *THE SOUL MARKET*

Olive Malvery

Source: Olive Malvery, 'Women Who Work and Babes Who Weep – 'What "Home Industries" Mean', in *The Soul Market* (New York, McClure, Phillips, and Company, 1907), pp. 182–201

So much for the sweating shops in the West End, and now to travel eastward, where our poorer sisters pay with life and sight and health – the price of this accursed system.

Since the days when Charles Kingsley, in "Alton Locke," threw a lurid light on the dark ways of "sweating," it would seem that very little headway has been made against this nefarious system, which still continues not only to exist, but to thrive, and that in spite of many enactments and Acts of Parliament dealing with the matter.

My knowledge of the existence of some of the evils of "sweating" is personal. The first time I came into actual touch with some of these slaves in England, I was startled at the ease with which it is possible to drive the proverbial "coach-and-four" through Acts of Parliament.

One day as I was returning home through a part of Brixton, I noticed in the window of one of the houses a card setting forth the fact that the dressmaker within (a German) required apprentices. As I passed, several girls came up from the area door and walked down the street in front of me. I heard some of their remarks. One said: "She's a regular beast, she is! The way she treats that girl's something shameful!" I did not follow the conversation further; but as I was waiting at the station, I bought a local paper, and glancing through the advertisements, I was struck by one which gave the address of the same house that I had lately passed, where the card in the window indicated that the lady who advertised in the paper was one and the same person. The advertisement stated that an apprentice would be received by a dressmaker and taught the trade for a small premium. With the memory of the

 DOI: 10.4324/9780429321078-27

scrap of conversation overheard in the street still ringing in my ears, I resolved that I would make an opportunity as soon as possible of investigating for myself the conditions of life in a dressmaker's shop.

A couple of weeks later I made my way to the same house, carrying the advertisement in my hand. I was admitted and interviewed by a stout, severe-looking woman, who spoke with a strong German accent. She asked me if I had done any work of the sort before. On being answered in the negative, she declared that "apprentices were more nuisance than they were worth," but added that if I could pay the premium down, she might take me in. I inquired how much this premium would be, and was informed that for £10 I would be given six months' training. The conditions were, that I must appear at eight o'clock every morning, and work nominally till 8 p.m., "but," said the lady who was to instruct me, "I don't have no nonsense – work is work, and it's got to be done." It did not require much intelligence to interpret this. I apprenticed myself.

The house where I worked was situated in one of those shabby-genteel streets that abound near the Brixton Road, a street in which poverty tries to hide itself behind clean but painfully cheap and mended lace curtains.

Before entering on a further description, it will be well to state that there are clauses in the Factory Act which limit the hours of work for children under fourteen; there are other sections of the same Act that protect young persons under the age of eighteen, employed in a factory. I knew these regulations, but desired to see how they worked in private places of employment. In the house in this delectable street where I apprenticed myself, I discovered a sufferer totally unprotected by any section of the Act.

"Madame Bavard," as I will call the German slave-driver who occupied this house, and with whom I made only too close an acquaintance, was a dressmaker in a small way. She employed, chiefly, apprentices who gave her a small premium, and worked for a certain time without wages. At the expiration of that period, they were discharged, and new apprentices took their places, so Madame Bavard's income never failed.

It is not with these young people, however, that I wish to deal, miserable as their lives undoubtedly were, for Madame Bavard took the utmost advantage of the long hours allowed her by Parliament to work her employees, and indeed we always worked overtime. But it is of the life of a little white-faced, worn-out child, just over fourteen, I want to write, who, ostensibly employed as a domestic servant, had to help in the workroom when not occupied with house-work.

She lived out, and every morning at 7 a.m., wet or fine, appeared at the house. Her duties commenced by lighting the fire and preparing the breakfast of her mistress. After tidying up, work in the dressmaking-room engaged her until it was time to prepare dinner. This meal finished, and its consequent cleaning-up done, there followed errands to shops for the matching of silks and ribbons; the taking home of finished work, and the catering for the household. Bed-making, scrubbing, window-cleaning, were the recreations of this factotum in the intervals of dressmaking – at which she toiled until 8 p.m. After this, having prepared our supper, she was allowed to go home – to reach which she had to traverse a low neighbourhood. For all this drudgery, she was rewarded with the munificent sum of two shillings a week and her food.

The hours she actually spent in the business of the "workshop" did not exceed those prescribed by the law, which takes no cognisance of time given to domestic work: besides, having just pased the age of fourteen, she was liable under the clauses of the "Domestic Workshop" sections of the Factory Acts, to work from 6 a.m. till 9 p.m. – the hours permitted for those under eighteen. Imagine such hours of work for girls! I tried to help the little creature when possible, but was kept so hard at work that I had little time to do anything beside sewing.

It has been realised in America that the creation of a public sentiment must precede any reform, and to this end an Association – the Consumers' League, to which I have referred – is working in New York City. It was formed with the object of rousing customers to a sense of responsibility for the treatment of workers, and also to enforce obedience to the State Factory Law. Under the "Sweatshop" Law of the State of New York, the manufacture of articles of wearing apparel is now specifically forbidden in any tenement house without a license. For this, application must be made to a Factory Inspector, who, after ascertaining by inspection that the premises are in a clean and sanitary condition, grants such license.

In England, not only is there no license necessary, but no lists need be kept by employers of outside workers, unless "so required by the Secretary of State." So that the inspection of these "domestic workshops" depends upon the order of the Secretary of State.

This half-hearted measure goes far towards explaining the existence of the many fever-dens of the East End – which, under a different system, would be summarily closed.

Within a stone's-throw of the inn chosen by Chaucer as the starting-place of his pilgrims, may be found a nest of the vilest courts in London. One morning I passed under an archway which leads from Tabard Street, on my way to investigate what I consider to be the very worst form of home industry that ever existed in this or any other country. An industry so bad that it attracts only the most destitute and hopeless, and them only at certain seasons of the year, and these must submit to the fate which forces them to toil for foreigners.

Fur-pulling is a terrible means for keeping body and soul together at any time; in the warm weather it is unbearable; therefore many who are driven to the filthy trade in the winter by want of food and lack of rent, desert it entirely in the summer, and seek more wholesome employment in the orchards and hop-fields of adjacent Kent. The trade is almost entirely in the hands of foreigners – Jews mostly – and they give out the work "on contract" to poor English workers. I do not personally know any foreigners engaged in the actual work.

Hare-skins and rabbit-skins are collected all over the country by dealers, and most of these find their way to this part of London. Many skins of this class are also imported from Australia, New Zealand, and elsewhere.

After they are plucked and cleaned, they are made up into bales under hydraulic pressure, and sent off to the manufacturing centres.

The work of a fur-puller consists in removing the long, coarse hairs from the skins, allowing the soft, down-like fur to remain: this is made into felt. Nothing, however, is wasted. The coarse hair that is torn out is used to stuff cheap mattresses, and the skin itself is boiled down to make glue and size.

After much inquiry, I at last found the home of a fur puller. She occupied a small, four-roomed cottage hidden away in a dark alley – a pestilential place indeed! On either side, the houses were overtopped by huge factory buildings which backed on to the cottages and shut them out from sunshine and fresh air. Perhaps it was for this reason that the place was chosen: fur-pullers object to too much air, the slightest draught makes their work almost impossible. It drives the fine hair and fluff with which the work-places of these people is impregnated into their eyes, nostrils, and lungs. It is in this impalpable dust that the chief danger of this unsavoury occupation lies, bronchial catarrh and "fur fever" are two diseases which attack the young worker, and are caused by inhaling this "fluff" and dust.

When I entered the cottage, I at once became acquainted with this distressing feature of the trade. The fluff was everywhere, on the floor, walls, ceilings, and staircases. The place also reeked with the sickly smell of decaying skins, which was so nauseating, that when I got into the room where the "pulling" was actually being done, I felt, for a moment, as if I could not breathe. Not only did the fine hair and dust enter my lungs at every breath, but the overpowering stench arising from the skins, that were heaped everywhere, made me almost sick. Skins were piled upon the table, on which also stood some crockery, denoting that food had been taken recently in this horrible place. In the corner stood a miserable bed – on which also was piled a heap of skins – and in the midst of all this filthy horror a little baby lay fast asleep.

To prevent draught, the window was tightly closed, and for the same reason the door had been tightly shut behind me. In this room three women were working. They were sitting on low stools with a rough wooden trough in front of them. By the side of each was piled a number of skins; those on which they worked were held in the left hand and between the knees, while the right hand grasped a short knife, and on the thumb was worn a kind of guard fastened like a finger-stall. Seizing the long, coarse hairs between the thumb and the edge of the knife, with a wrench they were torn out, and thrown into the trough in front. Afterwards, this hair is carefully collected and taken to the factory. Sixty skins are supposed to produce two pounds of "fluff," as this hair is called. The pay for this work, notwithstanding its unpleasant nature, is extremely poor. An experienced puller can only earn about one and sixpence a day when engaged on some of the skins; a bundle of sixty is called a "turn," and the pullers receive from sevenpence to one and sixpence a "turn." The average price paid is about elevenpence or a shilling. For "furriners," as the Australian and New Zealand furs are called, a slightly higher rate is given, as they take longer to "pull."

The women have to provide their knives and finger-guards from their wages, and the occasional sharpening of the knives is also paid for by the workers. The work is taken home at midday, and is paid for on delivery.

It is a wretched, ill-paid, unhealthy trade. May Heaven help those engaged in it! Many fur-pullers, however, do not consider their trade unhealthy. "Uncomfortable at first, but you soon get used to it," one woman said. "Dust! lor, we don't mind that. We eats it, drinks it, and sleeps on it," said another. "And die on it," she might have added.

"People employing others in this trade ought to be prosecuted by the Society for the Prevention of Cruelty to Animals," said a man from whom I inquired the way to the home of a fur-puller.

There is an industry, however, which brings some beauty into the lives of those engaged at it – albeit their purses may be no heavier than those of others who have enlisted our sympathies.

Artificial flower-making, as practised in France, becomes an art; in England it is too often a bondage, and rarely more than a poorly-paid trade. A Parisian girl wishing to learn this business is taught something of botany, and studies natural flowers, to gain a knowledge of their structure and tints. She learns to copy faithfully every part of a flower – leaf, bud, and blossom. Herein probably lies the secret of French supremacy in this particular line. For years the world has looked to France for artificial flowers. Only once during the last half century has she disappointed her clients, and that was during the dark days of the Franco-Prussian War, when Paris was besieged, and London became the centre of the artificial flower trade. That was a golden time for English manufacturers! Prosperity, however, in this line did not last. The lack of taste and talent in England enabled France to recover the trade directly the war was over, and in London it fell away to what we now find it, a second-rate and poorly-paid one.

I am aware that a healthy interest is at present being taken in this industry, and that several firms are endeavouring to raise the tone of the English flower market. It is to be hoped they will succeed; for the making of artificial flowers is a trade pre-eminently suited to women and home-work.

I have two young friends in Islington, who earn a living at this trade, and it was to them I went, when seeking to enter the "Profession." A description of their home and manner of working may be interesting. They are cousins and live together, occupying two unfurnished rooms, for which they pay seven shillings a week. One room they use as a bedroom, the other as a sitting and work room. They are employed by a wholesale firm whose business premises are situated at Clerkenwell. As they are very clever and very diligent, they earn a fairly good living. Their day commences about 7.30 a.m. Having cooked and eaten their breakfast, they start work, adhering to the same hours they used to keep in the days when they both made flowers in a factory, although, as they point out, they really work fewer hours now, because they spend no time going to or coming from business.

My friends are chiefly engaged in cheap rose-making; this is the best paid branch of that class of work, and only clever hands are engaged upon it. It is paid for at the rate of two and sixpence a gross, and each flower must have leaves, and at least one bud. Out of this money glue has to be provided, as well as several other necessary odds and ends.

By working hard for about ten hours a day, they are able, each, to earn an average of fifteen shilling a week. Not an enormous sum for an artistic trade that requires skill and patience!

Through their introduction I became acquainted with a poor woman who worked on the cheapest and commonest kinds of artificial flowers, assisted by a crippled daughter. Their home was one of the neatest, brightest little places I have ever seen amongst the poor homes I have visited. As is usual with the respectable poor, it contained two rooms. I have generally found that where a number of persons are content to live in one room without an effort to acquire more, it is either that they have put themselves into bondage with the publican and money-lender, and have lost all ambition and strength of character, or they live in a neighbourhood where the property is in the hands of dishonest landlords – aliens mostly. It is not, however, always poverty that drives a family into one room – a cabinet-maker who did small work at home, regularly moved into one room in the winter, "because he did not like to go to bed in the cold." It did not seem to occur to the man that a fire in the bedroom would have obviated this inconvenience – had he given up his beer, he could have afforded the fire and two rooms.

To return to the widow and her daughter: as I say, they occupied two rooms, one of which they used as their workplace. The afternoon I called on them, this room looked quite gay with the coloured material on which they were working. The daughter was seated on a sofa, surrounded with pillows, busily engaged making bunches of violets – this is the worst paid of all the branches – she received 1½d. only for a gross of blossoms. It was interesting to watch the thin white fingers of this poor crippled girl deftly forming the pretty blooms, while her mother occupied herself in making cornflowers, paid for at the rate of one and sixpence a gross. By working early and late, they were able to earn about fifteen shillings a week, and had but one complaint – trade was slack! "We had to sit idle two days last week," said the daughter, with a wan smile.

"I don't know," said the mother, "if they will give me any more out this week when I take these back. We don't mind if we can earn enough to pay the rent; it takes such a little to keep us, and anything is better than the 'big house.'"

I have found that the fear of the big house – that is, the Union – is a large factor in modern commercialism. To take work at any price rather than go into the workhouse is the resolve of many a poor worker, and the employer often trades on this, and endeavours to find out just how low he can cut the price before his employé is forced into the Union.

The Saturday morning after, when I called on my poor friends, I found them in great distress. The mother had taken the flowers to the factory, but had unfortunately offended the forewoman, whose duty it is to take in and examine the flowers made by the outworkers. This person had spitefully refused to pass more than half the poor woman's work, therefore she had returned home with scarcely any money, as from the amount due to her for the work accepted, there had to be deducted the cost of the material used on the flowers which were condemned.

Both mother and daughter were in tears. I determined to help them, and after a deal of persuasion I induced the mother to return with me and interview her employer. We insisted on seeing this gentleman. I put the flowers before him and asked him to point out in what way they were defective. He proved to be not altogether an unreasonable man. After demurring, not so much at the quality of the work, as on the grounds of his having "to keep up the authority of the forewoman, don't you know!" he finally passed the work himself, and the widow got her mite.

In this trade, as in many others of the same class, the facilities for employing children is a great temptation to the poor home-worker. School is often neglected, and the School Board visitor is met with every excuse and subterfuge imaginable. "If the kids don't help, I can't make both ends meet," is a remark one often hears. And Tommy and Lizzie, the home-worker's babies, become conscripts in the army of labour at an age when the children of the rich have barely started at the kindergarten class.

If one visits the streets in the houses of which much home-work is being done, one will only notice – during the interval of school-time – the smallest children playing; the others are busy helping to earn their dinners.

An amusing story is told of a little girl from Hoxton, who saw real roses for the first time, and wanted to know who made them. Being told "God," she answered that "Gawd made better flowers than her Aunt Poll; 'spects He has more time to stick'em together."

Take, for instance, match-box making. Few fingers are too old and few too tiny to help the match-box maker; children and old people, therefore, are engaged in this occupation perhaps more than in any other. It is a trade that requires but little training, and is very quickly learned. Much diligence and industry – but little skill – is required to earn a scanty livelihood. The pay for this work is so mean that an adult, unassisted by children, could not earn a living, and few makers work without this help. This industry is the last resource of the very poor, and the first occupation of their children.

That matches are too cheap, is the verdict of every person to whom I have spoken on the subject. No one would mind, as far as I can discover, if matches cost twice as much as they do now. If twice as much was paid for box-making, the lives of many poor women and numbers of children would be rendered more endurable. Matches are cheapened at the cost of human happiness. Weary, ill-fed women, and mirthless, playless children – these are the prices to be added to the cheap box of matches.

Some economists tell us that we cannot pay more for our match manufacture because of foreign competitors, that we have to sell matches cheap, not because the consumers will not pay more, but because the foreign manufacturer supplies his so cheaply. If this is so, the sooner some check is put upon this dumping, so that the trade may be in a position to pay a living wage to those engaged in it, the better it will be for many of our women and children.

My friend, Mrs. R., is a match-box maker, and she lives in a small street near Bow Road. She is a married woman with five children. Her husband describes himself as a "casual labourer." I think a better description would be "confirmed loafer." The woman supports herself and her children by her match-box making. Her husband earns but little, and what he earns is spent in beer and tobacco. Mrs. R. rents three rooms for six shillings per week. In one room a lodger sleeps with two of her boys; for this accommodation he pays two shillings a week, thus reducing her rent to four shillings. Her average earnings, when all her children are well, she estimates to be about fourteen shillings a week.

"It runs a bit more when the children 'ave their 'olidays," was one of her remarks. I took a room in a house next to hers and joined her for a little time at her trade.

The daily work in this house commenced as early as 6.30 a.m. A little work was done and then breakfast had to be prepared. We did not fare sumptuously. Weak tea, bread and treacle for the children, and bread and margarine for the elder ones. This eaten, the children went off to school and the man to "loaf." Mrs. R. and I worked at box-making all the morning. Any tidying up or domestic duties were left to the children to do.

A short time after twelve noon, the little ones used to return from school. One of the tables was cleared of the materials used in the box-making, and a meagre dinner hurriedly prepared and placed upon it – prepared not by the woman, for she had to continue working, but by one of the elder children. After bolting their food, these victims of toil began work at once. The dinner usually consisted of bread and cheese. On rare occasions there was a bit of bacon or fried fish; at times, in the winter, the children told me they fetched soup from a neighbouring charitable institution. Very little time was spent over meals in this house: the table was cleared, and the children continued work until the last minute before departing for school. The youngest, a tot of five years old, "'elped muvver" by pressing down the pasted tissue-paper which is fastened round the boxes to keep them together.

Every one of the family, except the lazy father, had his or her particular work to do on the boxes. The mother folded the material into shape, and put on the printed paper; another made the "drawer," as the inside is called. One of the biggest children fastened on sand-papers on which the match is struck. This is the work that the little ones most object to, "it 'urts yer fingers so!" Poor little fingers, that ought to have been making daisy-chains, or picking meadow flowers on those warm June days I was with them working – or rather slaving – for existence in a hot, stuffy room.

One of the very smallest of the children "boxed up," as fitting the "drawers" into the "covers" is called. This is absolutely wasted labour, because they have to be separated in the factory before they can be filled. Match-box makers in factories are not asked to do this, but home workers are obliged to deliver theirs so fitted.

The price that Mrs. R. was paid for her work is the price that rules throughout the trade – 2¼d. per gross. Think of it! 288 separate articles, from the drawer to

THE MATCHMAKER'S HOME—BABES WHO TOIL.

THE OLD CLOTHES MARKET AT ROME, WHERE INTENDING EMIGRANTS FIND THEIR OUTFITS.

the cover, to be handled for 2¼d! The price is monstrous! Even the deft fingers of this woman could not earn a penny an hour unless she was assisted by her children, and then, all she could hope to make was about twopence an hour. Out of this, she had to provide fire to dry the boxes, paste for fastening, and hemp to bind the boxes up in parcels when finished, for that is how they must be delivered at the factory. Then there is the time taken up in carrying the finished work there, the waiting while the parcels are counted and the work examined, and for fresh work to be given out. Mrs. R. was known as a "steady hand." She always returned her work at the time she was asked to do, therefore she obtained regular employment – but what an employment! A veritable life of slavery. No time for motherhood, affection, or pleasure. Life one continual struggle, with the wolf "Hunger" ever on her very hearth-stone! Home a factory, her children human machines, deprived of all that makes child-life rosy and bright, their health undermined by long hours spent in the close confinement of overfull rooms – work, school, and work again till bed-time – that was the daily routine.

"We've got to work, or we will starve," Mrs. R. impressed on me. Why? Well, perhaps first, because there is no law to compel men of the drunken, loafing type of this father, to work and support their families in a proper manner. Secondly, because of the curse of the foreign competition which forces the wages of this industry down below a living margin.

Surely it is a disgrace to our civilisation that any commodity should be produced at the expense of the health, strength, and happiness of frail women and children, who have to work long hours at a starving wage, in order that the consumer may be supplied at a cheap rate.

"Oh, God, to think that bread's so dear,
And flesh and blood so cheap."
– HOOD.

"But the child's sob curseth deeper in the silence,
Than the strong man in his wrath."
– *Cry of the Children.*

I was much struck during the descents I made into Poverty Kingdom to find in how many cases the distress, overwork, and evilly bad pay was due to the trades worked in being monopolised by foreigners. And then again, the utter misery of the lives of the workers caused by overcrowding, insanitary condition of the houses, inability to claim a sufficient water supply, and all the ugly results of desperate over-population in certain districts, was due almost entirely to the fact that the property in those neighbourhoods had been, bit by bit, acquired by our alien friends.

If I have to use severe language in describing the lives of the poverty-stricken creatures who are engaged in home industries, it must not be supposed that I believe the blame rests with them, though I am bound to admit, sorrowfully enough, what will, I am sure, be acknowledged by every philanthropic society in England to be true, that a great deal of the want and destitution is caused by the fact that the men who ought to be supporting healthy and happy families by legitimate work, spend 95 per cent. of their earnings in the public-house – that is, if they are earning at all, as for the most part, the husbands of the women engaged in home employments are irredeemable loafers. The public-houses are very often held by foreigners, though this is not by any means universal. But there exists an evil as great, I deem it, as the public-house, which is virtually the invention and monopoly of aliens. This is the sister institution of the public-house – I speak of the pawn-shop, of which almost every street boasts one.

I found, during my life with the home-workers, that it was a usual practice of these distressed and over-driven people to walk out with a bundle containing almost all their worldly possessions on the Monday morning, to leave them on their way to work, at the pawn-shop – from which place they were redeemed on Saturday evening. In return for these clothes and household goods, they received small sums of money, for which I have known them to pay 100 and even 200 per cent.; but not being able to calculate, they could never be brought to see how fearfully expensive this manner of raising money was.

Among the several branches of the home industry trade into which I entered for the purpose of learning the conditions under which people employed in them live, was that of making petticoats – the silk petticoats and blouses one sees in most drapers' shops in London.

These two articles are made partly at home and partly in the workshops. I knew a woman who was in the petticoat trade, and another in the blouse-making industry. These workers allowed me to stay with them for a little time and find out how the work was done. The woman who made blouses lived in a room in one of the streets off the Euston Road; about this locality there are a great many tailors' shops which are run by Germans, Poles, and Jews. The woman lived alone – she was a widow – and she procured for me a small room in the same house in order that I might be able to help her with her work. The room was a mere cupboard made of match-boarding. For this den I was obliged to pay half-a-crown a week. The house contained fifty people. I promised to pay my friend two and sixpence a week for teaching me the trade, and giving me work besides. I knew, of course, that I could not be a very valuable hand. I settled myself in the room one afternoon, and spent the evening with the woman, turning down the hems of the endless lengths of silk frills which were to be sewn on to the petticoats. It was agreed that in the morning I was to accompany the woman to the shop, and get from the "boss" some more work.

The tiny room was furnished with a small stove, upon which simple cooking might be done; but as long as I was there I did not see the woman cook anything except a bit of bacon.

She generally went out and got a meal "of sorts" at some cheap eating-house in the neighbourhood – it saved time, she said. I have described these eating-houses before, they are all more or less alike. But what the woman always did have ready was an enamelled tea-pot, full of an awful decoction she called tea, which rested on the stove all day and half the night, and was replenished with water from time to time. This drink the woman took while she worked. It kept her awake, she said, and "was comforting-like."

That night she worked till 2 a.m., and before I left the room we had folded up and made ready seven petticoats. Into these garments she had put literally hundreds of yards of stitching, providing the cotton herself, had made three buttonholes for fastening the plaquet-hole of each one, sewing on three buttons to match, and putting two drawing ribbons into each garment. For each of these finished petticoats she received the magnificent sum of fourpence, the materials, except the sewing cotton, were provided, the garments and frills were cut out at the shop.

Next morning we went together to the shop. The woman handed in her work, which was minutely examined by the "boss" himself. He gave out to her another half-dozen petticoats, the cut-out silk for each being carefully folded together. Then she introduced me. I was so desperately anxious to find out where this man was sending the garments for final sale, that I forgot myself so far as to ask him where he sold them and for what price. I shall never forget the look he gave me – his face was absolutely distorted with passion. He poured forth such a volume of abuse, that I was really afraid he would commit some act of violence. My poor friend was frightened almost out of her wits. He threatened to turn us both out of the shop, but after a great deal of persuasion and humble apologies, he calmed down a little. I explained I was anxious for work myself, and thinking that he mightn't have any for me, hoped he might be able to recommend me to the people with whom he dealt. This seemed to make matters all right, for he gave the woman two extra petticoats for me to sew, remarking politely that as "I was such a – fool," I wouldn't be able to do more, and also threatening that if the work was not up to the mark, she would have to pay for the material spoilt. The materials, I suppose, at the most liberal estimation, could not have cost, at wholesale prices, above five shillings. We took home our work. I think, even when I was engaged once in cutting tin during a visit to a tin factory, my fingers have never ached more than they did after sixteen hours of almost continuous work at those detestable petticoats. For me there was a hope of change, but for the other poor toiler, nothing in the world to look forward to but death.

It would, of course, be extremely difficult to control this sort of work – the very employees themselves would endeavour to hide the evils of the system for fear of losing their only means of livelihood. It would be in such cases as these that the Consumers' League would set its machinery in motion – follow the petticoats from the Jew's shop back to the women's rooms where they were made, and then to the large houses which bought them wholesale. These garments would then be condemned as having been manufactured with what might be called the price of blood. Let us hope that no decent woman would purchase them.

I found afterwards that these very petticoats made by us were sold to a large, well-known West End firm, who, in their turn, sold them to customers for prices ranging from fifteen shillings to thirty shillings. What the Jew's profit was I am unable to say, but my experience with the class would convince me that he made an enormous profit on each. I have found that almost invariably the middleman, who is really the actual sweater, is a foreigner – either German or Polish.

My next essay with the needle was when I joined forces with a woman who made blouses. She lived near Paddington, and also worked for a Jew. He had a shop in which he employed twenty-two women – all English – nearly all of them took away work to do at home besides. In the shop the blouses were cut out and sewn together – at home the finishing was done, any trimming that might be necessary, the making of button-holes, putting on of buttons or hooks, and folding the goods.

For work that occupied her from eight in the morning till eight at night, in the shop, with forty minutes for dinner in the middle of the day and half an hour for tea, and again the whole evening – except the hour that was spent in lighting her fire and getting some sort of meal ready, and in tidying her room – till one and two in the morning, my friend earned sixteen shillings a week. She turned out on an average from five to eight blouses a day. These were not of the very plain, cheap kind, but were made of pretty muslins and silk, were trimmed more or less elaborately with lace, and sold from six shillings to twenty shillings in a shop not far off.

26

MARRIAGE AS A TRADE

Cecily Hamilton

Source: Cecily Hamilton, *Marriage as a Trade* (New York, Moffat, Yard and Company, 1909)

PREFACE

THE only excuse for this book is the lack of books on the subject with which it deals – the trade aspect of marriage. That is to say, wifehood and motherhood considered as a means of livelihood for women.

I shall not deny for an instant that there are aspects of matrimony other than the trade aspect; but upon these there is no lack of a very plentiful literature – the love of man and woman has been written about since humanity acquired the art of writing.

The love of man and woman is, no doubt, a thing of infinite importance; but also of infinite importance is the manner in which woman earns her bread and the economic conditions under which she enters the family and propagates the race. Thus an inquiry into the circumstances under which the wife and mother plies her trade seems to me quite as necessary and justifiable as an inquiry into the conditions of other and less important industries – such as mining or cotton-spinning. It will not be disputed that the manner in which a human being earns his livelihood tends to mould and influence his character – to warp or to improve it. The man who works amidst brutalizing surroundings is apt to become brutal; the man from whom intelligence is demanded is apt to exercise it. Particular trades tend to develop particular types; the boy who becomes a soldier will not turn out in all respects the man he would have been had he decided to enter a stockbroker's office. In the same way the trade of marriage tends to produce its own particular type, and my contention is that woman, as we know her, is largely the product of the conditions imposed upon her by her staple industry.

I am not of those who are entirely satisfied with woman as she is; on the contrary, I consider that we are greatly in need of improvement, mental, physical and moral. And it is because I desire such improvement – not only in our own interests but in that of the race in general – that I desire to see an alteration in the conditions of our staple industry. I have no intention of attacking the institution of marriage in itself – the life companionship of man and woman; I merely wish to point out

 DOI: 10.4324/9780429321078-28

that there are certain grave disadvantages attaching to that institution as it exists to-day. These disadvantages I believe to be largely unnecessary and unavoidable; but at present they are very real and the results produced by them are anything but favourable to the mental, physical and moral development of women.

MARRIAGE AS A TRADE

I

THE sense of curiosity is, as a rule, aroused in us only by the unfamiliar and the unexpected. What custom and long usage has made familiar we do not trouble to inquire into but accept without comment or investigation; confusing the actual with the inevitable, and deciding, slothfully enough, that the thing that is is, likewise the thing that was and is to be. In nothing is this inert and slothful attitude of mind more marked than in the common, unquestioning acceptance of the illogical and unsatisfactory position occupied by women. And it is the prevalence of that attitude of mind which is the only justification for a book which purports to be nothing more than the attempt of an unscientific woman to explain, honestly and as far as her limitations permit, the why and wherefore of some of the disadvantages under which she and her sisters exist – the reason why their place in the world into which they were born is often so desperately and unnecessarily uncomfortable.

I had better, at the outset, define the word "woman" as I understand and use it, since it is apt to convey two distinct and differing impressions, according to the sex of the hearer. My conception of woman is inevitably the feminine conception; a thing so entirely unlike the masculine conception of woman that it is eminently needful to define the term and make my meaning clear; lest, when I speak of woman in my own tongue, my reader, being male, translate the expression, with confusion as the result.

By a woman, then, I understand an individual human being whose life is her own concern; whose worth, in my eyes (worth being an entirely personal matter) is in no way advanced or detracted from by the accident of marriage; who does not rise in my estimation by reason of a purely physical capacity for bearing children, or sink in my estimation through a lack of that capacity. I am quite aware, of course, that her life, in many cases, will have been moulded to a great extent by the responsibilities of marriage and the care of children; just as I am aware that the lives of most of the men with whom I am acquainted have been moulded to a great extent by the trade or profession by which they earn their bread. But my judgment of her and appreciation of her are a personal judgment and appreciation, having nothing to do with her actual or potential relations, sexual or maternal, with other people. In short, I never think of her either as a wife or as a mother – I separate the woman from her attributes. To me she is an entity in herself; and if, on meeting her for the first time, I inquire whether or no she is married, it is only because I wish to know whether I am to address her as Mrs. or Miss.

That, frankly and as nearly as I can define it, is my attitude towards my own sex; an attitude which, it is almost needless to say, I should not insist upon if I did not believe that it was fairly typical and that the majority of women, if they analyzed their feelings on the subject, would find that they regarded each other in much the same way .

It is hardly necessary to point out that the mental attitude of the average man towards woman is something quite different from this. It is a mental attitude reminding one of that of the bewildered person who could not see the wood for the trees. To him the accidental factor in woman's life is the all-important and his conception of her has never got beyond her attributes – and certain only of these. As far as I can make out, he looks upon her as something having a definite and necessary physical relation to man; without that definite and necessary relation, she is, as the cant phrase goes "incomplete." That is to say, she is not woman at all – until man has made her so. Until the moment when he takes her in hand she is merely the raw material of womanhood – the undeveloped and unfinished article.

Without sharing in the smallest degree this estimate of her own destiny, any fair-minded woman must admit its advantages from the point of view of the male – must sympathize with the pleasurable sense of importance, creative power, even of artistry, which such a conviction must impart. To take the imperfect and undeveloped creature and, with a kiss upon her lips and a ring upon her finger, to make of her a woman, perfect and complete – surely a prerogative almost divine in its magnificence, most admirable, most enviable!

It is this consciousness, expressed or unexpressed, (frequently the former) of his own supreme importance in her destiny that colours every thought and action of man towards woman. Having assumed that she is incomplete without him, he draws the quite permissible conclusion that she exists only for the purpose of attaining to completeness through him – and that where she does not so attain it, the unfortunate creature is, for all practical purposes, non-existent. To him womanhood is summed up in one of its attributes – wifehood, or its unlegalized equivalent. Language bears the stamp of the idea that woman is a wife, actually, or in embryo. To most men – perhaps to all – the girl is some man's wife that is to be; the married woman some man's wife that is; the widow some man's wife that was; the spinster some man's wife that should have been – a damaged article, unfit for use, unsuitable. Therefore a negligible quantity.

I have convinced myself, by personal observation and inquiry, that my description of the male attitude in this respect is in no way exaggerated. It has, for instance, fallen to my lot, over and over again, to discuss with men – most of them distinctly above the average in intelligence – questions affecting the welfare and conditions of women. And over and over again, after listening to their views for five minutes or so, I have broken in upon them and pulled them up with the remark that they were narrowing down the subject under discussion – that what they were considering was not the claim of women in general, but the claim of a particular class – the class of wives and mothers. I may add that the remark has invariably been received with an expression of extreme astonishment. And is it not on record that Henley once dashed across a manuscript the terse pronouncement, "I take no interest in childless women"? Comprehensive; and indicating a confusion in the author's mind between the terms woman and breeding-machine. Did it occur to him, I wonder, that the poor objects of his scorn might venture to take some interest in themselves? Probably he did not credit them with so much presumption.

The above has, I hope, explained in how far my idea of woman differs from male ideas on the same subject and has also made it clear that I do not look upon women as persons whose destiny it is to be married. On the contrary, I hold, and hold very strongly, that the narrowing down of woman's hopes and ambitions to the sole pursuit and sphere of marriage is one of the principal causes of the various disabilities, economic and otherwise, under which she labours to-day. And I hold, also, that this concentration of all her hopes and ambitions on the one object was, to a great extent, the result of artificial pressure, of unsound economic and social conditions – conditions which forced her energy into one channel, by the simple expedient of depriving it of every other outlet, and made marriage practically compulsory.

To say the least of it, marriage is no more essentially necessary to woman than to man – one would imagine that it was rather the other way about. There are a good many drawbacks attached to the fulfilment of a woman's destiny; in an unfettered state of existence it is possible that they might weigh more heavily with her than they can do at present – being balanced, and more than balanced, by artificial means. I am inclined to think that they would. The institution of marriage by capture, for instance, has puzzled many inquirers into the habits of primitive man. It is often, I believe, regarded as symbolic; but why should it not point to a real reluctance to be reduced to permanent servitude on the part of primitive woman – a reluctance comprehensible enough, since, primitive woman's wants being few and easily supplied by herself, there was no need for her to exchange possession of her person for the means of existence?

It is Nietzsche, if I remember rightly, who has delivered himself of the momentous opinion that everything in woman is a riddle, and that the answer to the riddle is child-bearing. Child-bearing certainly explains some qualities in woman – for instance, her comparative fastidiousness in sexual relations – but not all. If it did, there would be no riddle – yet Nietzsche admits that one exists. Nor is he alone in his estimate of the "mysterious" nature of woman; her unfathomable and erratic character, her peculiar aptitude for appearing "uncertain, coy, and hard to please", has been insisted upon time after time – insisted upon alike as a charm and a deficiency. A charm because of its unexpected, a deficiency because of its unreasonable, quality. Woman, in short, is not only a wife and mother, but a thoroughly incomprehensible wife and mother.

Now it seems to me that a very simple explanation of this mystery which perpetually envelops our conduct and impulses can be found in the fact that the fundamental natural laws which govern them have never been ascertained or honestly sought for. Or rather – since the fundamental natural laws which govern us are the same large and simple laws which govern other animals, man included –

though they have been ascertained, the masculine intellect has steadfastly and stubbornly refused to admit that they can possibly apply to us in the same degree as to every other living being. As a substitute for these laws, he suggests explanations of his own – for the most part flattering to himself. He believes, apparently, that we live in a world apart, governed by curious customs and regulations of our own – customs and regulations which "have no fellow in the universe." Once the first principle of natural law was recognized as applying to us, we should cease to be so unfathomable, erratic, and unexpected to the wiseacres and poets who spend their time in judging us by rule of thumb, and expressing amazement at the unaccountable and contradictory results.

I do not know whether it is essentially impossible for man to approach us in the scientific spirit, but it has not yet been done. (To approach motherhood or marriage in the scientific spirit is, of course, not in the least the same thing.) His attitude towards us has been by turns – and sometimes all at once – adoring, contemptuous, sentimental, and savage – anything, in short, but open-minded and deductive. The result being that different classes, generations, and peoples have worked out their separate and impressionistic estimates of woman's meaning in the scheme of things – the said estimates frequently clashing with those of other classes, generations, and peoples. The Mahometan, for instance, after careful observation from his point of view, decided that she was flesh without a soul, and to be treated accordingly; the troubadour seems to have found in her a spiritual incentive to aspiration in deed and song. The early Fathers of the Church, who were in the habit of giving troubled and nervous consideration to the subject, denounced her, at spasmodic intervals, as sin personified. What the modern man understands by woman I have already explained; and he further expects his theory to materialize and embody itself in a being who combines the divergent qualities of an inspiration and a good general servant. He is often disappointed.

All these are rule of thumb definitions, based on insufficient knowledge and inquiry, which, each in its turn, has been accepted, acted upon, and found wanting. Each of the generations and classes mentioned – and many more beside – has worked out its own theory of woman's orbit (round man); and has subsequently found itself in the position of the painstaking astronomer who, after having mapped the pathway of a newly-discovered heavenly body to his own satisfaction, suddenly finds his calculations upset, and the heavenly body swerving off through space towards some hitherto unexpected centre of attraction. The theory of the early Fathers was upset before it was enunciated – for sin personified had wept at the foot of the Cross, and men adored her for it. The modern angel with the cookery-book under her wing has expressed an open and pronounced dislike to domestic service, and cheerfully discards her wings to fight her way into the liberal professions. And those who hold fast to the Nietzschean theory that motherhood is the secret and justification of woman's existence, must be somewhat bewildered by latter-day episcopal lamentations over the unwillingness of woman to undergo the pains and penalties of childbirth, and by the reported intention of an American State Legislature to stimulate a declining birth-rate by the payment of one dollar for each child born. One feels that the strength of an instinct that has, in an appreciable number of cases, to be stimulated by the offer of four shillings and twopence must have been somewhat overestimated. No wonder woman is a mystery in her unreliability; she has broken every law of her existence, and does so day by day.

As a matter of fact, the various explanations which have been given for woman's existence can be narrowed down to two – her husband and her child. Male humanity has wobbled between two convictions – the one, that she exists for the entire benefit of contemporary mankind; the other, that she exists for the entire benefit of the next generation. The latter is at present the favourite. One consideration only male humanity has firmly refused to entertain – that she exists in any degree whatsoever for the benefit of herself. In consequence, woman is the one animal from whom he demands that it shall deviate from, and act in defiance of, the first law of nature – self-preservation.

It seems baldly ridiculous, of course, to state in so many words the that first and iron law applies to women as well as to men, birds, and beetles. No one in cold blood or cold ink would contradict the obvious statement; but all the same, I maintain that I am perfectly justified in asserting that the average man does mentally and unconsciously except the mass of women from the workings of that universal law.

To give a simple and familiar instance. Year by year there crops up in the daily newspapers a grumbling and sometimes acrid correspondence on the subject of the incursion of women into a paid labour market formerly monopolized by their brothers. (The unpaid labour market, of course, has always been open to them.) The tone taken by the objector is instructive and always the same. It is pointed out to us that we are working for less than a fair wage; that we are taking the bread out of the mouths of men; that we are filching the earnings of a possible husband and thereby lessening, or totally destroying, our chances of matrimony.

The first objection is, of course, legitimate, and is shared by the women to whom it applies; from the others one can only infer that it is an impertinence in a woman to be hungry, and that, in the opinion of a large number of persons who write to the newspapers, the human female is a creature capable of living on air and the hopes of a possible husband. The principle that it is impolite to mention a certain organ of the body which requires to be replenished two or three times a day is, in the case of a woman, carried so far that it is considered impolite of her even to possess that organ; and as a substitute for the wages wherewith she buys food to fill it, she is offered the lifting of a hat and the resignation of a seat in a tramcar. She rejects the offer, obeys the first law of nature, and is rebuked for it – the human male, bred in the conviction that she lives for him alone, standing aghast. Some day he will discover that woman does not support life only in order to obtain a husband, but frequently obtains a husband only in order to support life.

The above is, to my mind, a clear and familiar instance of the manner in which man is accustomed to take for granted our exemption from a law from which there is no exemption. It matters not whether or no he believes, in so many words, that we need not eat in order that we may not die; the point is, that he acts as if he believed it. (The extreme reluctance of local authorities to spend any of the money at their disposal on unemployed women is a case in point. It would be ridiculous to ascribe it to animosity towards the women themselves – it must arise, therefore, from a conviction that the need of the foodless woman is not so pressing as the need of the foodless man.) And it is because I have so often come in contact with the state of mind that makes such delusions possible, that I have thought it necessary to insist on the fact that self-preservation is the first law of our being. The purpose of race-preservation, which is commonly supposed to be the excuse for our existence, is, and must be, secondary and derivative; it is quite impossible for a woman to bring children into the world unless she has first obtained the means of supporting her own life. How to eat, how to maintain existence, is the problem that has confronted woman, as well as man, since the ages dawned for her. Other needs and desires may come later; but the first call of life is for the means of supporting it.

To support life it is necessary to have access to the fruits of the earth, either directly – as in the case of the agriculturist – or indirectly, and through a process of exchange as the price of work done in other directions. And in this process of exchange woman, as compared with her male fellow-worker, has always been at a disadvantage. The latter, even where direct access to the earth was denied to him, has usually been granted some measure of choice as to the manner in which he would pay for the necessities the earth produced for him – that is to say, he was permitted to select the trade by which he earned his livelihood. From woman, who has always been far more completely excluded from direct access to the necessities of life, who has often been barred, both by law and by custom, from the possession of property, one form of payment was demanded, and one only. It was demanded of her that she should enkindle and satisfy the desire of the male, who would thereupon admit her to such share of the property he possessed or earned as should seem good to him. In other words, she exchanged, by the ordinary process of barter, possession of her person for the means of existence.

Whether such a state of things is natural or unnatural I do not pretend to say; but it is, I understand, peculiar to women, having no exact counterpart amongst the females of other species. Its existence, at any rate, justifies us in regarding marriage as essentially (from the woman's point of view) a commercial or trade undertaking. By marriage she earned her bread; and as the instinct of self-preservation drove man forth to hunt, to till the soil, to dig beneath it – to cultivate his muscles and his brain so that he might get the better of nature and his rivals – so brute necessity and the instinct of self-preservation in woman urged and enjoined on her the cultivation of those narrow and particular qualities of mind and body whereby desire might be excited and her wage obtained.

A man who was also a poet has thoughtfully explained that

> "Man's love is of man's life a thing apart,
> 'Tis woman's whole existence."

(It must be very pleasant to be a man and to entertain that conviction.) Translated into feminine and vulgar prose, the effusion runs something like this -

The housekeeping trade is the only one open to us – so we enter the housekeeping trade in order to live. This is not always quite the same as entering the housekeeping trade in order to love.

No one can imagine that it is the same who has ever heard one haggard, underpaid girl cry to another, in a burst of bitter confidence -

"I would marry any one, to get out of this."

Which, if one comes to think of it, is hard on "any one."

VII

ONE peculiarity of the trade at which so many women earn their livelihood I have, as yet, hardly touched upon. It is this: that however arduous and exacting the labour that trade entails – and the rough manual work of most households is done by women – it is not paid except by a wage of subsistence. There may be exceptions, of course, but, as a general rule, the work done by the wife and mother in the home is paid for merely by supplying her with the necessaries of existence – food, lodging, and clothing. She is fed and lodged on the same principle as a horse is fed and lodged – so that she may do her work, her cooking, her cleaning, her sewing, and the tending and rearing of her children. She may do it very well or she may do it very badly; but beyond food, lodging, and a certain amount of clothing, she can claim no wage for it. In short, her work in the home is not recognized either by the State or by the individual citizen (except in occasional instances) as work which has any commercial value.

There must, of course, be some reason why such intrinsically important work as the rearing of children and ministering to the comfort of the community should be held in such poor esteem that it is paid for at the lowest possible rate – subsistence rate. (Which means, of course, that wages in that particular branch of work have been forced just as low as they can go, since human beings cannot continue to exist without the means of supporting life.) And the principal reason for this state of things I take to be the compulsory nature of the trade. Given a sufficiently large number of persons destined and educated from birth for one particular calling, with no choice at all in the matter, and with every other calling and means of livelihood sternly barred to them, and you have all the conditions necessary for the forcing down of wages to the lowest possible point to which they will go – subsistence point. In that calling labour will be as cheap as the heart of the employer could desire; and incidentally it will tend to become what ill-paid labour always tends to become – inefficient. Exactly the same condition of affairs would prevail in any other trade – mining or boiler-making, for instance – if immense numbers of boys were brought up to be miners or boiler-makers, and informed that whatever their needs or desires, whatever the state of the labour market in those particular callings, they could not turn their abilities into any other direction. Under those circumstances miners and boiler-makers would probably work for their keep and nothing more, as the ordinary wife has to do.

I shall be told, of course, that the position of a husband is not that of an ordinary employer of labour, and that the financial relations of a man and his wife are complicated by considerations of affection and mutual interest which make it quite impossible to estimate the exact wage-earning value of the wife's services in the household, or the price which she receives for them in other things than money. Even if, for the sake of argument, this be admitted as a general rule, it does not invalidate my point, which is that the compulsory nature of woman's principal trade is quite sufficient, in itself, to account for the fact that the workers in that trade are not deemed worthy of anything more than a wage of subsistence. Considerations of sentiment and affection may help to keep her direct monetary remuneration down; but to bring it down in the first instance nothing more was needed than compulsory overcrowding of the "domestic service" market.

That the wage of subsistence – the board, lodging, and clothing – dealt out to a married woman is often board, lodging, and clothing on a very liberal and comfortable scale, does not alter the fact that it is essentially a wage of subsistence, regulated by the idea of what is necessary for subsistence in the particular class to which she may happen to belong. The plutocrat who wishes his wife to entertain cannot habitually feed her on fish and chips from round the corner, or renew her wardrobe in an old-clothes shop. But she does not get twelve-course dinners and dresses from the Rue de la Paix because she has earned them by extra attention to her duties as a wife and mother, but because they are necessary qualifications for the place in his household which her husband wishes her to take – because, without them, she could not fulfil the duties that he requires of her. The monetary reward of wifehood and motherhood depends entirely on the life, the good luck and the good nature of another person; the strictest attention to duty on the part of a wife and mother is of no avail without that. The really hard labour of housework and rearing children is done in those households where the wage of subsistence is lowest; and the women who receive most money from their husbands are precisely those who pass on the typical duties of a wife and mother to other persons – housekeepers, cooks, nurses, and governesses. Excellence in the trade is no guarantee of reward, which is purely a matter of luck; work, however hard, will not bring about that measure of independence, more or less comparative, which is attained by successful work in other trades. Dependence, in short, is the essence of wifehood as generally understood by the masculine mind.

Under normal and favourable conditions, then, a married woman without private means of her own obtains a wage of subsistence for the fulfillment of the duties required of her in her husband's household. Under unfavourable (but not very abnormal) conditions she does not even obtain that. In the case of the large army of married women who support idle or invalid husbands by paid labour outside the home, the additional work inside the home is carried on gratis, and without a suggestion of payment of any kind.

I am inclined to believe that the principle that payment should be made for domestic service rendered does not really enter into the question of a wife's wages; that those wages (of subsistence) are paid simply for the possession of her person, and that the other arts and accomplishments she may possess are not supposed to have any exchange value. At any rate, a mistress, from whom the domestic arts are not expected, is often just as expensively kept as a wife – which seems to point to my conclusion. What Mr. John Burns has called a woman's "duty and livelihood" is, in the strict sense of the term, not her livelihood at all. Her livelihood, as an ordinary wife, is a precarious dependence upon another person's life; should that other person die, she could not support herself and her children by remaining in "woman's sphere" – cooking, tending the house, and looking after her young family. That sort of work having no commercial value, she and her young family would very shortly starve. The profession of the prostitute is a livelihood; the profession of the wife and mother is not. A woman can support her children by prostitution; she cannot do so by performing the duties ordinarily associated with motherhood.

That marriage has another side than the economic I should be the last to deny, as I should be the last to deny that there are many households in which subjection and dependence in the wife is not desired by her husband – households in which there is a sharing of material, as well as of intellectual, interests. But that does not alter the fact that the position of a great many other married women is simply that of an unpaid domestic servant on the premises of a husband. The services that, rendered by another, would command payment, or at least thanks, from her are expected as a matter of course. They are supposed to be natural to her; she is no more to be paid for them than she is to be paid for breathing or feeling hungry. (One wonders why it should be "natural" in woman to do so many disagreeable things. Does the average man really believe that she has an instinctive and unquenchable craving for all the unpleasant and unremunerative jobs? or is that only a polite way of expressing his deeply-rooted conviction that when once she has got a husband she ought to be so thoroughly happy that a little dirty work more or less really cannot matter to her?)

It may be argued that in the greater number of cases marriage, for the husband, means the additional labour and expense of supporting a wife and children; and that this added labour and expense is expected from him as a matter of course, and that neither does he receive any thanks for it. Quite so; but, as I pointed out at the beginning of this book, marriage is a voluntary matter on the part of a man. He does not earn his living by it; he is under no necessity to undertake its duties and responsibilities should he prefer not to do so. He has other interests in life, and no social stigma attaches to him if he does not take to himself a wife and beget children. He enters the marriage state because he wishes to enter it, and is prepared to make certain necessary sacrifices in order to maintain a wife and family; whereas the position of the woman is very different. She very often enters the married state because she has to – because more lucrative trades are barred to her, because to remain unmarried will be to confess failure. This state of things in itself gives the man an advantage, and enables him to ensure (not necessarily consciously) that his share of the bargain shall be advantageous to himself – to ensure, in short, that he gets his money's worth. With his wife, on the other hand, it has often been a case of take it or leave it; since she knows that, if she does leave it, she will not be able to strike any more advantageous bargain elsewhere.

These being the conditions under which, consciously or unconsciously, the average wife strikes her bargain, it follows that in the ensuing division of labour she generally gets the worst of the transaction, the duties assigned to her being those which her husband would prefer not to perform. They are handed over to her as a matter of course, and on the assumption that they enter into what is commonly known as her "sphere." And it is this principle – that woman's work is the kind of work which man prefers not to do – which regulates and defines not only the labour of a woman in her own household, but the labour of women generally.

I am quite aware that this principle is not openly admitted in assigning to woman her share of the world's work – that, on the contrary, the results of its application are explained away on the theory that there is a "natural" division of labour between the two sexes. But when one comes to examine that theory, dispassionately and without prejudice, one finds that it does not hold water – or very little – since the estimate of woman's "natural" work is such an exceedingly variable quantity. One nation, people, or class, will esteem it "natural" in woman to perform certain duties which, in another nation, people, or class, are entirely left to men – so much so, that woman's sphere, like morality, seems to be defined by considerations "purely geographical." Unless we grasp the underlying principle that woman's "natural" labour in any given community is the form of labour which the men of that community do not care to undertake, her share in the world's work must appear to be regulated by sheer and arbitrary chance.

INDEX

Note: Numbers in **bold** indicate a table.

www.ingramcontent.com/pod-product-compliance
Lightning Source LLC
LaVergne TN
LVHW010629300926
849162LV00001B/100
9780367336585